THE TRANSFORMERS
SPOTLIGHT
REVELATION

Cover by
Nick Roche

Collection Edits by
Justin Eisinger

Collection Design by
Chris Mowry

Special thanks to Hasbro's Aaron Archer, Michael Kelly, Amie Lozanski,
Val Roca, Ed Lane, Michael Provost, Erin Hillman, Samantha Lomow, and
Michael Verrecchia for their invaluable assistance.

IDW Publishing
Operations
Moshe Berger, Chairman
Ted Adams, Chief Executive Officer
Greg Goldstein, Chief Operating Officer
Matthew Ruzicka, CPA, Chief Financial Officer
Alan Payne, VP of Sales
Lorelei Bunjes, Dir. of Digital Services
Marci Hubbard, Executive Assistant
Alonzo Simon, Shipping Manager

Editorial
Chris Ryall, Publisher/Editor-in-Chief
Scott Dunbier, Editor, Special Projects
Andy Schmidt, Senior Editor
Justin Eisinger, Editor
Kris Oprisko, Editor/Foreign Lic.
Denton J. Tipton, Editor
Tom Waltz, Editor
Mariah Huehner, Assistant Editor

Design
Robbie Robbins, EVP/Sr. Graphic Artist
Ben Templesmith, Artist/Designer
Neil Uyetake, Art Director
Chris Mowry, Graphic Artist
Amauri Osorio, Graphic Artist

Licensed by:

25 YEARS
1984-2009

ISBN: 978-1-60010-421-3
12 11 10 09   1 2 3 4
www.IDWPUBLISHING.com

CYCLONUS

For someone so mercurial, so unpredictable, CYCLONUS craves, above all, order. To him, the universe is as chaotic and maddening as his own nature, and he feels if he could just impose structure and control upon it his own volatility would diminish accordingly. NOVA PRIME'S dream of expansion, his wish to impose the Cybertronian ideal on the larger universe, jibes perfectly with Cyclonus' own needs. Fiercely, demonstrably patriotic, Cyclonus believes utterly in Cybertron (and the Cybertronian race as some kind of universal template for existence) and those he deems responsible for its decline and fall are just… the enemy!

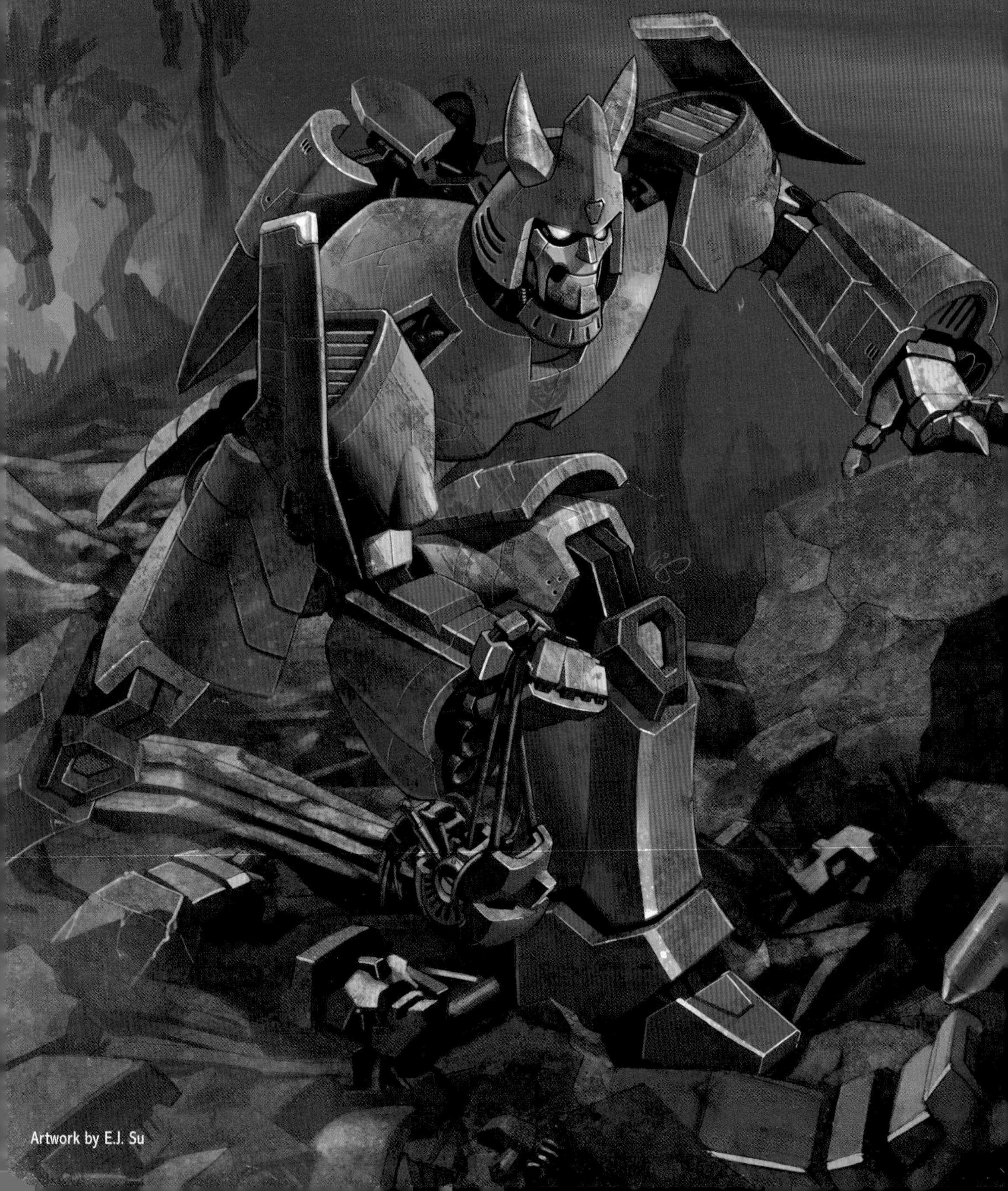

Artwork by E.J. Su

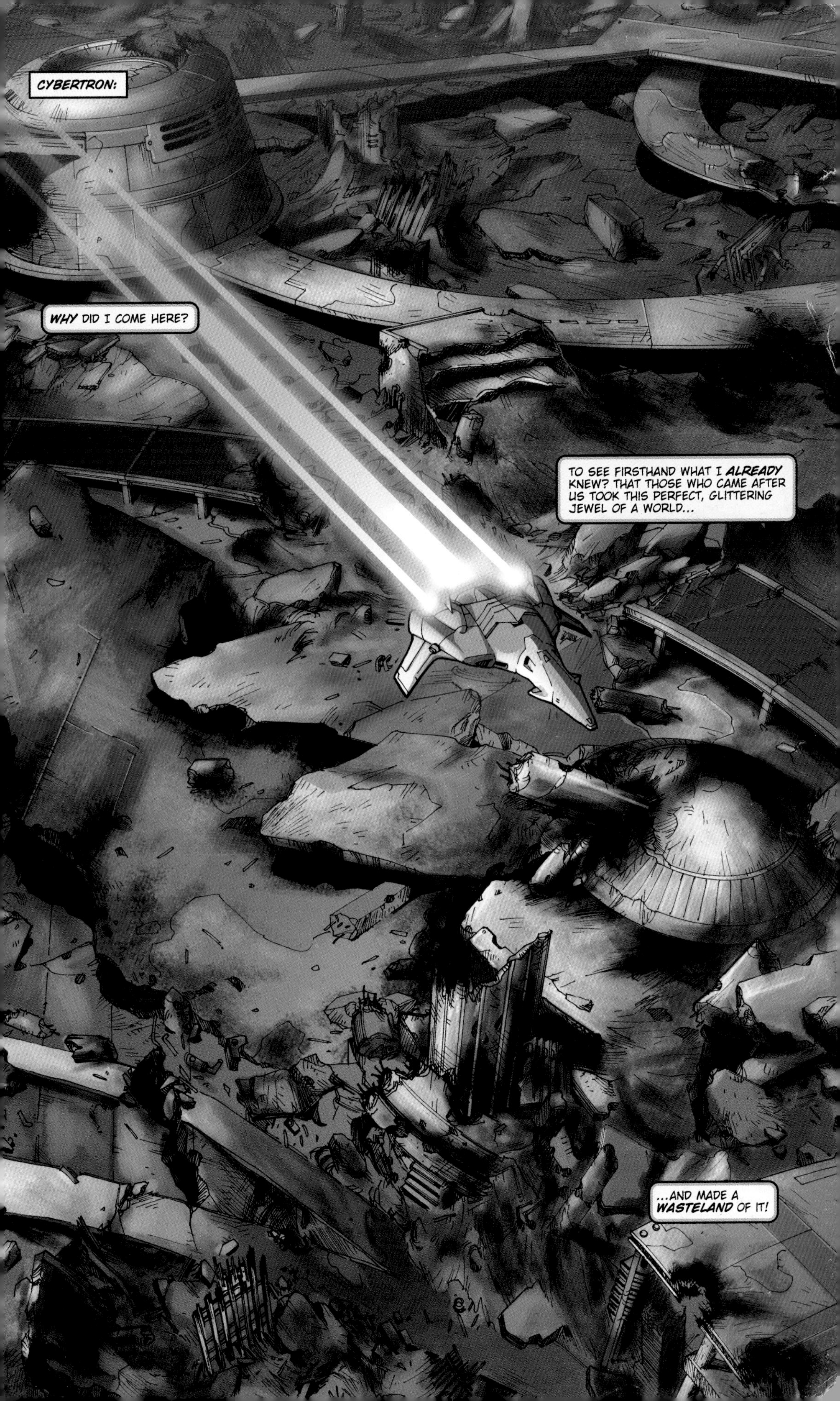
CYBERTRON:
WHY DID I COME HERE?
TO SEE FIRSTHAND WHAT I ALREADY KNEW? THAT THOSE WHO CAME AFTER US TOOK THIS PERFECT, GLITTERING JEWEL OF A WORLD...
...AND MADE A WASTELAND OF IT!

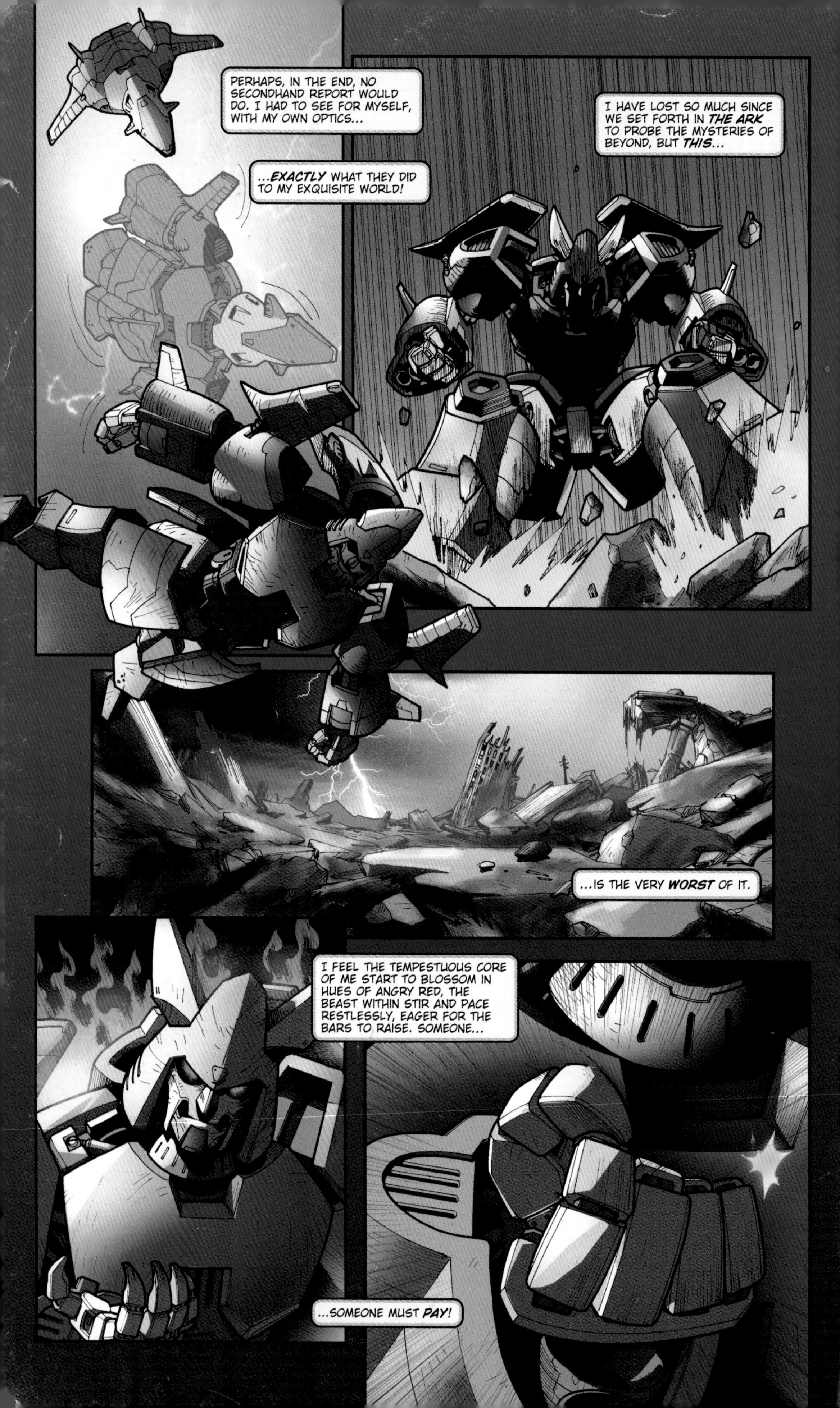
PERHAPS, IN THE END, NO SECONDHAND REPORT WOULD DO. I HAD TO SEE FOR MYSELF, WITH MY OWN OPTICS...
...EXACTLY WHAT THEY DID TO MY EXQUISITE WORLD!
I HAVE LOST SO MUCH SINCE WE SET FORTH IN THE ARK TO PROBE THE MYSTERIES OF BEYOND, BUT THIS...
...IS THE VERY WORST OF IT.
I FEEL THE TEMPESTUOUS CORE OF ME START TO BLOSSOM IN HUES OF ANGRY RED, THE BEAST WITHIN STIR AND PACE RESTLESSLY, EAGER FOR THE BARS TO RAISE. SOMEONE...
...SOMEONE MUST PAY!

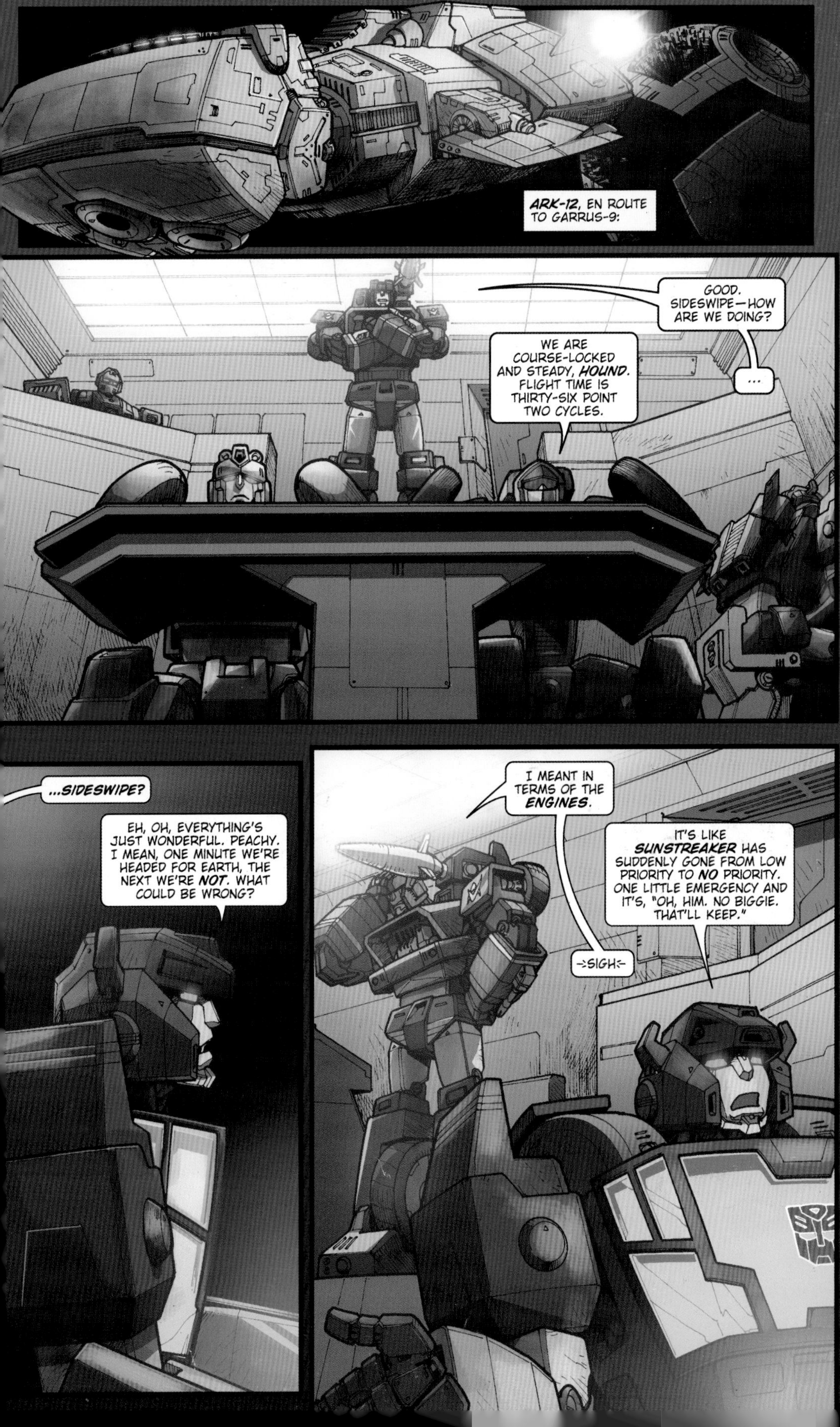

ARK-12, EN ROUTE TO GARRUS-9:
GOOD. SIDESWIPE—HOW ARE WE DOING?
WE ARE COURSE-LOCKED AND STEADY, HOUND. FLIGHT TIME IS THIRTY-SIX POINT TWO CYCLES.
...
...SIDESWIPE?
EH, OH, EVERYTHING'S JUST WONDERFUL. PEACHY. I MEAN, ONE MINUTE WE'RE HEADED FOR EARTH, THE NEXT WE'RE NOT. WHAT COULD BE WRONG?
I MEANT IN TERMS OF THE ENGINES.
-SIGH-
IT'S LIKE SUNSTREAKER HAS SUDDENLY GONE FROM LOW PRIORITY TO NO PRIORITY. ONE LITTLE EMERGENCY AND IT'S, "OH, HIM. NO BIGGIE. THAT'LL KEEP."

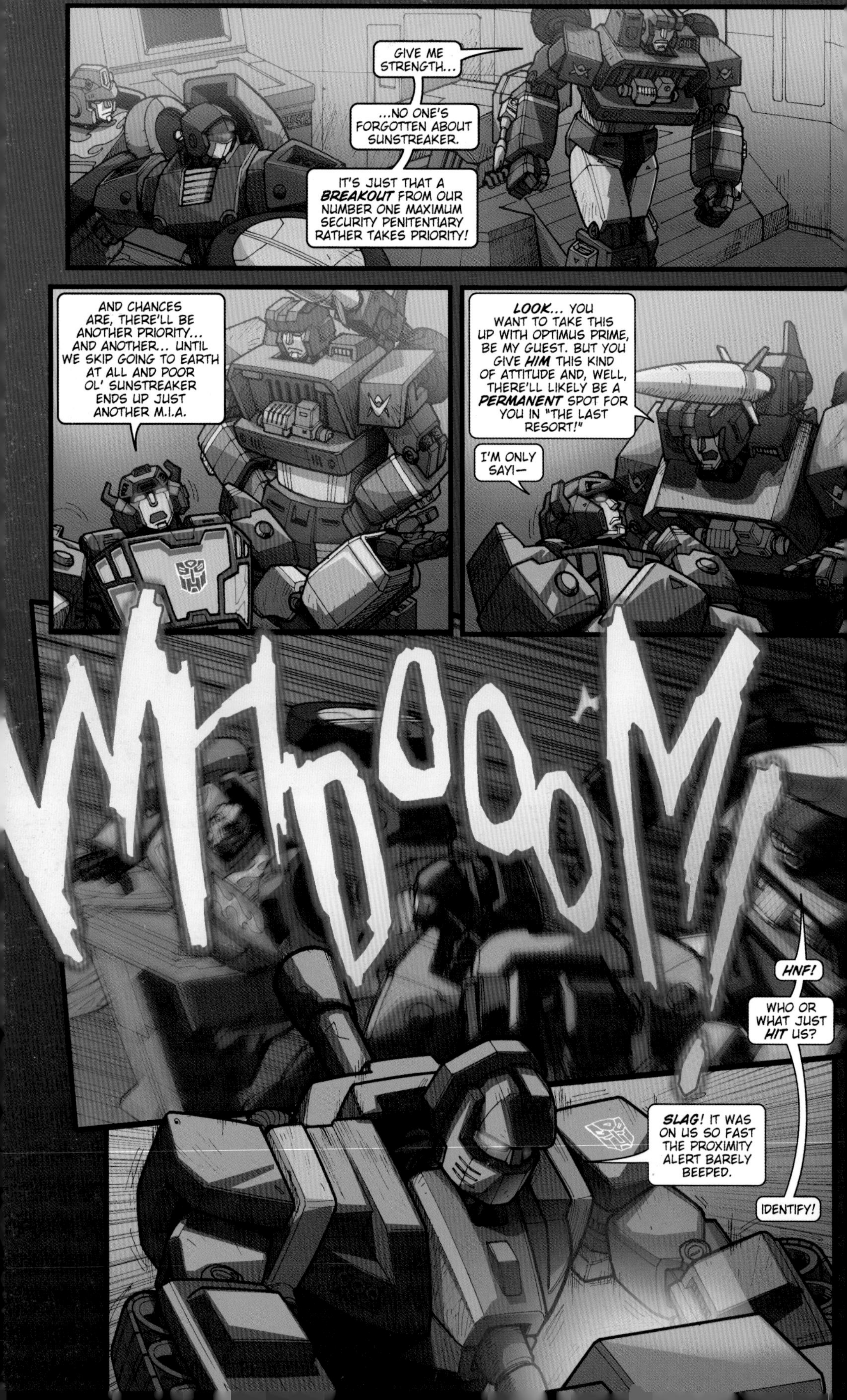
GIVE ME STRENGTH...
...NO ONE'S FORGOTTEN ABOUT SUNSTREAKER.
IT'S JUST THAT A **BREAKOUT** FROM OUR NUMBER ONE MAXIMUM SECURITY PENITENTIARY RATHER TAKES PRIORITY!
AND CHANCES ARE, THERE'LL BE ANOTHER PRIORITY... AND ANOTHER... UNTIL WE SKIP GOING TO EARTH AT ALL AND POOR OL' SUNSTREAKER ENDS UP JUST ANOTHER M.I.A.
LOOK... YOU WANT TO TAKE THIS UP WITH OPTIMUS PRIME, BE MY GUEST. BUT YOU GIVE **HIM** THIS KIND OF ATTITUDE AND, WELL, THERE'LL LIKELY BE A **PERMANENT** SPOT FOR YOU IN "THE LAST RESORT!"
I'M ONLY SAY!—
WHOOOM
HNF!
WHO OR WHAT JUST **HIT** US?
SLAG! IT WAS ON US SO FAST THE PROXIMITY ALERT BARELY BEEPED.
IDENTIFY!

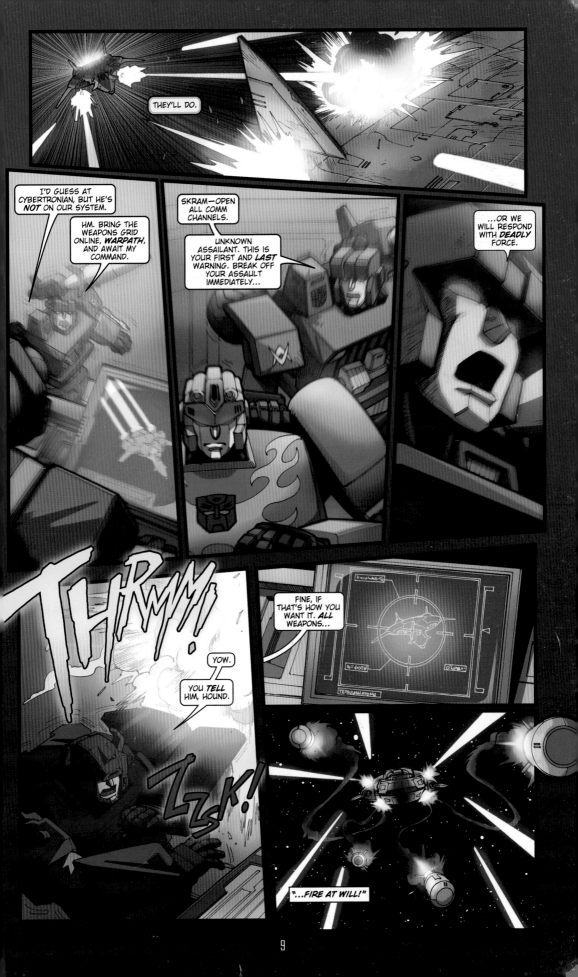

THEY'LL DO.

I'D GUESS AT CYBERTRONIAN, BUT HE'S *NOT* ON OUR SYSTEM.

HM. BRING THE WEAPONS GRID ONLINE, *WARPATH*, AND AWAIT MY COMMAND.

SKRAM—OPEN ALL COMM CHANNELS.

UNKNOWN ASSAILANT. THIS IS YOUR FIRST AND *LAST* WARNING. BREAK OFF YOUR ASSAULT IMMEDIATELY...

...OR WE WILL RESPOND WITH *DEADLY* FORCE.

THRMM!

YOW.

YOU *TELL* HIM, HOUND.

ZZK!

FINE, IF THAT'S HOW YOU WANT IT. ALL WEAPONS...

"...FIRE AT WILL!"

9

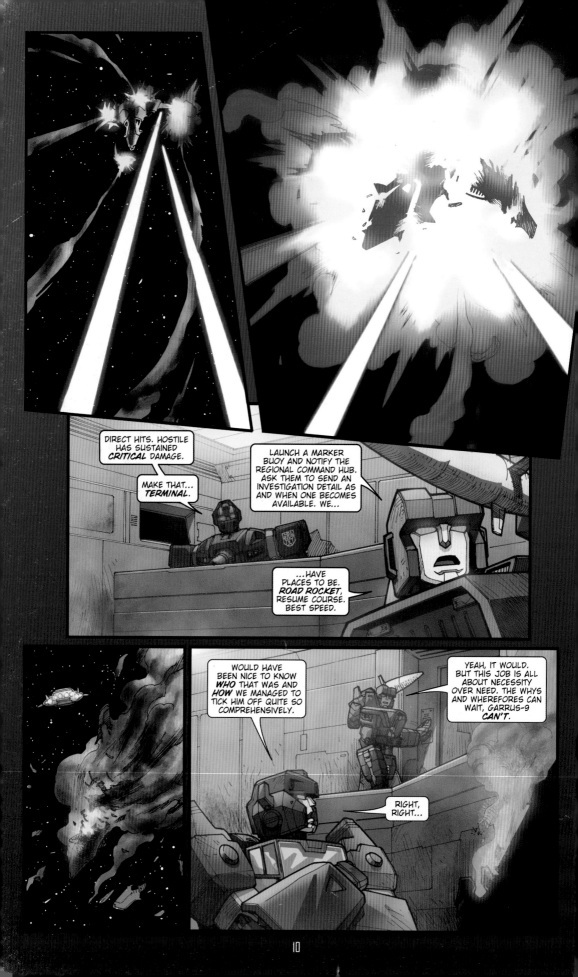

DIRECT HITS. HOSTILE HAS SUSTAINED *CRITICAL* DAMAGE.

MAKE THAT... *TERMINAL*.

LAUNCH A MARKER BUOY AND NOTIFY THE REGIONAL COMMAND HUB. ASK THEM TO SEND AN INVESTIGATION DETAIL AS AND WHEN ONE BECOMES AVAILABLE. WE...

...HAVE PLACES TO BE. *ROAD ROCKET*, RESUME COURSE. BEST SPEED.

WOULD HAVE BEEN NICE TO KNOW *WHO* THAT WAS AND *HOW* WE MANAGED TO TICK HIM OFF QUITE SO COMPREHENSIVELY.

YEAH, IT WOULD. BUT THIS JOB IS ALL ABOUT NECESSITY OVER NEED. THE WHYS AND WHEREFORES CAN WAIT, GARRUS-9 *CAN'T*.

RIGHT, RIGHT...

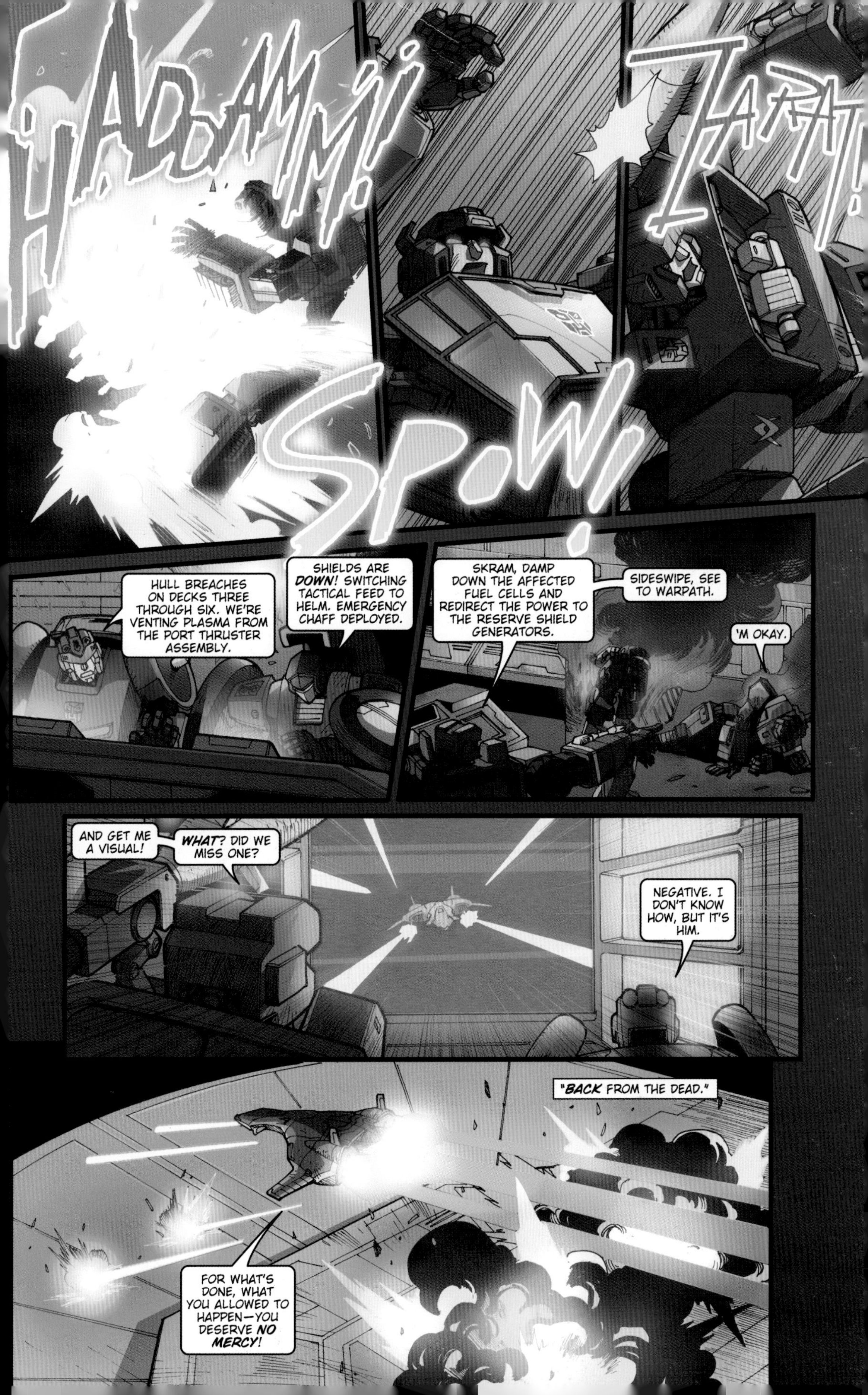

KADOAMM!
TAPAT!
SPOW!
HULL BREACHES ON DECKS THREE THROUGH SIX. WE'RE VENTING PLASMA FROM THE PORT THRUSTER ASSEMBLY.
SHIELDS ARE **DOWN**! SWITCHING TACTICAL FEED TO HELM. EMERGENCY CHAFF DEPLOYED.
SKRAM, DAMP DOWN THE AFFECTED FUEL CELLS AND REDIRECT THE POWER TO THE RESERVE SHIELD GENERATORS.
SIDESWIPE, SEE TO WARPATH.
'M OKAY.
AND GET ME A VISUAL!
WHAT? DID WE MISS ONE?
NEGATIVE. I DON'T KNOW HOW, BUT IT'S HIM.
"**BACK** FROM THE DEAD."
FOR WHAT'S DONE, WHAT YOU ALLOWED TO HAPPEN—YOU DESERVE **NO MERCY**!

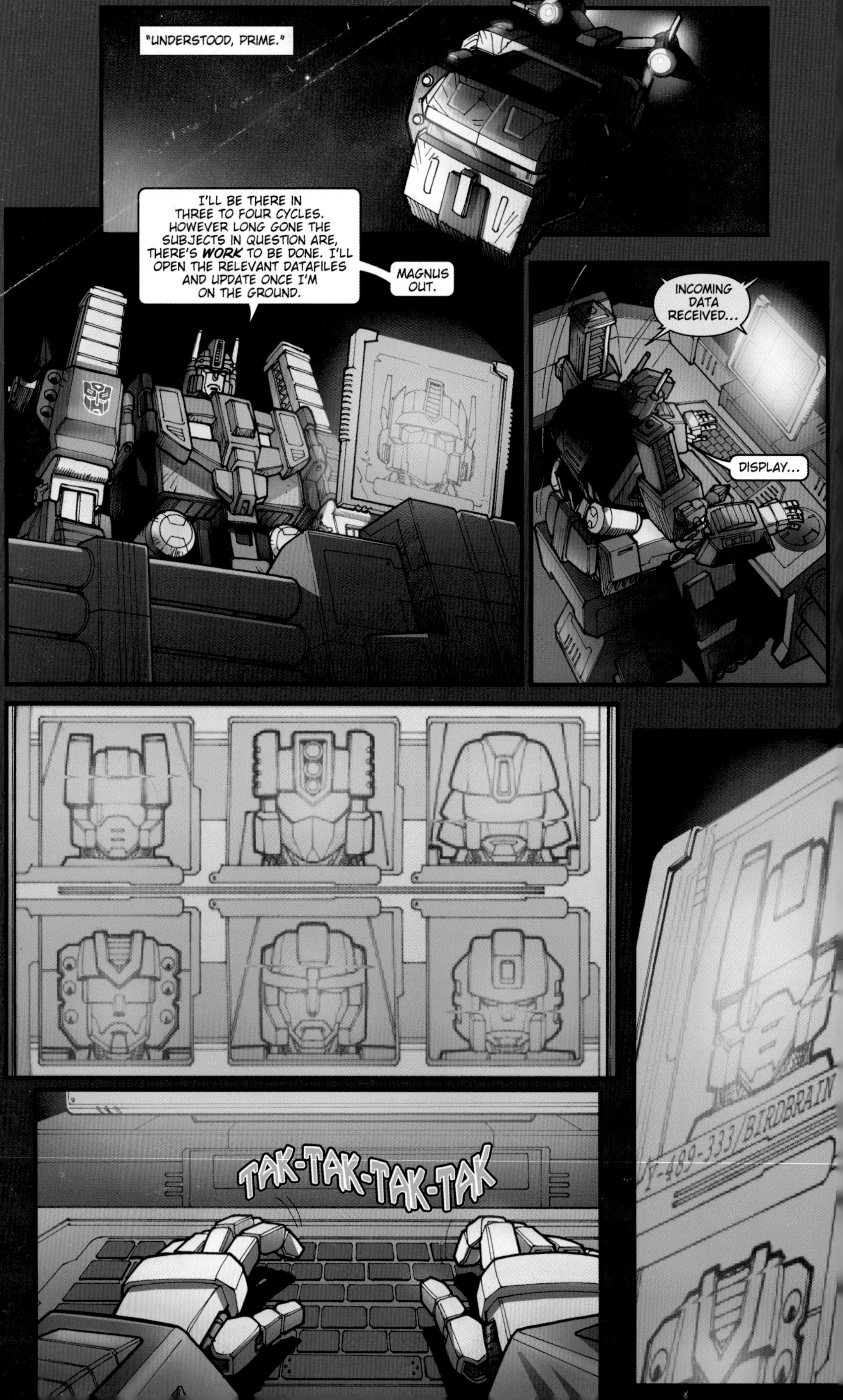
"UNDERSTOOD, PRIME."
I'LL BE THERE IN THREE TO FOUR CYCLES. HOWEVER LONG GONE THE SUBJECTS IN QUESTION ARE, THERE'S WORK TO BE DONE. I'LL OPEN THE RELEVANT DATAFILES AND UPDATE ONCE I'M ON THE GROUND.
MAGNUS OUT.
INCOMING DATA RECEIVED...
DISPLAY...
Y-489-333/BIRDBRAIN
TAK-TAK-TAK-TAK

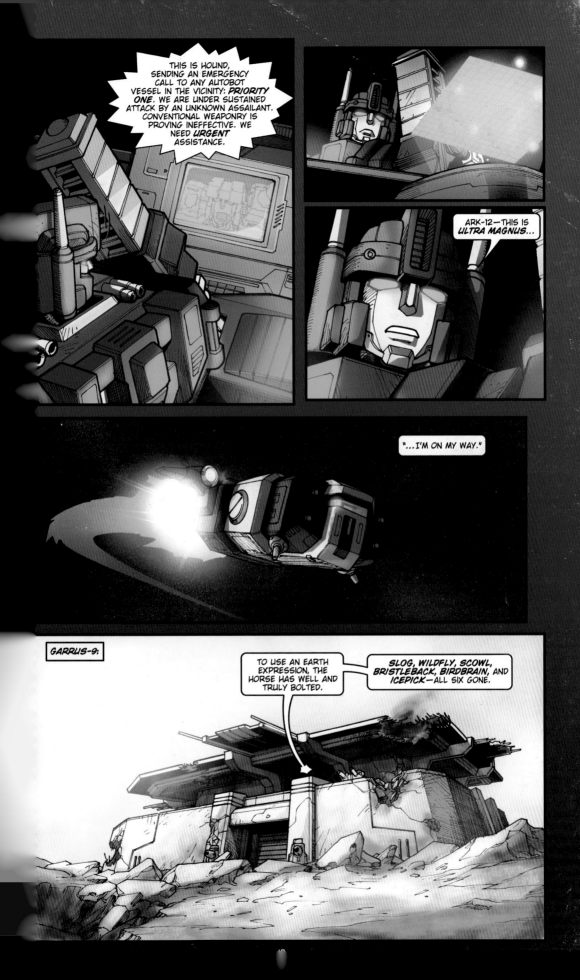

THIS IS HOUND, SENDING AN EMERGENCY CALL TO ANY AUTOBOT VESSEL IN THE VICINITY: *PRIORITY ONE*. WE ARE UNDER SUSTAINED ATTACK BY AN UNKNOWN ASSAILANT. CONVENTIONAL WEAPONRY IS PROVING INEFFECTIVE. WE NEED *URGENT* ASSISTANCE.

ARK-12—THIS IS *ULTRA MAGNUS*...

"...I'M ON MY WAY."

GARRUS-9:

TO USE AN EARTH EXPRESSION, THE HORSE HAS WELL AND TRULY BOLTED.

SLOG, WILDFLY, SCOWL, BRISTLEBACK, BIRDBRAIN, AND *ICEPICK*—ALL SIX GONE.

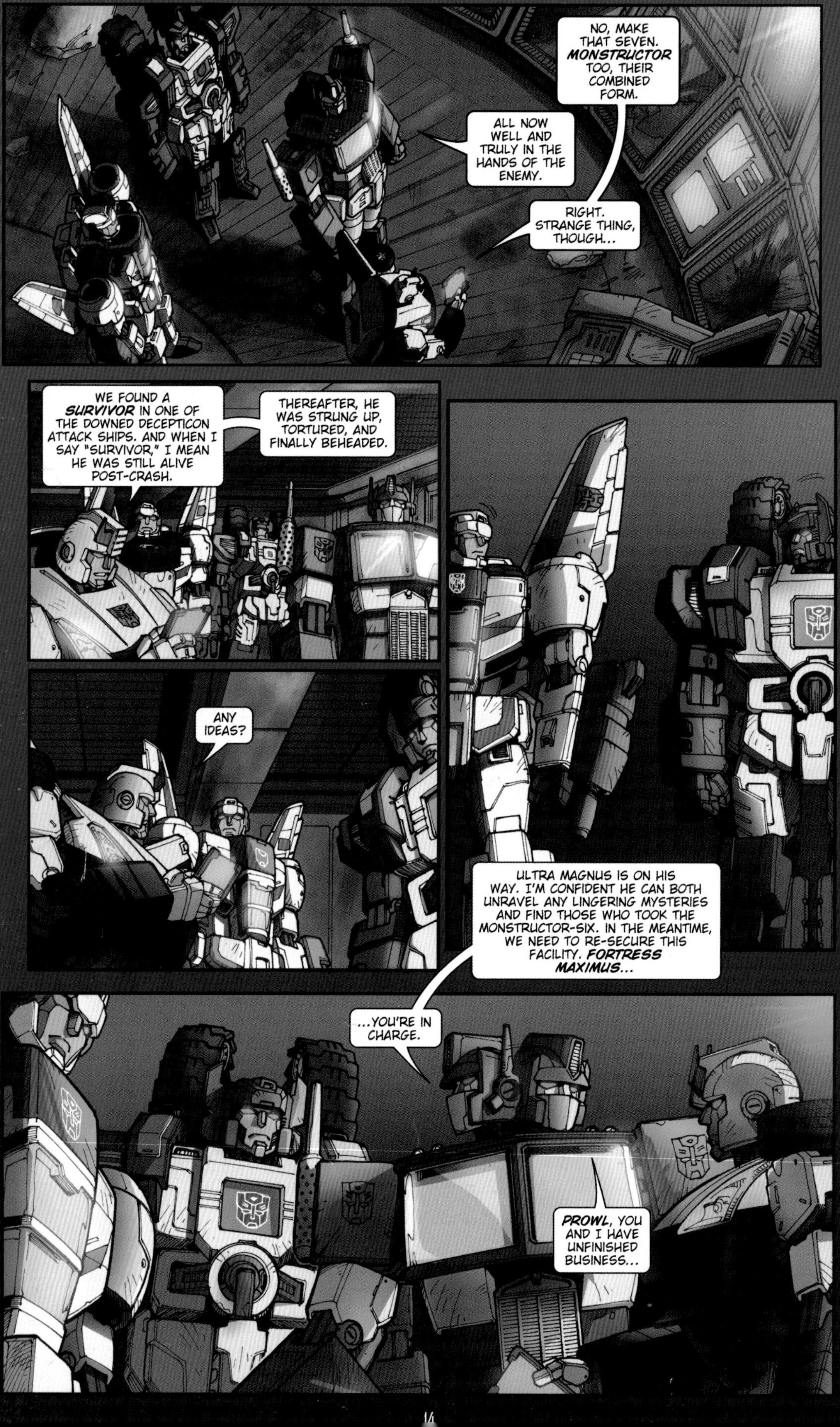
NO, MAKE THAT SEVEN. MONSTRUCTOR TOO, THEIR COMBINED FORM.
ALL NOW WELL AND TRULY IN THE HANDS OF THE ENEMY.
RIGHT. STRANGE THING, THOUGH...
WE FOUND A SURVIVOR IN ONE OF THE DOWNED DECEPTICON ATTACK SHIPS. AND WHEN I SAY "SURVIVOR," I MEAN HE WAS STILL ALIVE POST-CRASH.
THEREAFTER, HE WAS STRUNG UP, TORTURED, AND FINALLY BEHEADED.
ANY IDEAS?
ULTRA MAGNUS IS ON HIS WAY. I'M CONFIDENT HE CAN BOTH UNRAVEL ANY LINGERING MYSTERIES AND FIND THOSE WHO TOOK THE MONSTRUCTOR-SIX. IN THE MEANTIME, WE NEED TO RE-SECURE THIS FACILITY. FORTRESS MAXIMUS...
...YOU'RE IN CHARGE.
PROWL, YOU AND I HAVE UNFINISHED BUSINESS...

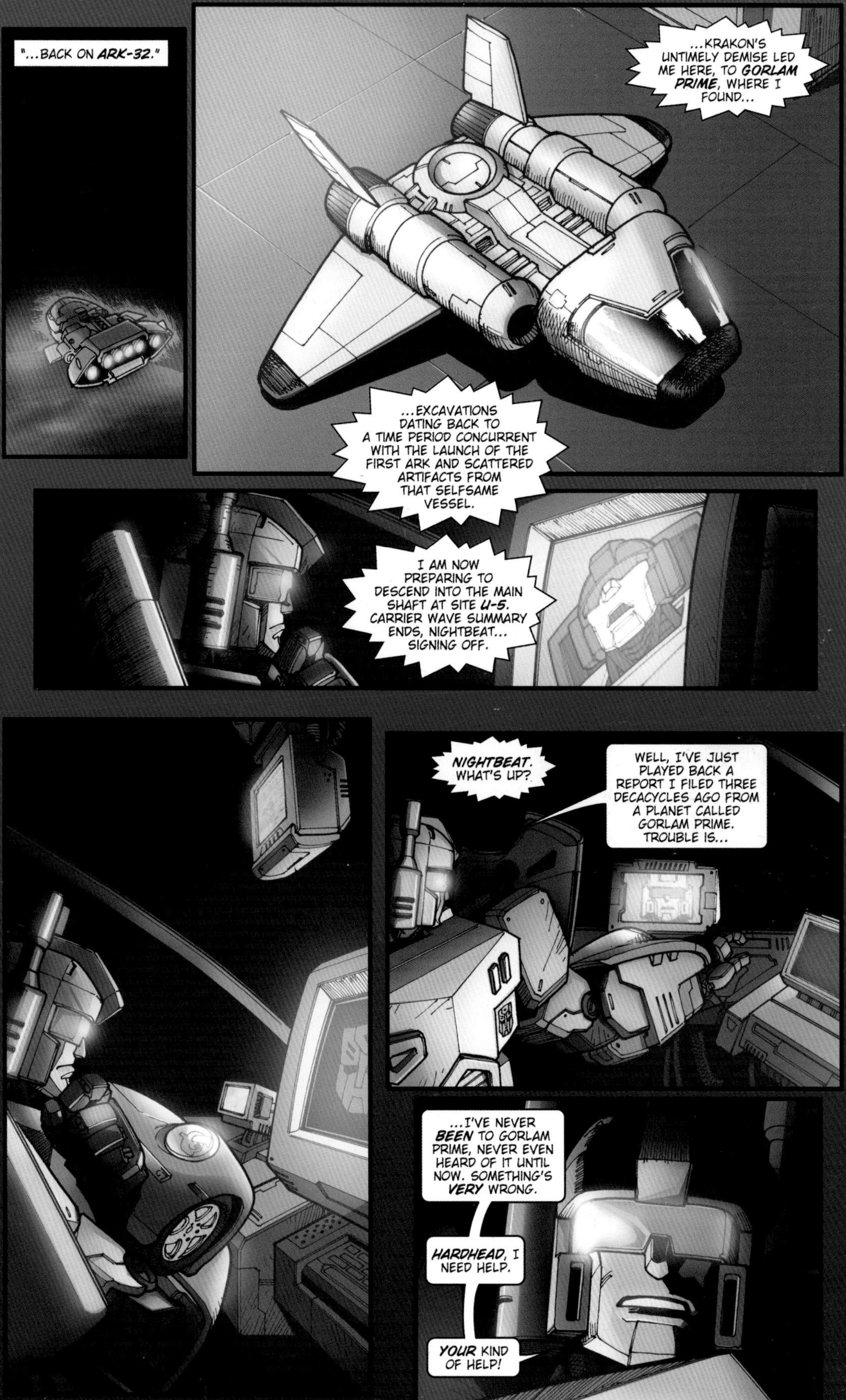
"...BACK ON ARK-32."
...KRAKON'S UNTIMELY DEMISE LED ME HERE, TO GORLAM PRIME, WHERE I FOUND...
...EXCAVATIONS DATING BACK TO A TIME PERIOD CONCURRENT WITH THE LAUNCH OF THE FIRST ARK AND SCATTERED ARTIFACTS FROM THAT SELFSAME VESSEL.
I AM NOW PREPARING TO DESCEND INTO THE MAIN SHAFT AT SITE U-5. CARRIER WAVE SUMMARY ENDS, NIGHTBEAT... SIGNING OFF.
NIGHTBEAT. WHAT'S UP?
WELL, I'VE JUST PLAYED BACK A REPORT I FILED THREE DECACYCLES AGO FROM A PLANET CALLED GORLAM PRIME. TROUBLE IS...
...I'VE NEVER BEEN TO GORLAM PRIME, NEVER EVEN HEARD OF IT UNTIL NOW. SOMETHING'S VERY WRONG.
HARDHEAD, I NEED HELP.
YOUR KIND OF HELP!

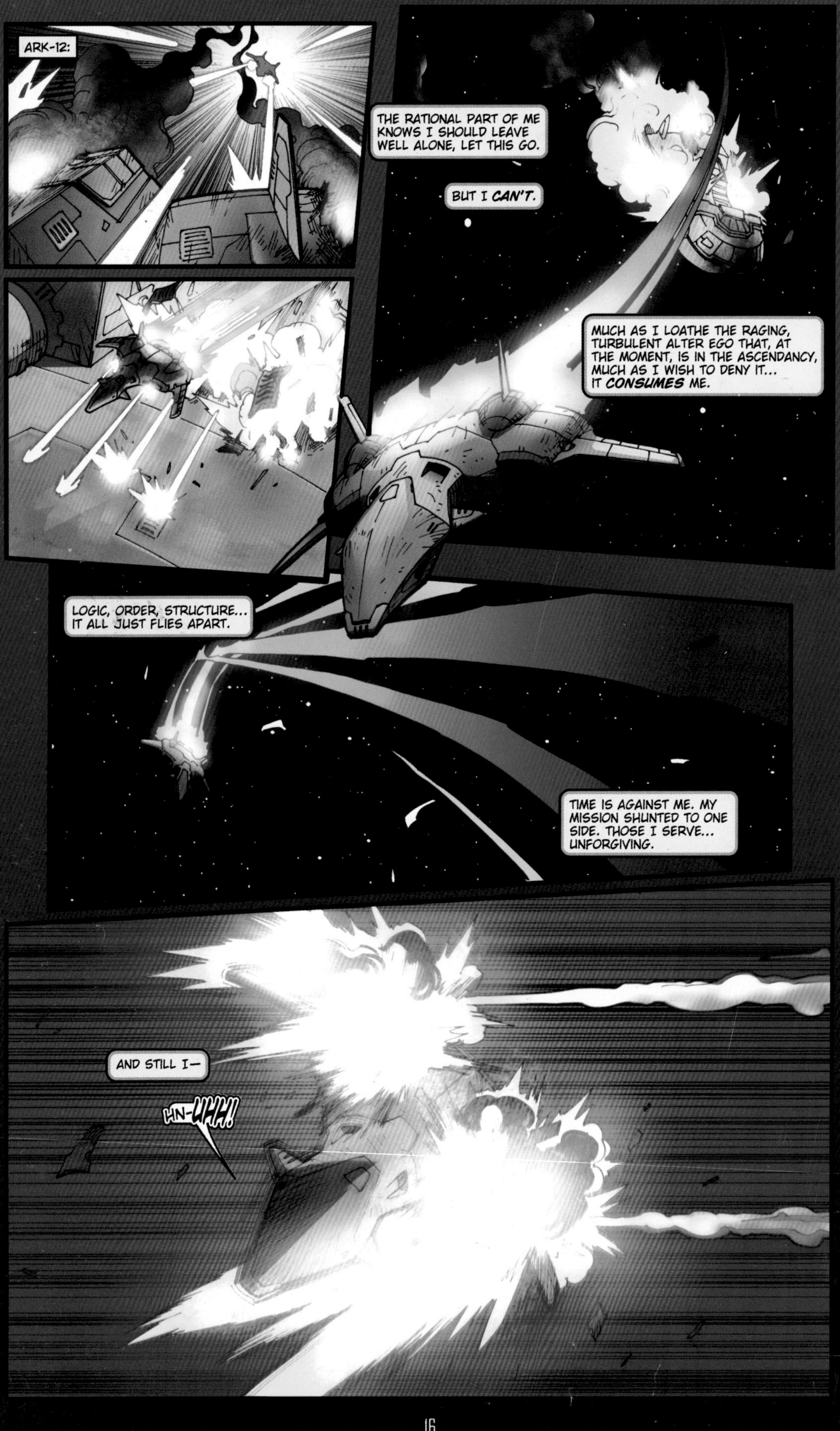
ARK-12:
THE RATIONAL PART OF ME KNOWS I SHOULD LEAVE WELL ALONE, LET THIS GO.
BUT I CAN'T.
MUCH AS I LOATHE THE RAGING, TURBULENT ALTER EGO THAT, AT THE MOMENT, IS IN THE ASCENDANCY, MUCH AS I WISH TO DENY IT... IT CONSUMES ME.
LOGIC, ORDER, STRUCTURE... IT ALL JUST FLIES APART.
TIME IS AGAINST ME. MY MISSION SHUNTED TO ONE SIDE. THOSE I SERVE... UNFORGIVING.
AND STILL I—
HN-UHH!

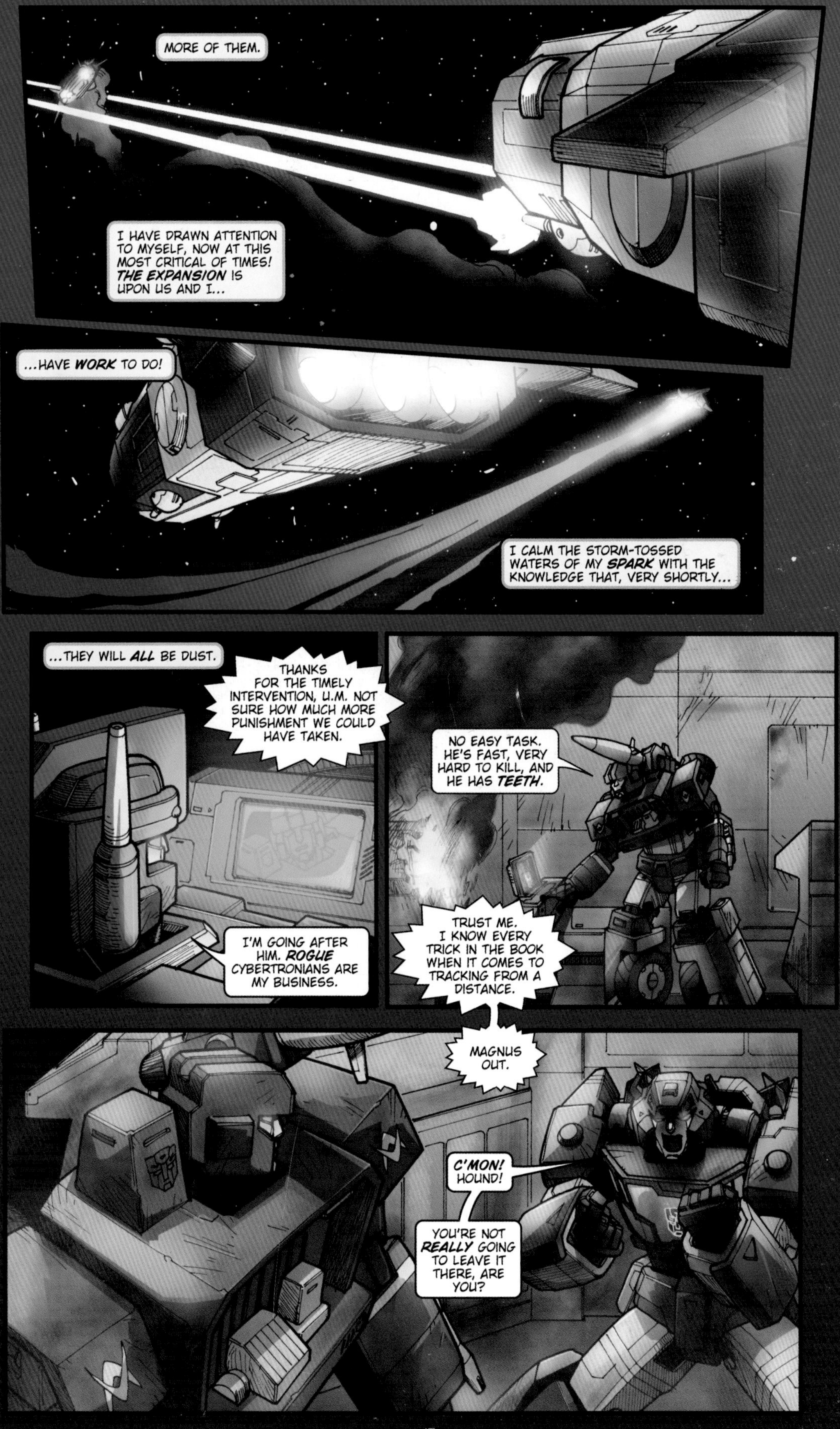
MORE OF THEM.
I HAVE DRAWN ATTENTION TO MYSELF, NOW AT THIS MOST CRITICAL OF TIMES! THE EXPANSION IS UPON US AND I...
...HAVE WORK TO DO!
I CALM THE STORM-TOSSED WATERS OF MY SPARK WITH THE KNOWLEDGE THAT, VERY SHORTLY...
...THEY WILL ALL BE DUST.
THANKS FOR THE TIMELY INTERVENTION, U.M. NOT SURE HOW MUCH MORE PUNISHMENT WE COULD HAVE TAKEN.
I'M GOING AFTER HIM. ROGUE CYBERTRONIANS ARE MY BUSINESS.
NO EASY TASK. HE'S FAST, VERY HARD TO KILL, AND HE HAS TEETH.
TRUST ME. I KNOW EVERY TRICK IN THE BOOK WHEN IT COMES TO TRACKING FROM A DISTANCE.
MAGNUS OUT.
C'MON! HOUND!
YOU'RE NOT REALLY GOING TO LEAVE IT THERE, ARE YOU?

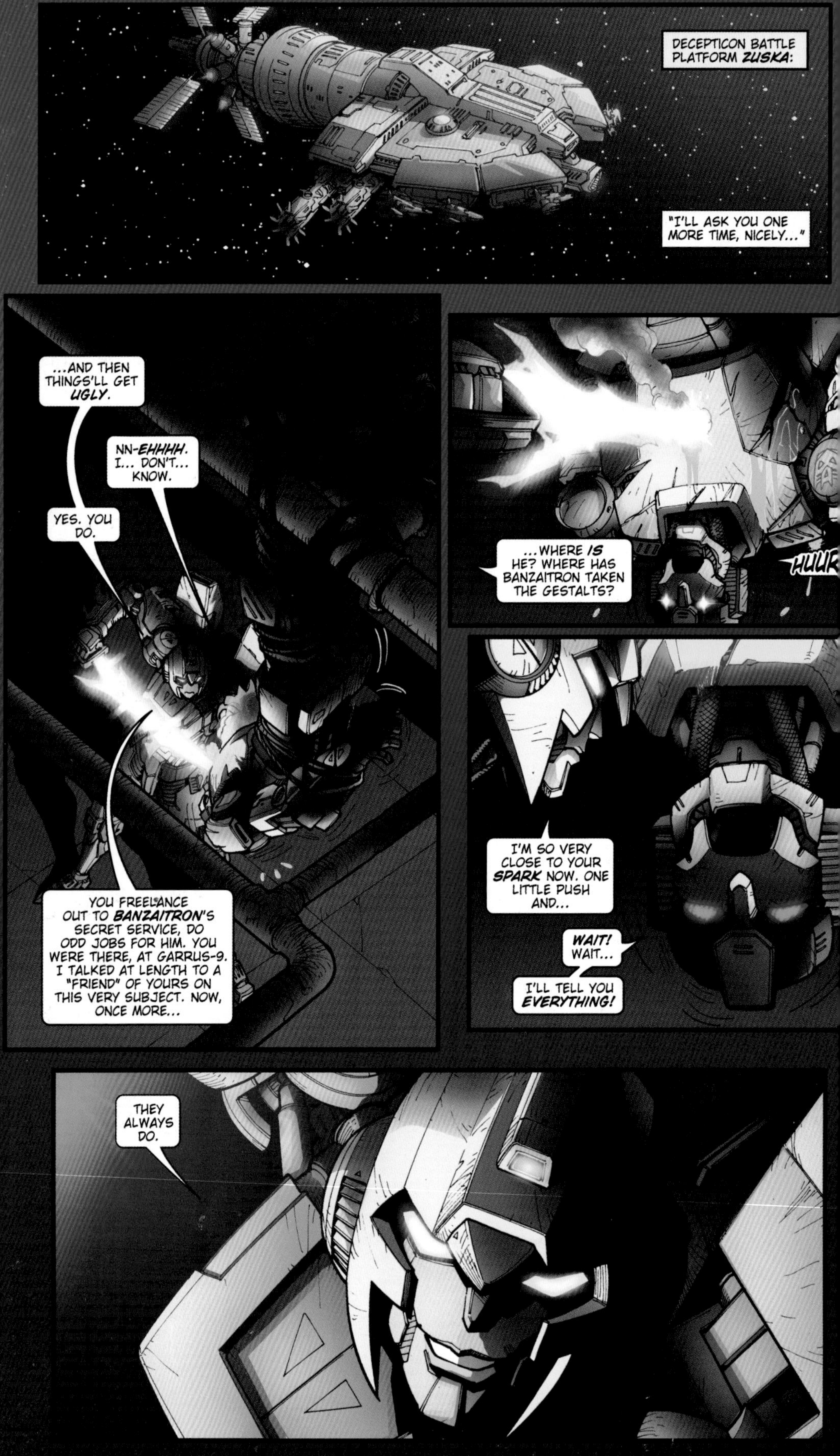
DECEPTICON BATTLE PLATFORM *ZUSKA*:
"I'LL ASK YOU ONE MORE TIME, NICELY..."
...AND THEN THINGS'LL GET *UGLY*.
NN-*EHHHH*. I... DON'T... KNOW.
YES. YOU DO.
YOU FREELANCE OUT TO *BANZAITRON*'S SECRET SERVICE, DO ODD JOBS FOR HIM. YOU WERE THERE, AT GARRUS-9. I TALKED AT LENGTH TO A "FRIEND" OF YOURS ON THIS VERY SUBJECT. NOW, ONCE MORE...
...WHERE *IS* HE? WHERE HAS BANZAITRON TAKEN THE GESTALTS?
HUUR
I'M SO VERY CLOSE TO YOUR *SPARK* NOW. ONE LITTLE PUSH AND...
WAIT! WAIT...
I'LL TELL YOU *EVERYTHING!*
THEY ALWAYS DO.

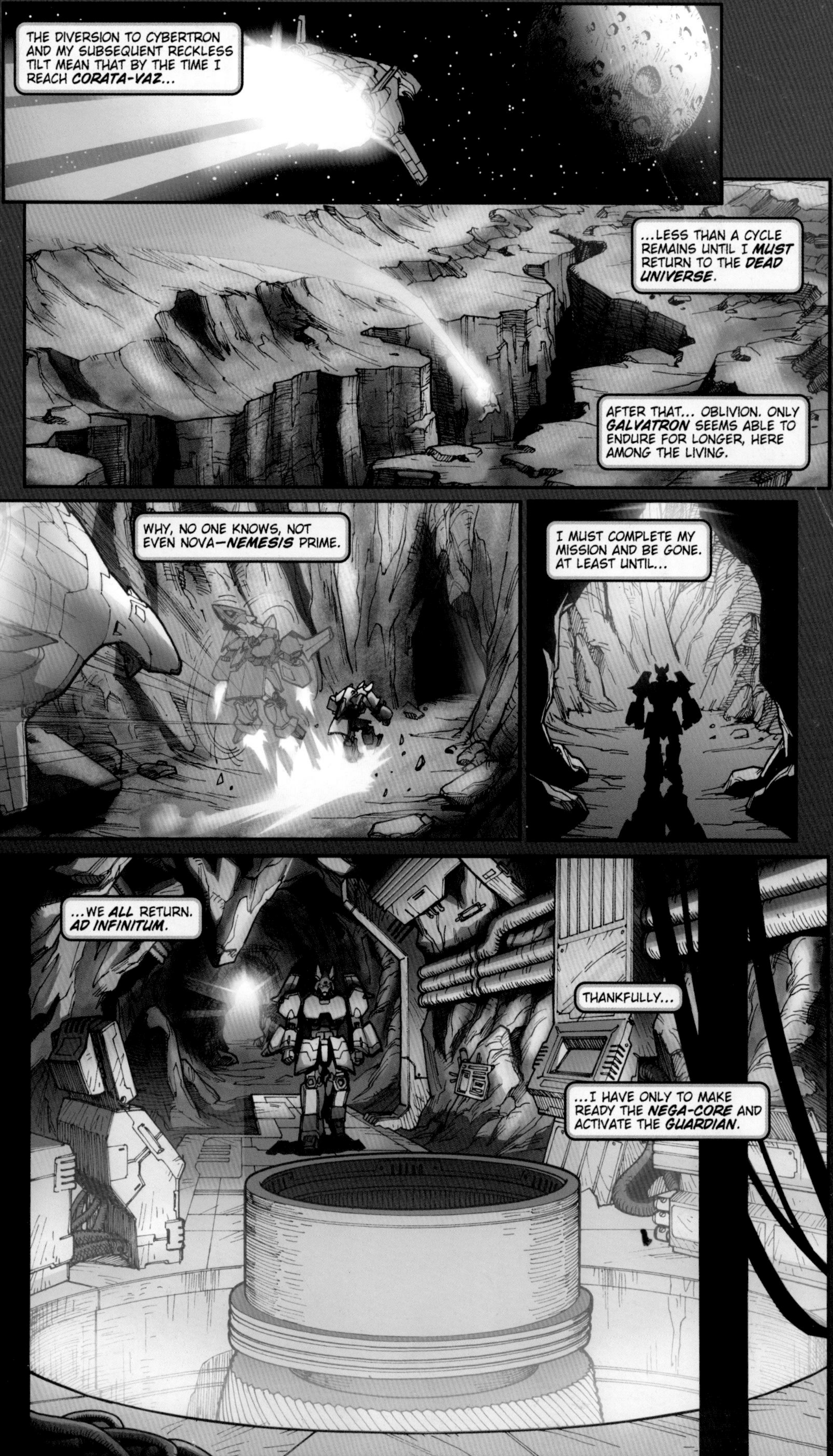
THE DIVERSION TO CYBERTRON AND MY SUBSEQUENT RECKLESS TILT MEAN THAT BY THE TIME I REACH CORATA-VAZ...
...LESS THAN A CYCLE REMAINS UNTIL I MUST RETURN TO THE DEAD UNIVERSE.
AFTER THAT... OBLIVION. ONLY GALVATRON SEEMS ABLE TO ENDURE FOR LONGER, HERE AMONG THE LIVING.
WHY, NO ONE KNOWS, NOT EVEN NOVA—NEMESIS PRIME.
I MUST COMPLETE MY MISSION AND BE GONE. AT LEAST UNTIL...
...WE ALL RETURN. AD INFINITUM.
THANKFULLY...
...I HAVE ONLY TO MAKE READY THE NEGA-CORE AND ACTIVATE THE GUARDIAN.

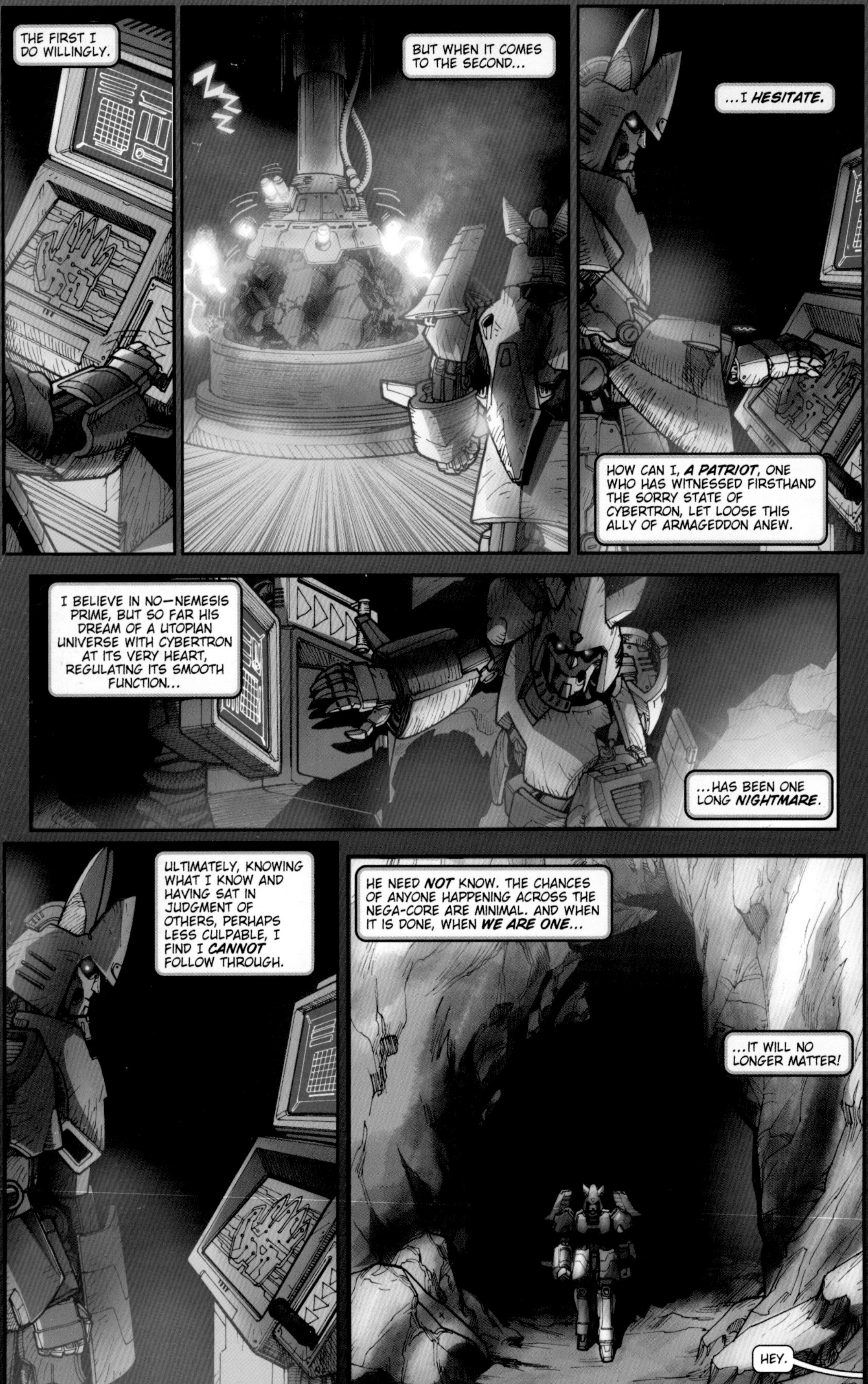
THE FIRST I DO WILLINGLY.
BUT WHEN IT COMES TO THE SECOND...
...I HESITATE.
HOW CAN I, A PATRIOT, ONE WHO HAS WITNESSED FIRSTHAND THE SORRY STATE OF CYBERTRON, LET LOOSE THIS ALLY OF ARMAGEDDON ANEW.
I BELIEVE IN NO—NEMESIS PRIME, BUT SO FAR HIS DREAM OF A UTOPIAN UNIVERSE WITH CYBERTRON AT ITS VERY HEART, REGULATING ITS SMOOTH FUNCTION...
...HAS BEEN ONE LONG NIGHTMARE.
ULTIMATELY, KNOWING WHAT I KNOW AND HAVING SAT IN JUDGMENT OF OTHERS, PERHAPS LESS CULPABLE, I FIND I CANNOT FOLLOW THROUGH.
HE NEED NOT KNOW. THE CHANCES OF ANYONE HAPPENING ACROSS THE NEGA-CORE ARE MINIMAL. AND WHEN IT IS DONE, WHEN WE ARE ONE...
...IT WILL NO LONGER MATTER!
HEY.

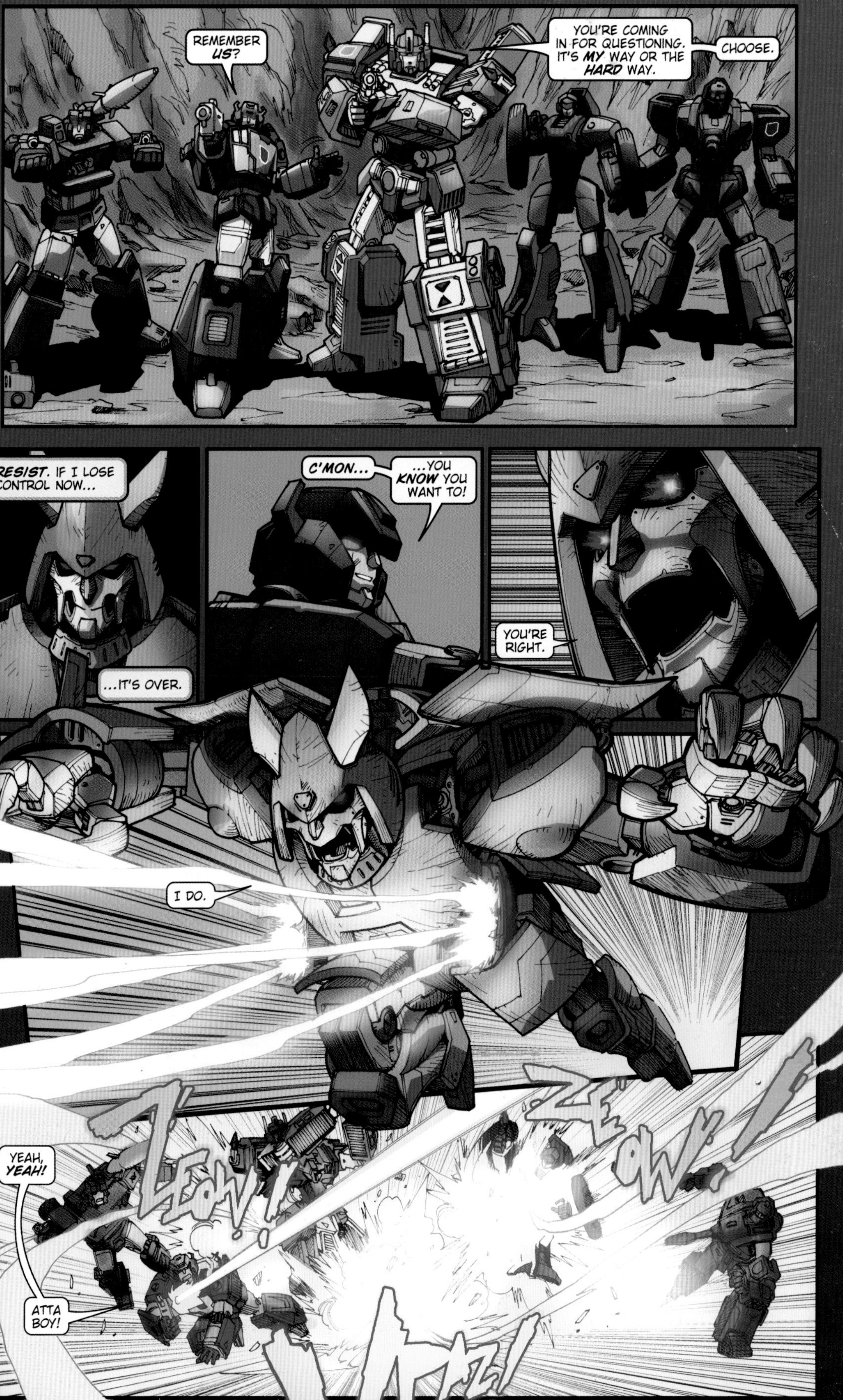
REMEMBER US?
YOU'RE COMING IN FOR QUESTIONING. IT'S MY WAY OR THE HARD WAY.
CHOOSE.
RESIST. IF I LOSE CONTROL NOW...
...IT'S OVER.
C'MON...
...YOU KNOW YOU WANT TO!
YOU'RE RIGHT.
I DO.
YEAH, YEAH!
ATTA BOY!
ZEOW!!
ZEOW!!
VZZZ!

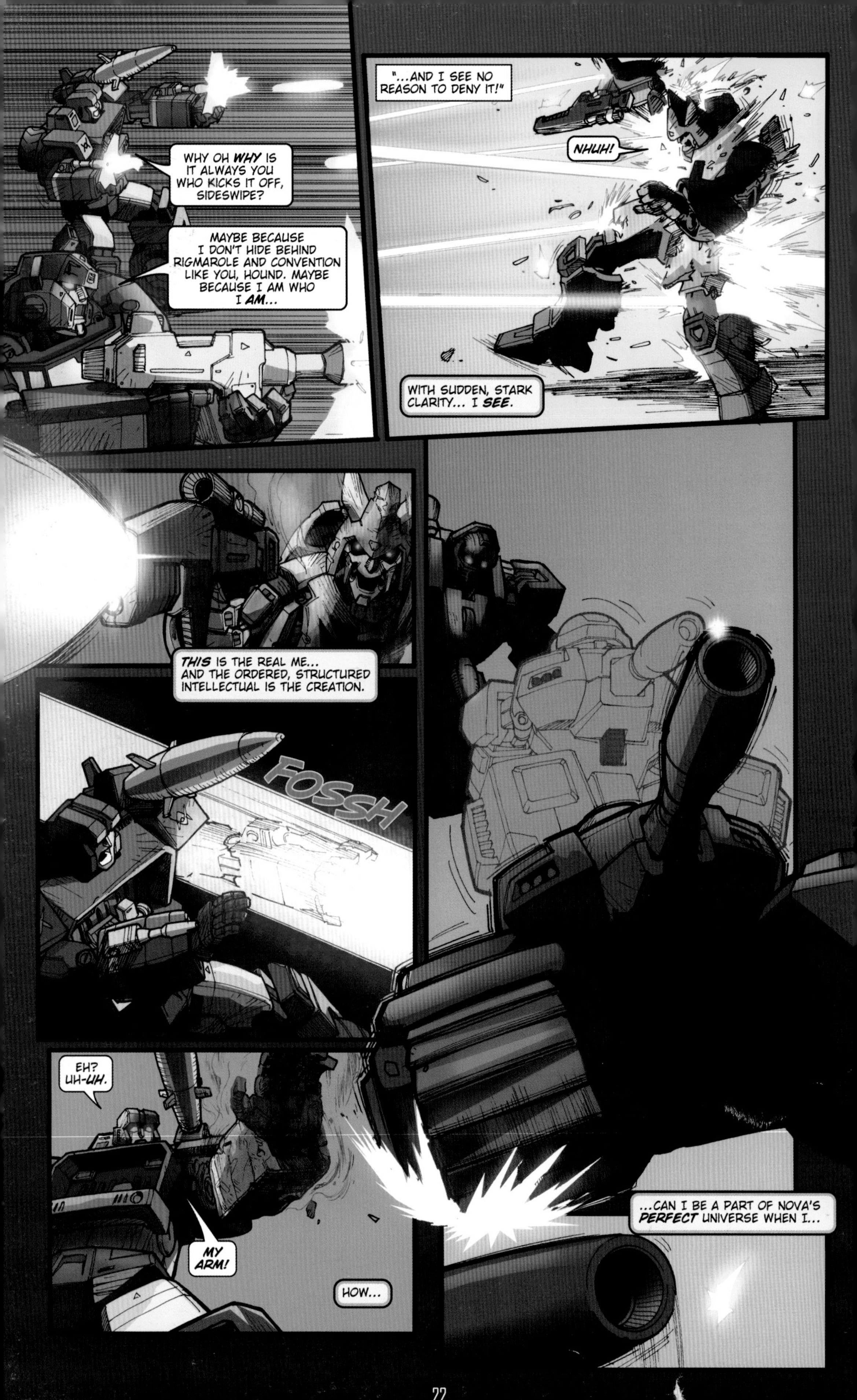
WHY OH *WHY* IS IT ALWAYS YOU WHO KICKS IT OFF, SIDESWIPE?
MAYBE BECAUSE I DON'T HIDE BEHIND RIGMAROLE AND CONVENTION LIKE YOU, HOUND. MAYBE BECAUSE I AM WHO I *AM*...
"...AND I SEE NO REASON TO DENY IT!"
NHUH!
WITH SUDDEN, STARK CLARITY... I *SEE*.
THIS IS THE REAL ME... AND THE ORDERED, STRUCTURED INTELLECTUAL IS THE CREATION.
FOSSH
EH? UH-*UH*.
MY ARM!
HOW...
...CAN I BE A PART OF NOVA'S *PERFECT* UNIVERSE WHEN I...

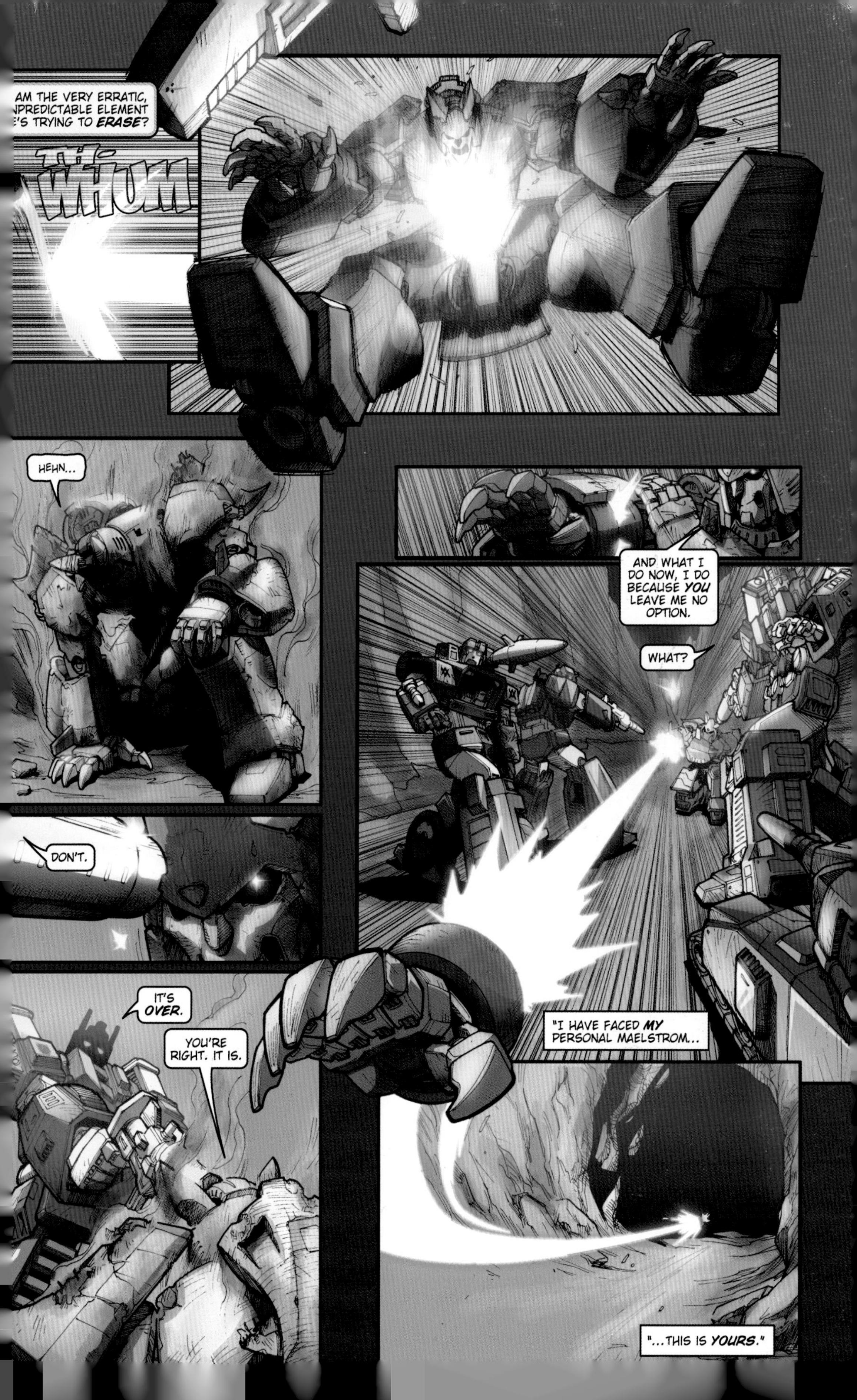

AM THE VERY ERRATIC, NPREDICTABLE ELEMENT E'S TRYING TO ERASE?
WHUM
HEHN...
AND WHAT I DO NOW, I DO BECAUSE YOU LEAVE ME NO OPTION.
WHAT?
DON'T.
IT'S OVER.
YOU'RE RIGHT. IT IS.
"I HAVE FACED MY PERSONAL MAELSTROM...
"...THIS IS YOURS."

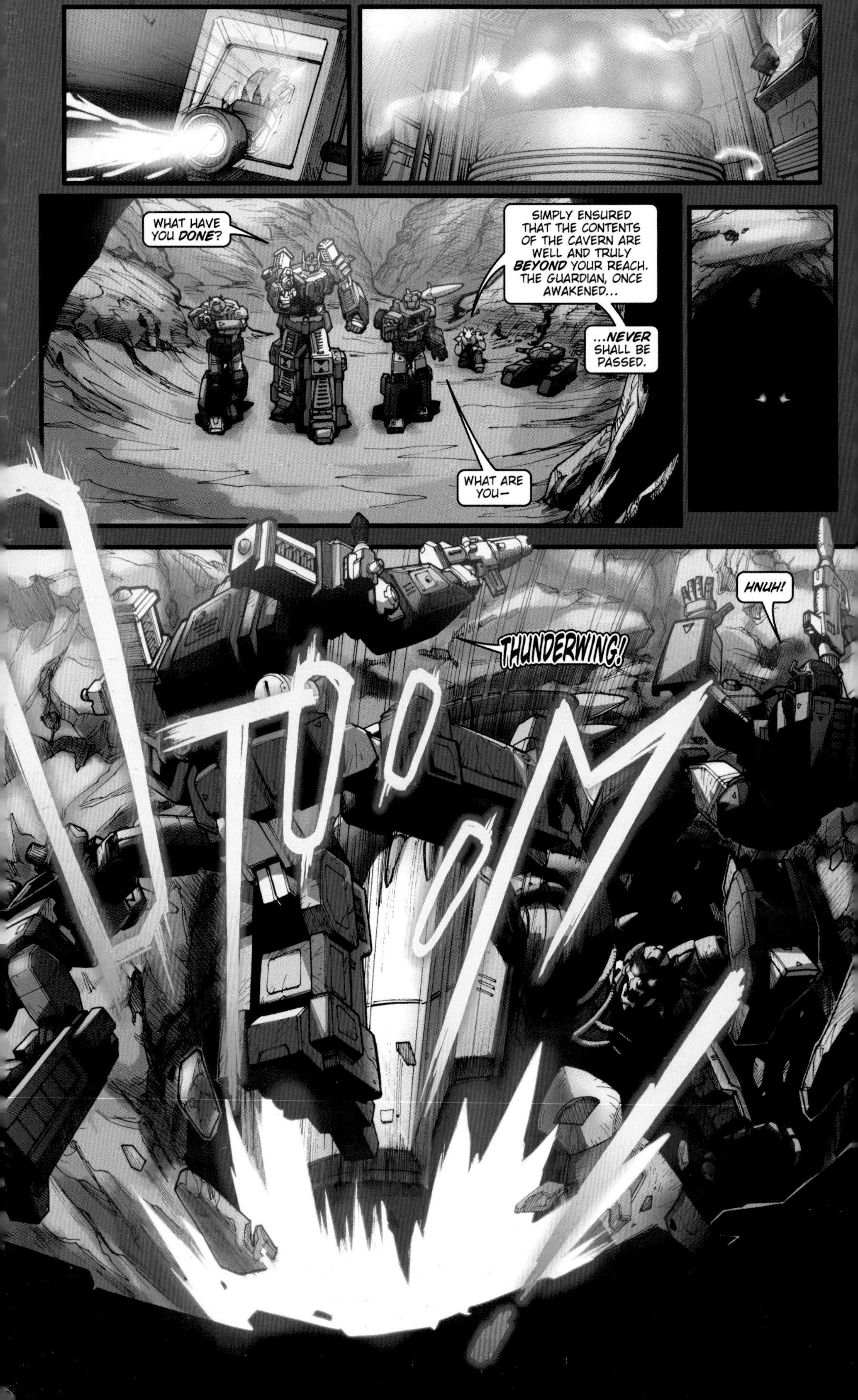
WHAT HAVE YOU DONE?
SIMPLY ENSURED THAT THE CONTENTS OF THE CAVERN ARE WELL AND TRULY BEYOND YOUR REACH. THE GUARDIAN, ONCE AWAKENED...
...NEVER SHALL BE PASSED.
WHAT ARE YOU–
THUNDERWING!
HNUH!
TOOOM

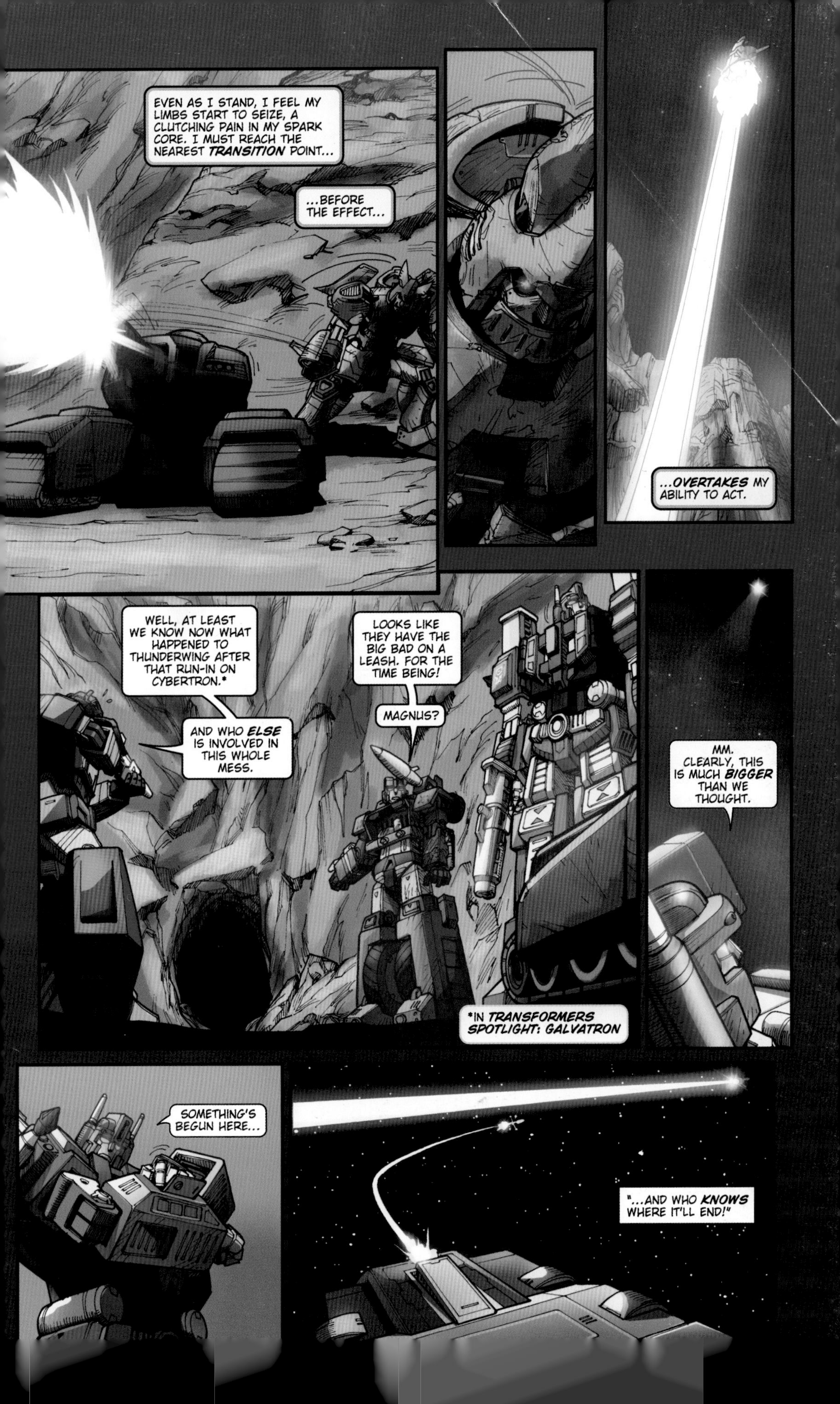
EVEN AS I STAND, I FEEL MY LIMBS START TO SEIZE, A CLUTCHING PAIN IN MY SPARK CORE. I MUST REACH THE NEAREST TRANSITION POINT...
...BEFORE THE EFFECT...
...OVERTAKES MY ABILITY TO ACT.
WELL, AT LEAST WE KNOW NOW WHAT HAPPENED TO THUNDERWING AFTER THAT RUN-IN ON CYBERTRON.*
AND WHO ELSE IS INVOLVED IN THIS WHOLE MESS.
LOOKS LIKE THEY HAVE THE BIG BAD ON A LEASH. FOR THE TIME BEING!
MAGNUS?
MM. CLEARLY, THIS IS MUCH BIGGER THAN WE THOUGHT.
*IN TRANSFORMERS SPOTLIGHT: GALVATRON
SOMETHING'S BEGUN HERE...
"...AND WHO KNOWS WHERE IT'LL END!"

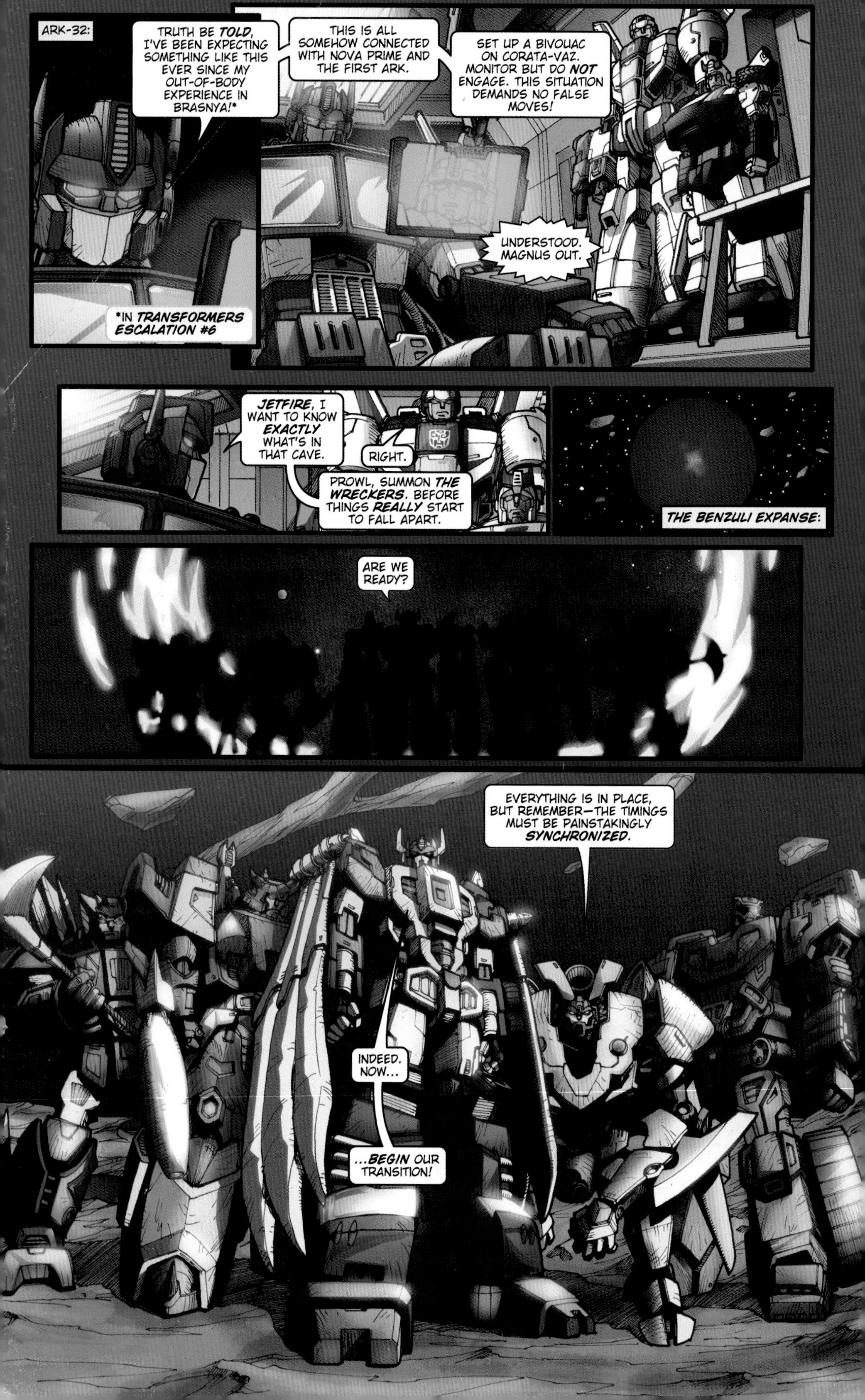

ARK-32:
TRUTH BE TOLD, I'VE BEEN EXPECTING SOMETHING LIKE THIS EVER SINCE MY OUT-OF-BODY EXPERIENCE IN BRASNYA!*
THIS IS ALL SOMEHOW CONNECTED WITH NOVA PRIME AND THE FIRST ARK.
SET UP A BIVOUAC ON CORATA-VAZ. MONITOR BUT DO NOT ENGAGE. THIS SITUATION DEMANDS NO FALSE MOVES!
UNDERSTOOD. MAGNUS OUT.
*IN TRANSFORMERS ESCALATION #6
JETFIRE, I WANT TO KNOW EXACTLY WHAT'S IN THAT CAVE.
RIGHT.
PROWL, SUMMON THE WRECKERS. BEFORE THINGS REALLY START TO FALL APART.
THE BENZULI EXPANSE:
ARE WE READY?
EVERYTHING IS IN PLACE, BUT REMEMBER—THE TIMINGS MUST BE PAINSTAKINGLY SYNCHRONIZED.
INDEED. NOW...
...BEGIN OUR TRANSITION!

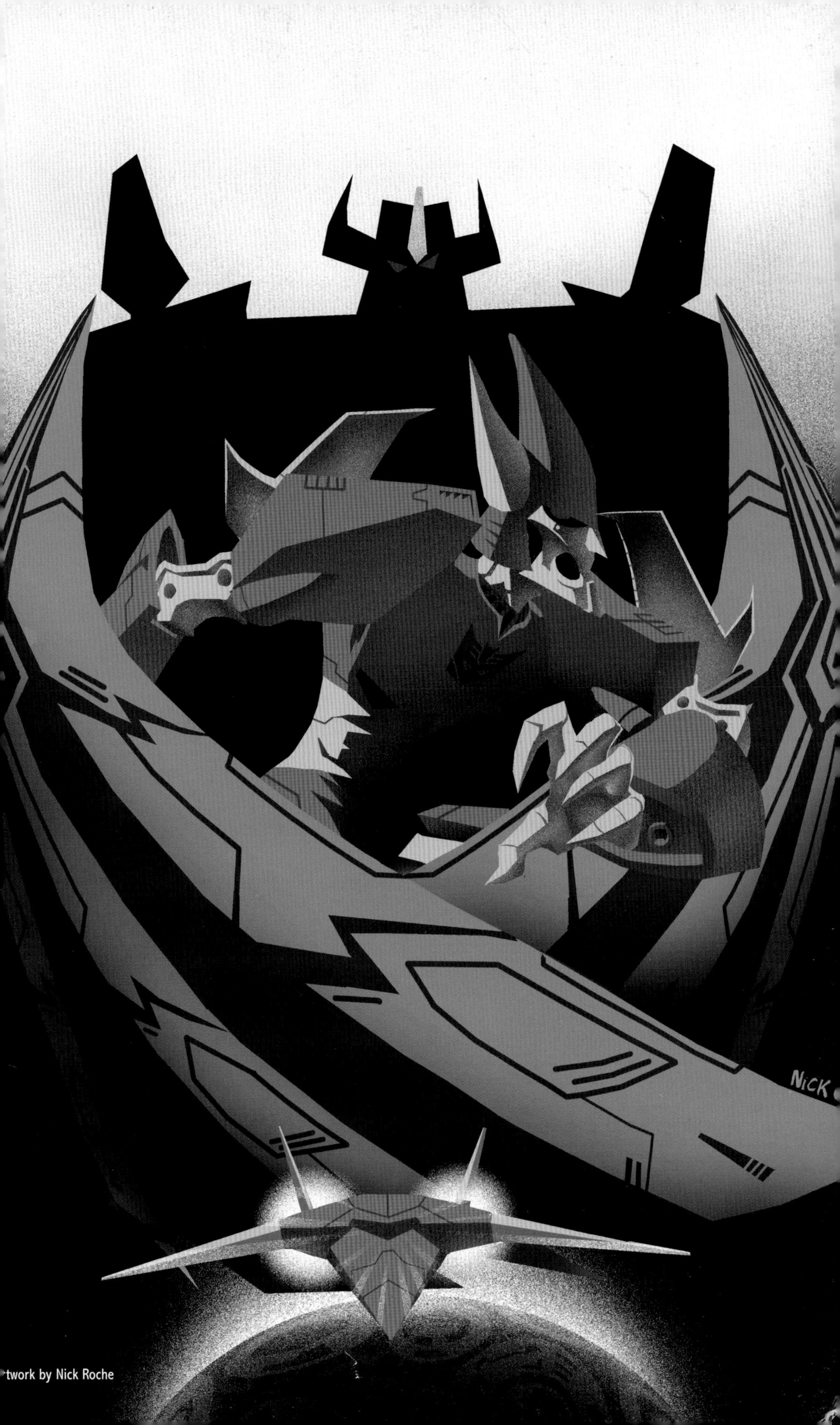
NICK

twork by Nick Roche

HARDHEAD

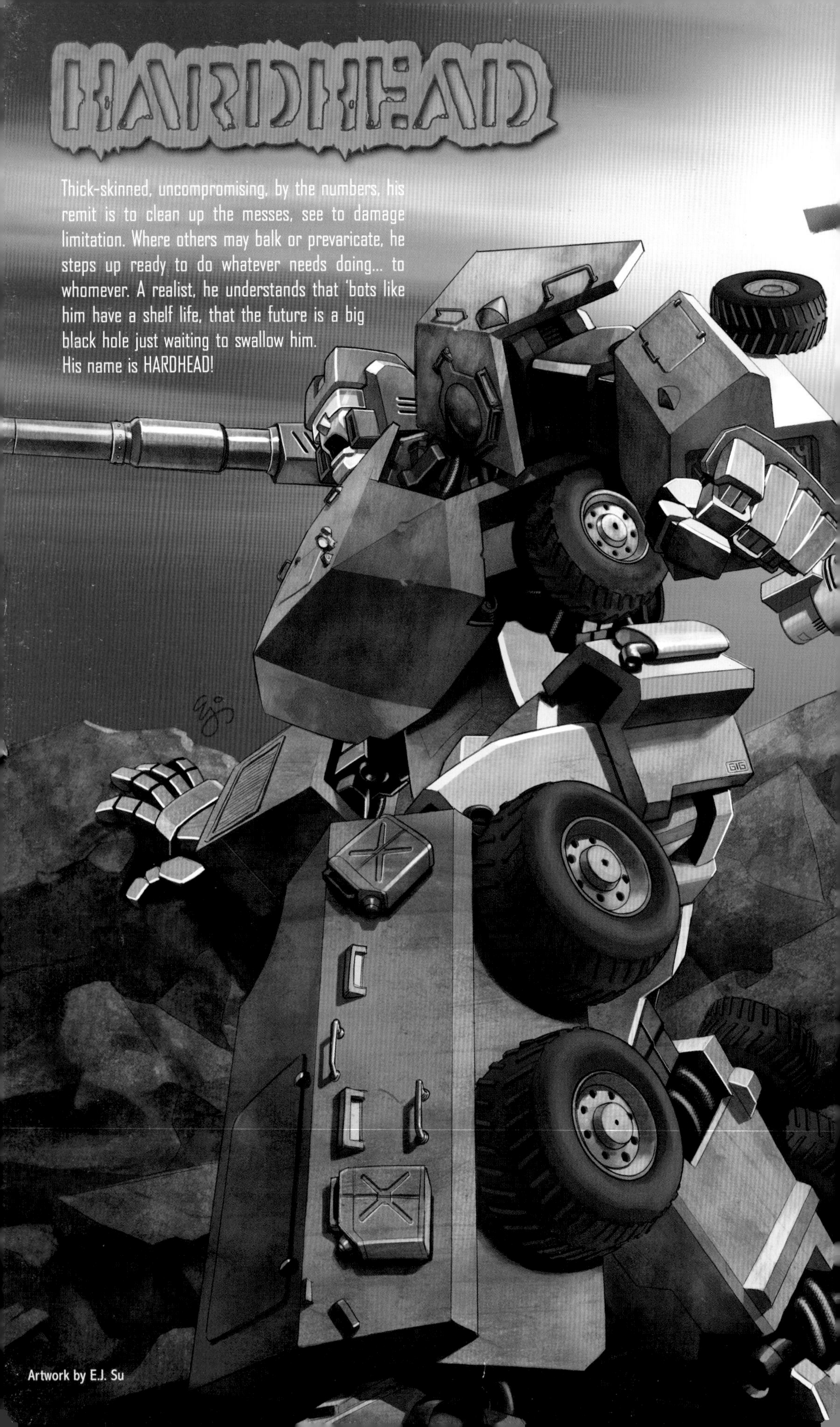

Thick-skinned, uncompromising, by the numbers, his remit is to clean up the messes, see to damage limitation. Where others may balk or prevaricate, he steps up ready to do whatever needs doing... to whomever. A realist, he understands that 'bots like him have a shelf life, that the future is a big black hole just waiting to swallow him.

His name is HARDHEAD!

Artwork by E.J. Su

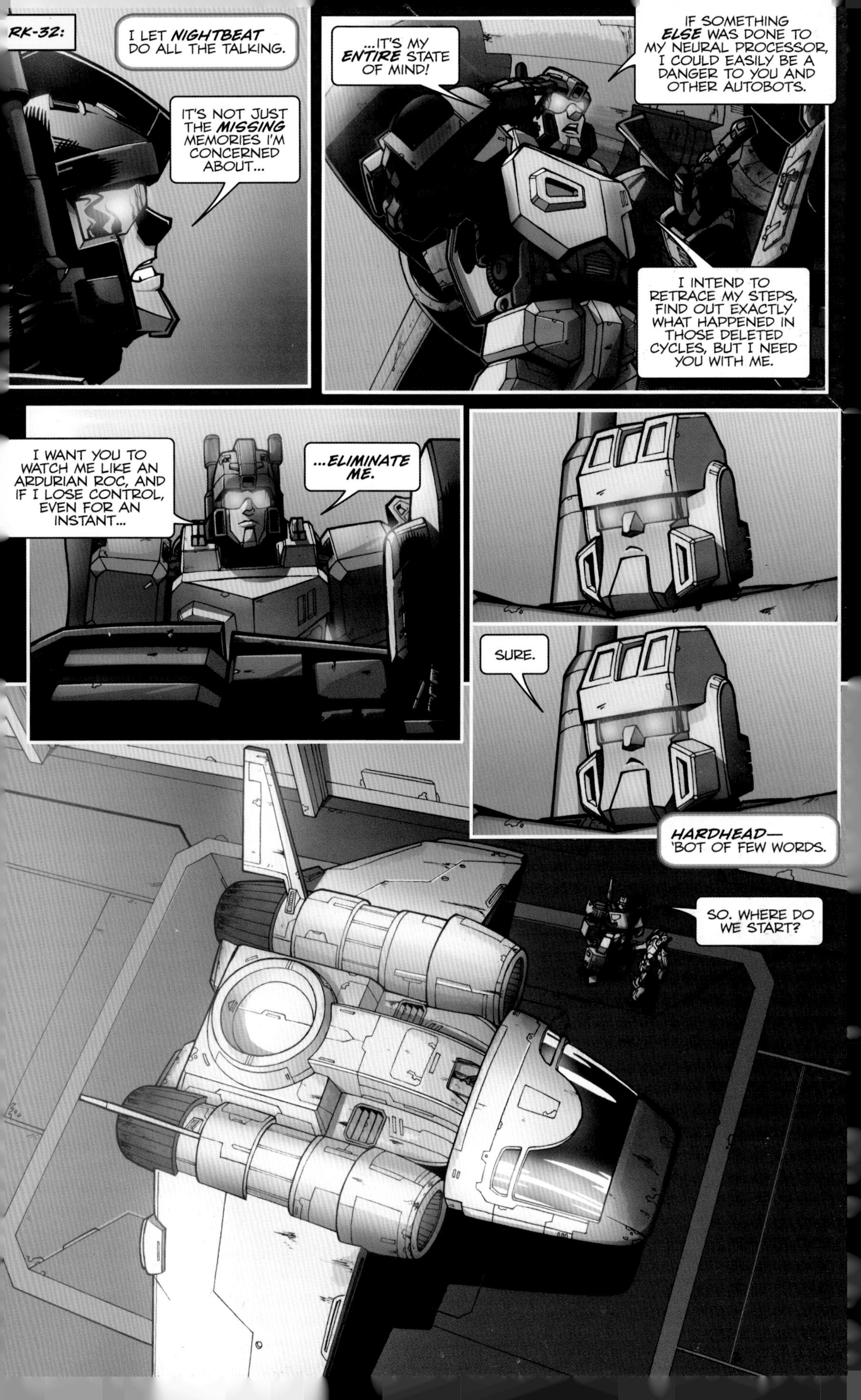
RK-32:
I LET NIGHTBEAT DO ALL THE TALKING.
IT'S NOT JUST THE MISSING MEMORIES I'M CONCERNED ABOUT...
...IT'S MY ENTIRE STATE OF MIND!
IF SOMETHING ELSE WAS DONE TO MY NEURAL PROCESSOR, I COULD EASILY BE A DANGER TO YOU AND OTHER AUTOBOTS.
I INTEND TO RETRACE MY STEPS, FIND OUT EXACTLY WHAT HAPPENED IN THOSE DELETED CYCLES, BUT I NEED YOU WITH ME.
I WANT YOU TO WATCH ME LIKE AN ARDURIAN ROC, AND IF I LOSE CONTROL, EVEN FOR AN INSTANT...
...ELIMINATE ME.
SURE.
HARDHEAD— 'BOT OF FEW WORDS.
SO. WHERE DO WE START?

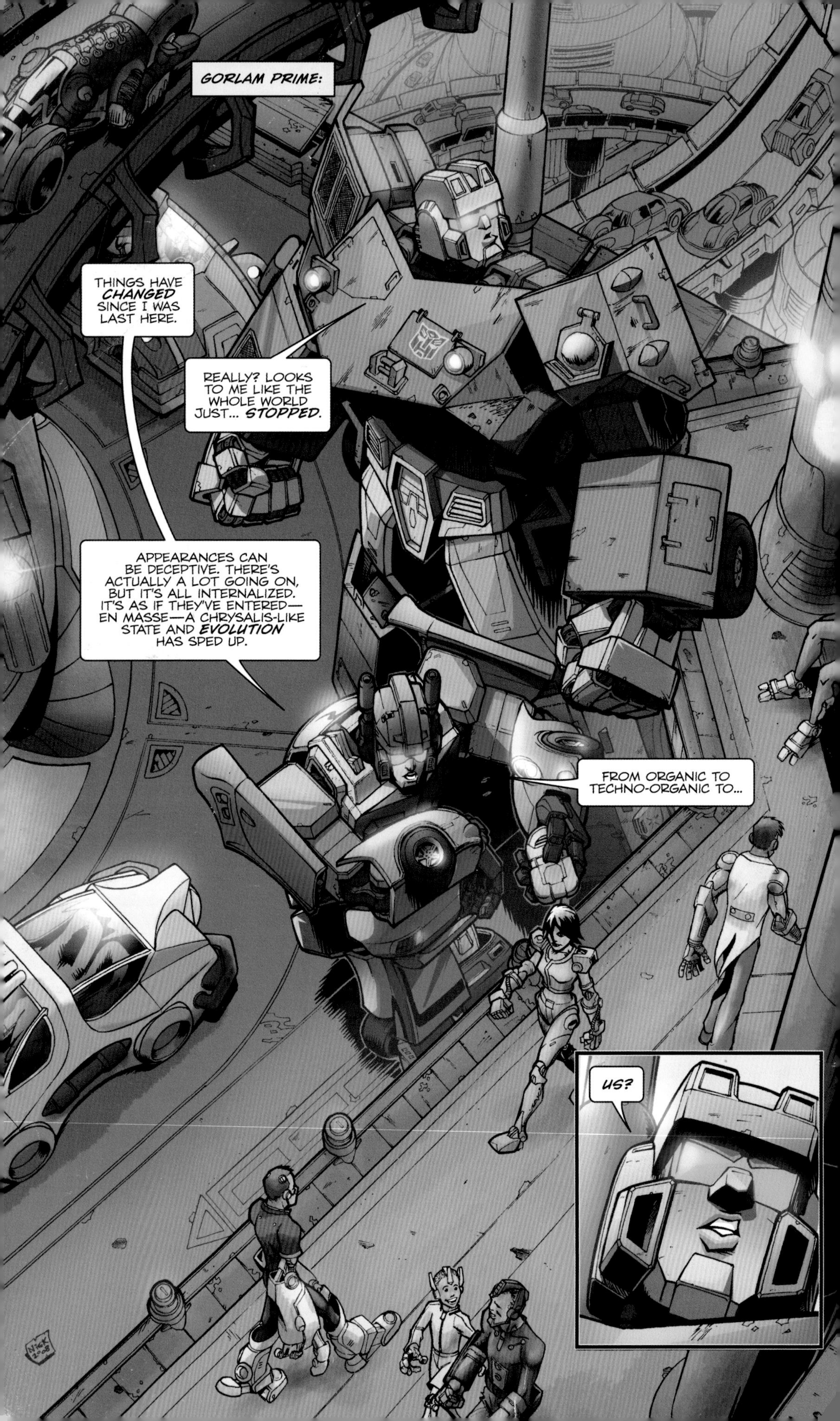
GORLAM PRIME:
THINGS HAVE CHANGED SINCE I WAS LAST HERE.
REALLY? LOOKS TO ME LIKE THE WHOLE WORLD JUST... STOPPED.
APPEARANCES CAN BE DECEPTIVE. THERE'S ACTUALLY A LOT GOING ON, BUT IT'S ALL INTERNALIZED. IT'S AS IF THEY'VE ENTERED—EN MASSE—A CHRYSALIS-LIKE STATE AND EVOLUTION HAS SPED UP.
FROM ORGANIC TO TECHNO-ORGANIC TO...
US?

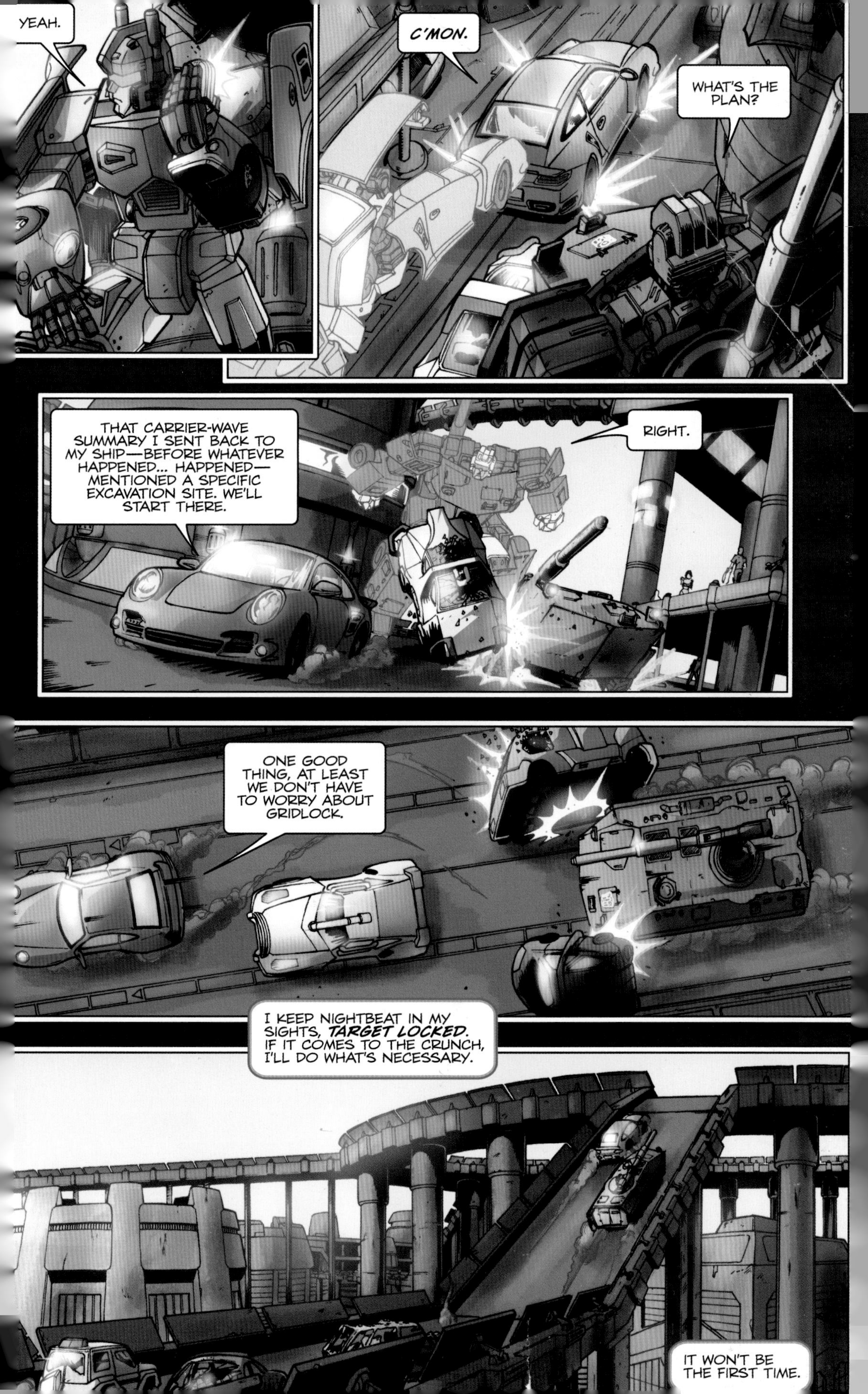

YEAH.
C'MON.
WHAT'S THE PLAN?
THAT CARRIER-WAVE SUMMARY I SENT BACK TO MY SHIP—BEFORE WHATEVER HAPPENED... HAPPENED—MENTIONED A SPECIFIC EXCAVATION SITE. WE'LL START THERE.
RIGHT.
ONE GOOD THING, AT LEAST WE DON'T HAVE TO WORRY ABOUT GRIDLOCK.
I KEEP NIGHTBEAT IN MY SIGHTS, ***TARGET LOCKED.*** IF IT COMES TO THE CRUNCH, I'LL DO WHAT'S NECESSARY.
IT WON'T BE THE FIRST TIME.

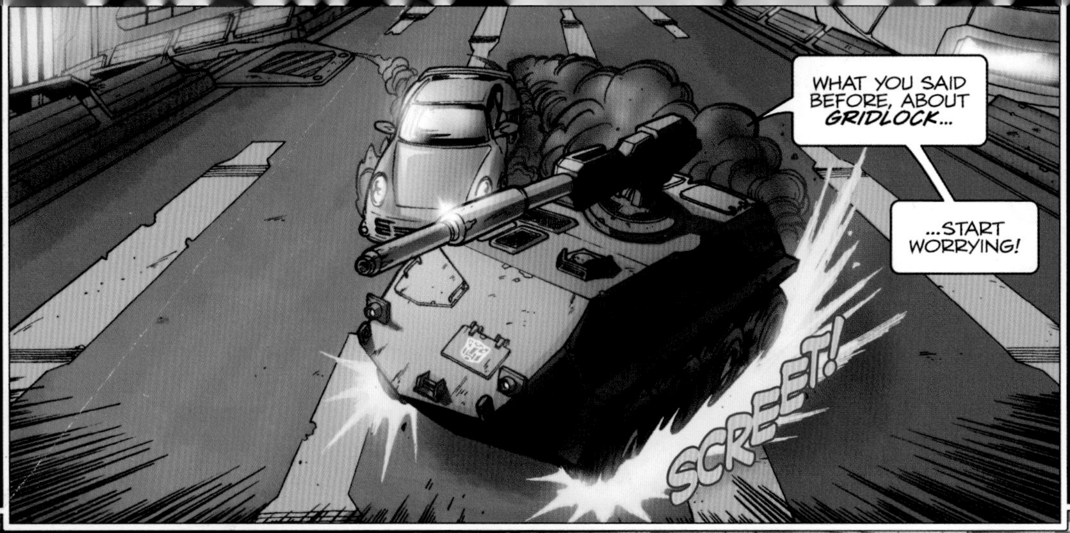
WHAT YOU SAID BEFORE, ABOUT GRIDLOCK...
...START WORRYING!
SCREEET!

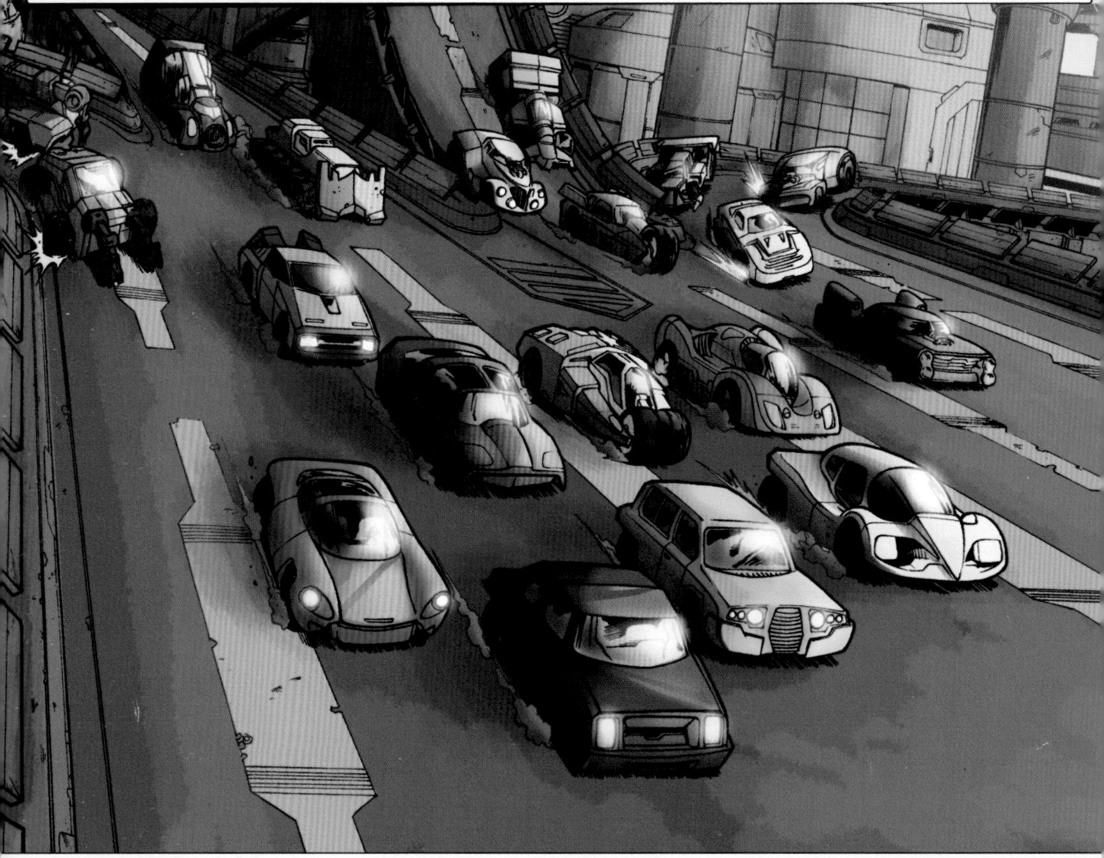

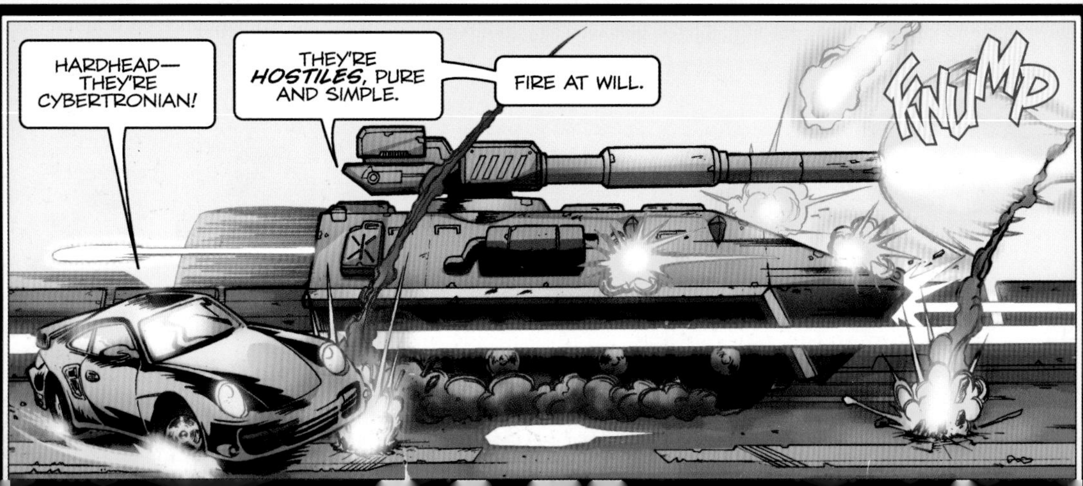
HARDHEAD— THEY'RE CYBERTRONIAN!
THEY'RE HOSTILES, PURE AND SIMPLE.
FIRE AT WILL.
FWUMP

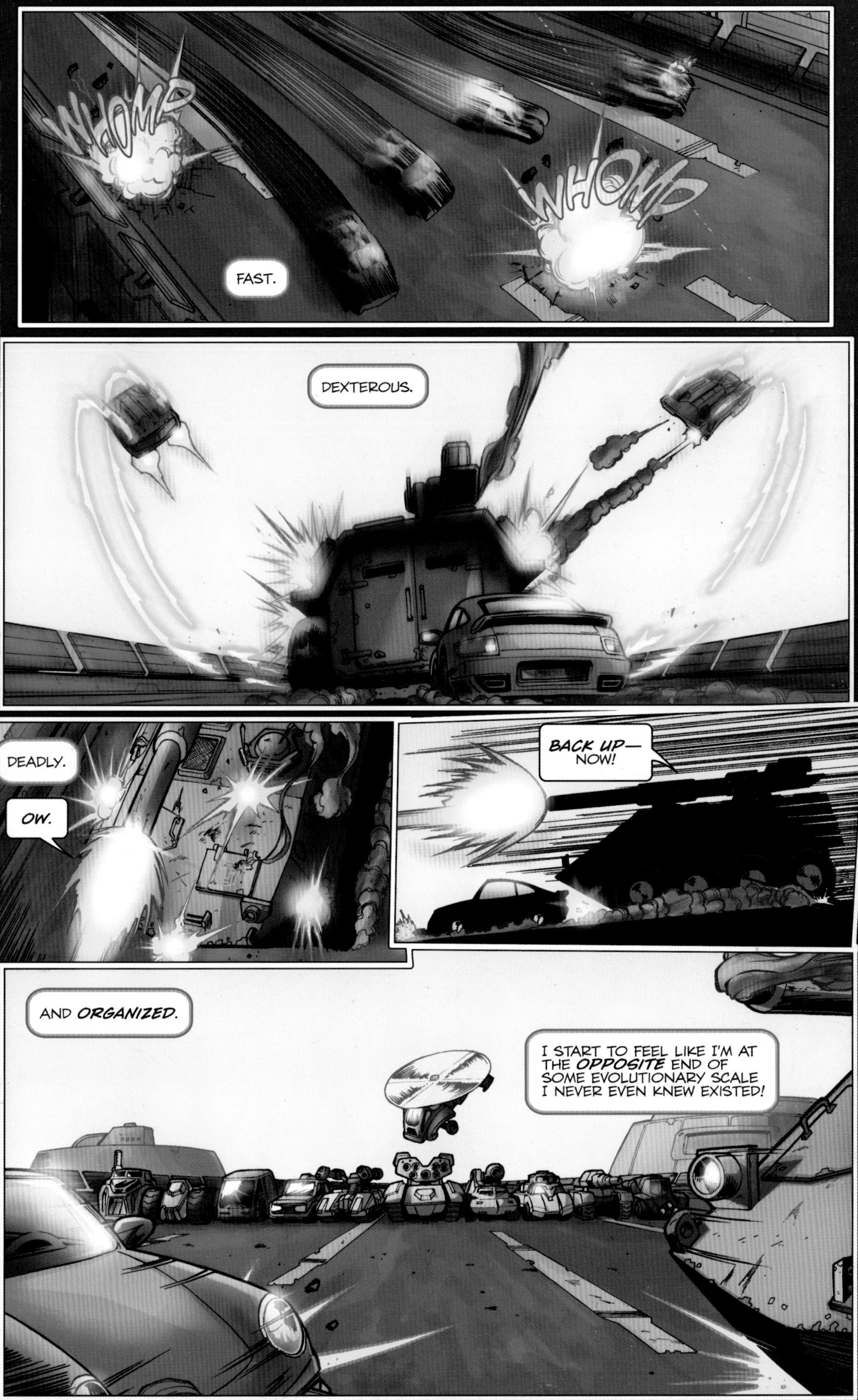
WHOMP
FAST.
WHOMP
DEXTEROUS.
DEADLY.
OW.
BACK UP— NOW!
AND ORGANIZED.
I START TO FEEL LIKE I'M AT THE OPPOSITE END OF SOME EVOLUTIONARY SCALE I NEVER EVEN KNEW EXISTED!

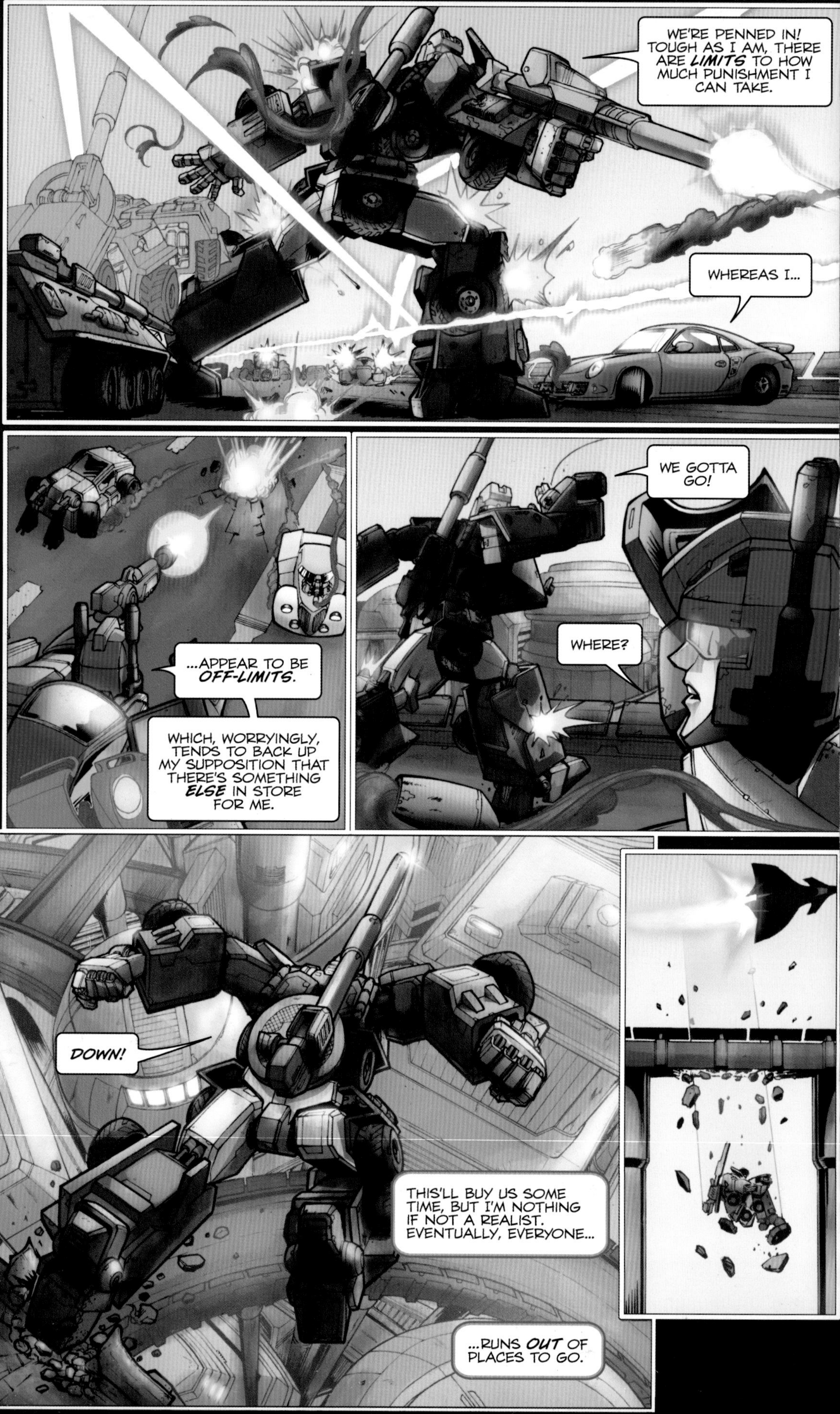
WE'RE PENNED IN! TOUGH AS I AM, THERE ARE LIMITS TO HOW MUCH PUNISHMENT I CAN TAKE.
WHEREAS I...
...APPEAR TO BE OFF-LIMITS.
WHICH, WORRYINGLY, TENDS TO BACK UP MY SUPPOSITION THAT THERE'S SOMETHING ELSE IN STORE FOR ME.
WE GOTTA GO!
WHERE?
DOWN!
THIS'LL BUY US SOME TIME, BUT I'M NOTHING IF NOT A REALIST. EVENTUALLY, EVERYONE...
...RUNS OUT OF PLACES TO GO.

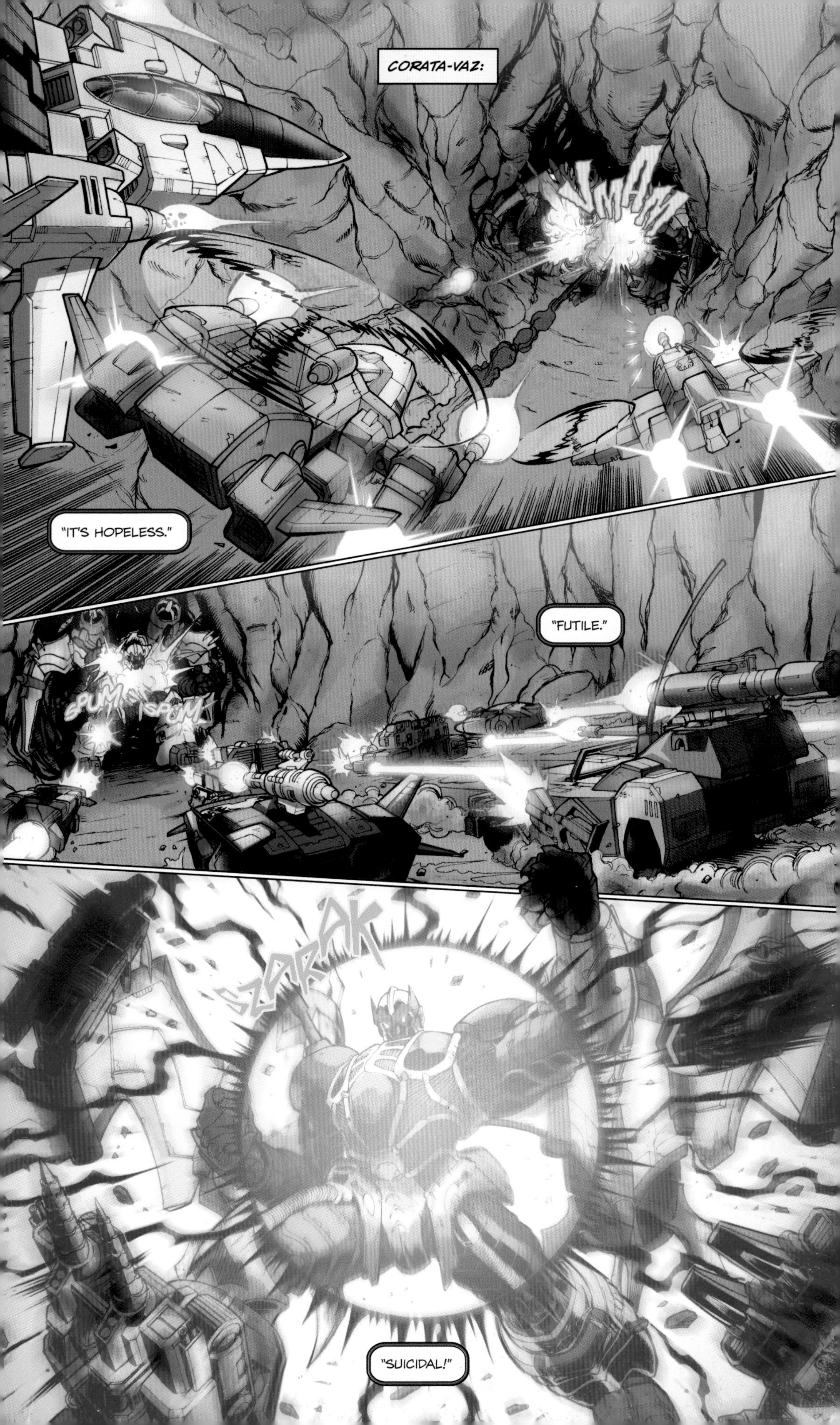
CORATA-VAZ:
"IT'S HOPELESS."
"FUTILE."
SPUM SPUM
"SUICIDAL!"

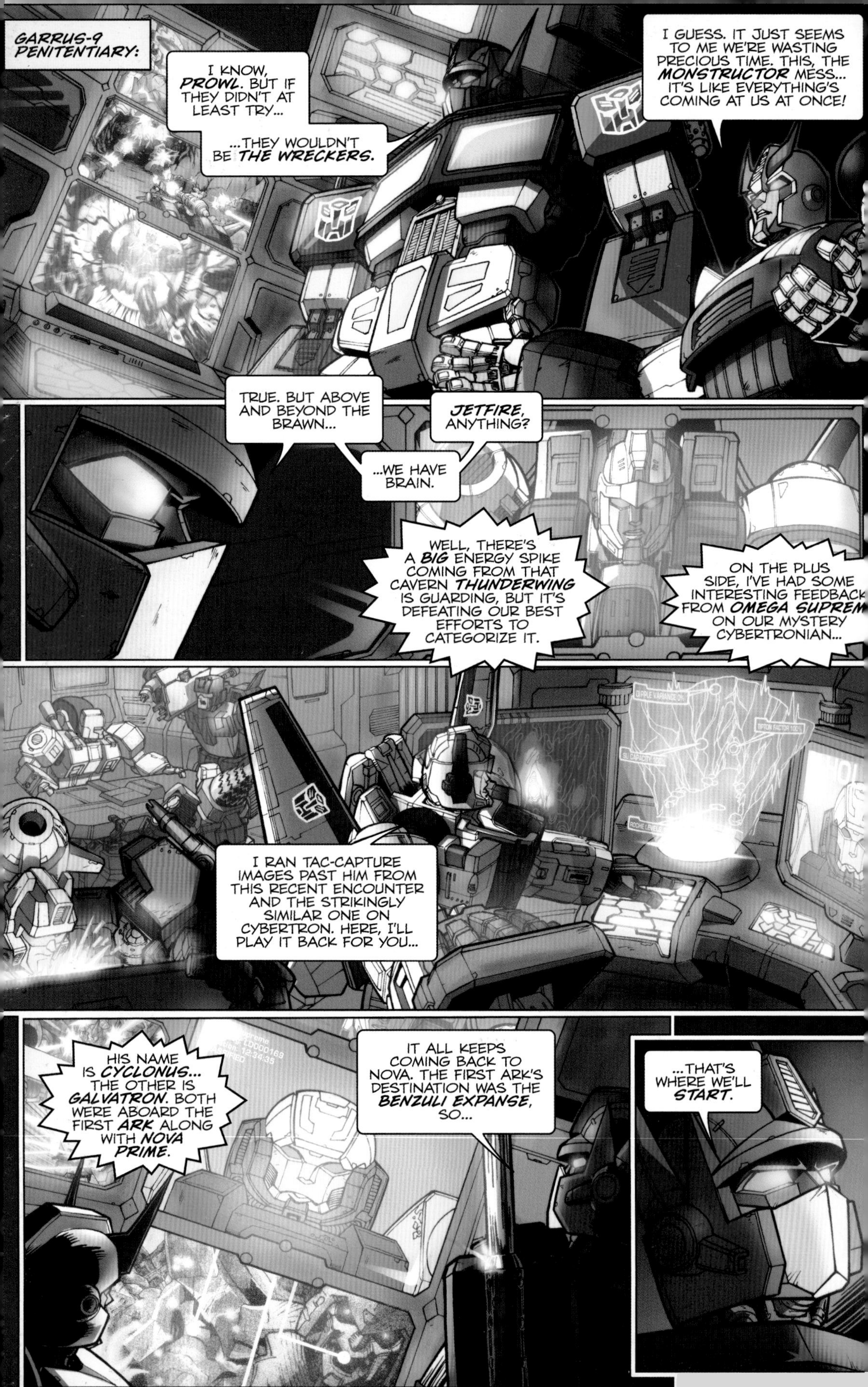
GARRUS-9 PENITENTIARY:
I KNOW, PROWL. BUT IF THEY DIDN'T AT LEAST TRY...
...THEY WOULDN'T BE THE WRECKERS.
I GUESS. IT JUST SEEMS TO ME WE'RE WASTING PRECIOUS TIME. THIS, THE MONSTRUCTOR MESS... IT'S LIKE EVERYTHING'S COMING AT US AT ONCE!
TRUE. BUT ABOVE AND BEYOND THE BRAWN...
...WE HAVE BRAIN.
JETFIRE, ANYTHING?
WELL, THERE'S A BIG ENERGY SPIKE COMING FROM THAT CAVERN THUNDERWING IS GUARDING, BUT IT'S DEFEATING OUR BEST EFFORTS TO CATEGORIZE IT.
ON THE PLUS SIDE, I'VE HAD SOME INTERESTING FEEDBACK FROM OMEGA SUPREME ON OUR MYSTERY CYBERTRONIAN...
I RAN TAC-CAPTURE IMAGES PAST HIM FROM THIS RECENT ENCOUNTER AND THE STRIKINGLY SIMILAR ONE ON CYBERTRON. HERE, I'LL PLAY IT BACK FOR YOU...
HIS NAME IS CYCLONUS... THE OTHER IS GALVATRON. BOTH WERE ABOARD THE FIRST ARK ALONG WITH NOVA PRIME.
IT ALL KEEPS COMING BACK TO NOVA. THE FIRST ARK'S DESTINATION WAS THE BENZULI EXPANSE, SO...
...THAT'S WHERE WE'LL START.

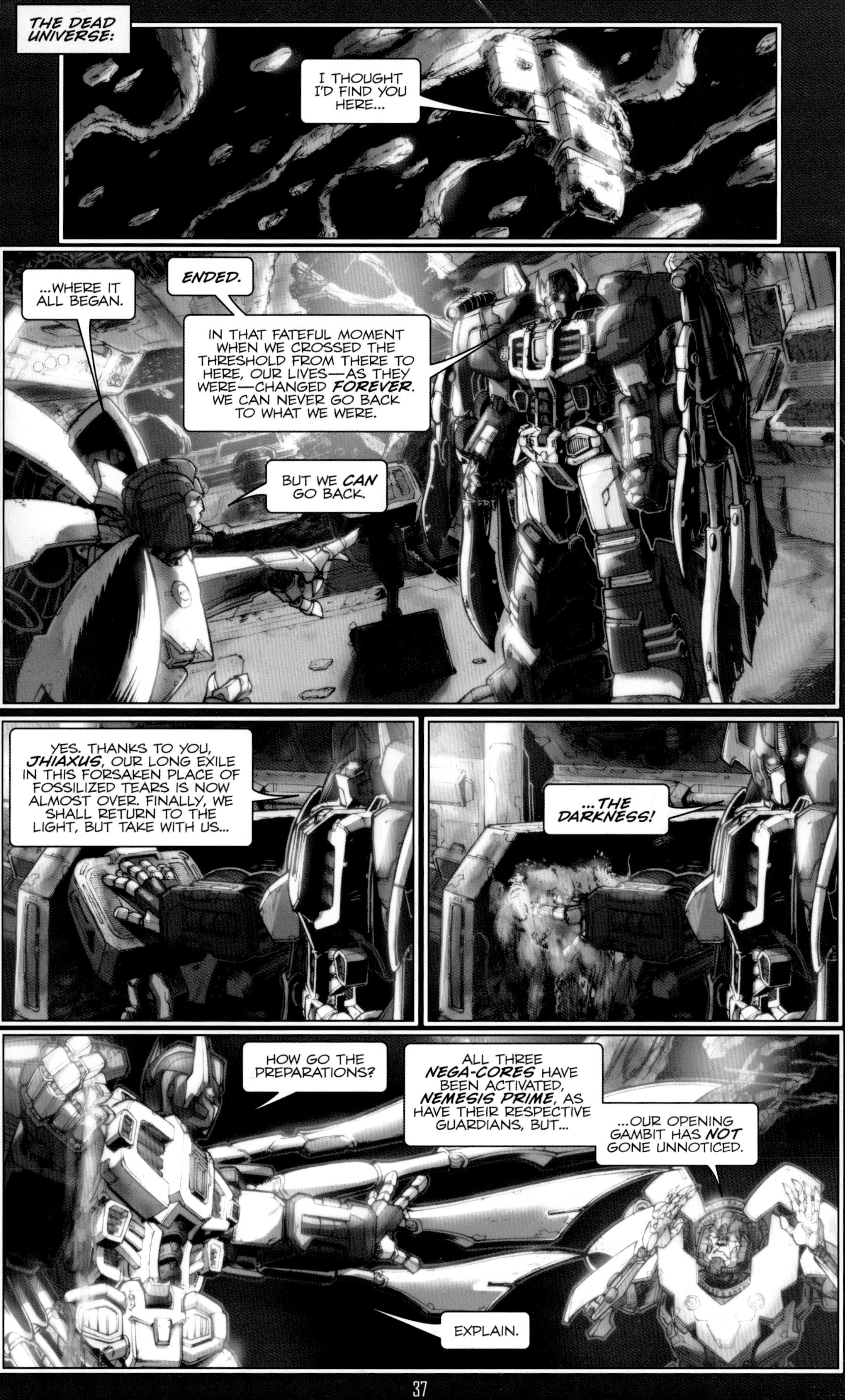
THE DEAD UNIVERSE:
I THOUGHT I'D FIND YOU HERE...
...WHERE IT ALL BEGAN.
ENDED.
IN THAT FATEFUL MOMENT WHEN WE CROSSED THE THRESHOLD FROM THERE TO HERE, OUR LIVES—AS THEY WERE—CHANGED FOREVER. WE CAN NEVER GO BACK TO WHAT WE WERE.
BUT WE CAN GO BACK.
YES. THANKS TO YOU, JHIAXUS, OUR LONG EXILE IN THIS FORSAKEN PLACE OF FOSSILIZED TEARS IS NOW ALMOST OVER. FINALLY, WE SHALL RETURN TO THE LIGHT, BUT TAKE WITH US...
...THE DARKNESS!
HOW GO THE PREPARATIONS?
ALL THREE NEGA-CORES HAVE BEEN ACTIVATED, NEMESIS PRIME, AS HAVE THEIR RESPECTIVE GUARDIANS, BUT...
...OUR OPENING GAMBIT HAS NOT GONE UNNOTICED.
EXPLAIN.

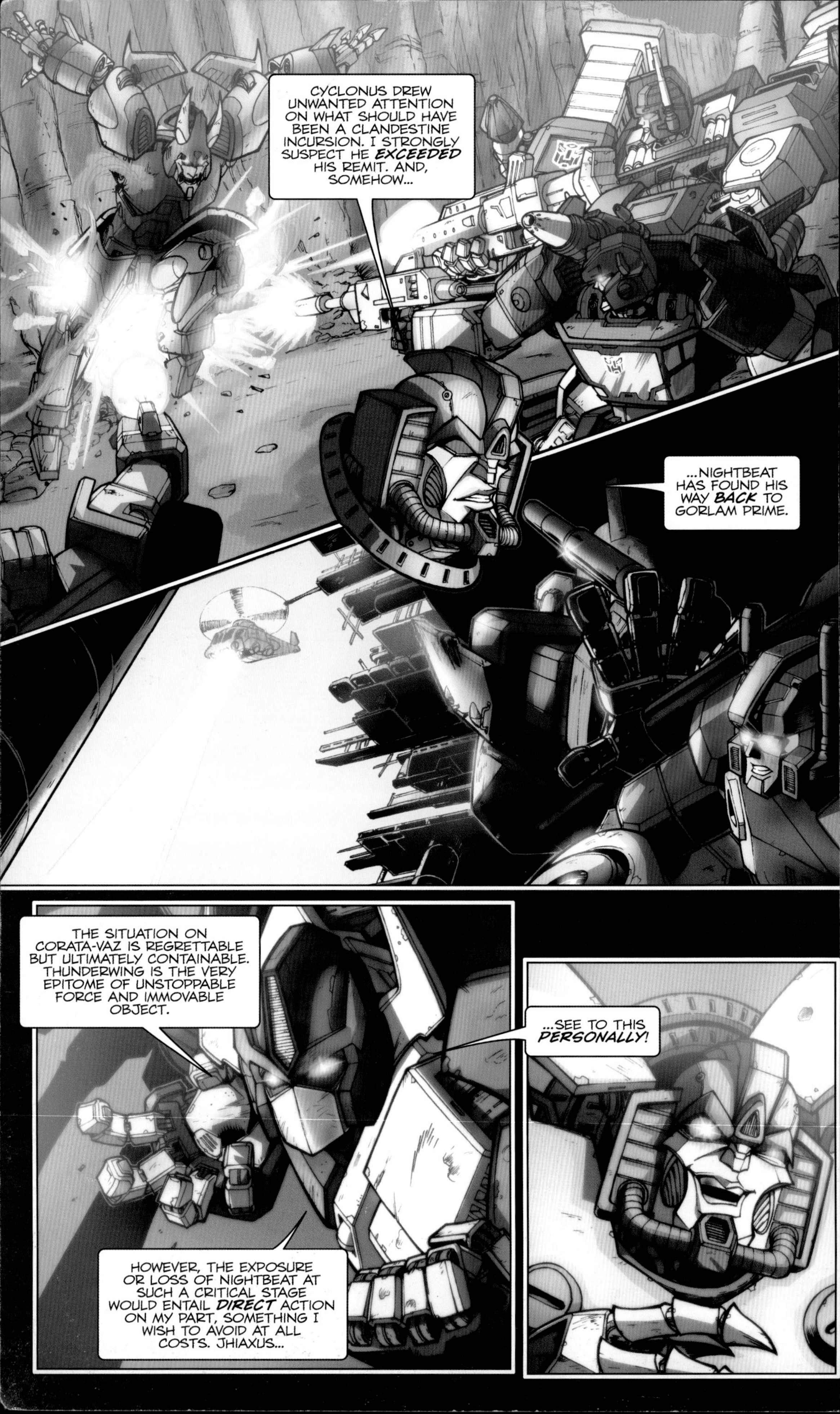

CYCLONUS DREW UNWANTED ATTENTION ON WHAT SHOULD HAVE BEEN A CLANDESTINE INCURSION. I STRONGLY SUSPECT HE EXCEEDED HIS REMIT. AND, SOMEHOW...
...NIGHTBEAT HAS FOUND HIS WAY BACK TO GORLAM PRIME.
THE SITUATION ON CORATA-VAZ IS REGRETTABLE BUT ULTIMATELY CONTAINABLE. THUNDERWING IS THE VERY EPITOME OF UNSTOPPABLE FORCE AND IMMOVABLE OBJECT.
HOWEVER, THE EXPOSURE OR LOSS OF NIGHTBEAT AT SUCH A CRITICAL STAGE WOULD ENTAIL DIRECT ACTION ON MY PART, SOMETHING I WISH TO AVOID AT ALL COSTS. JHIAXUS...
...SEE TO THIS PERSONALLY!

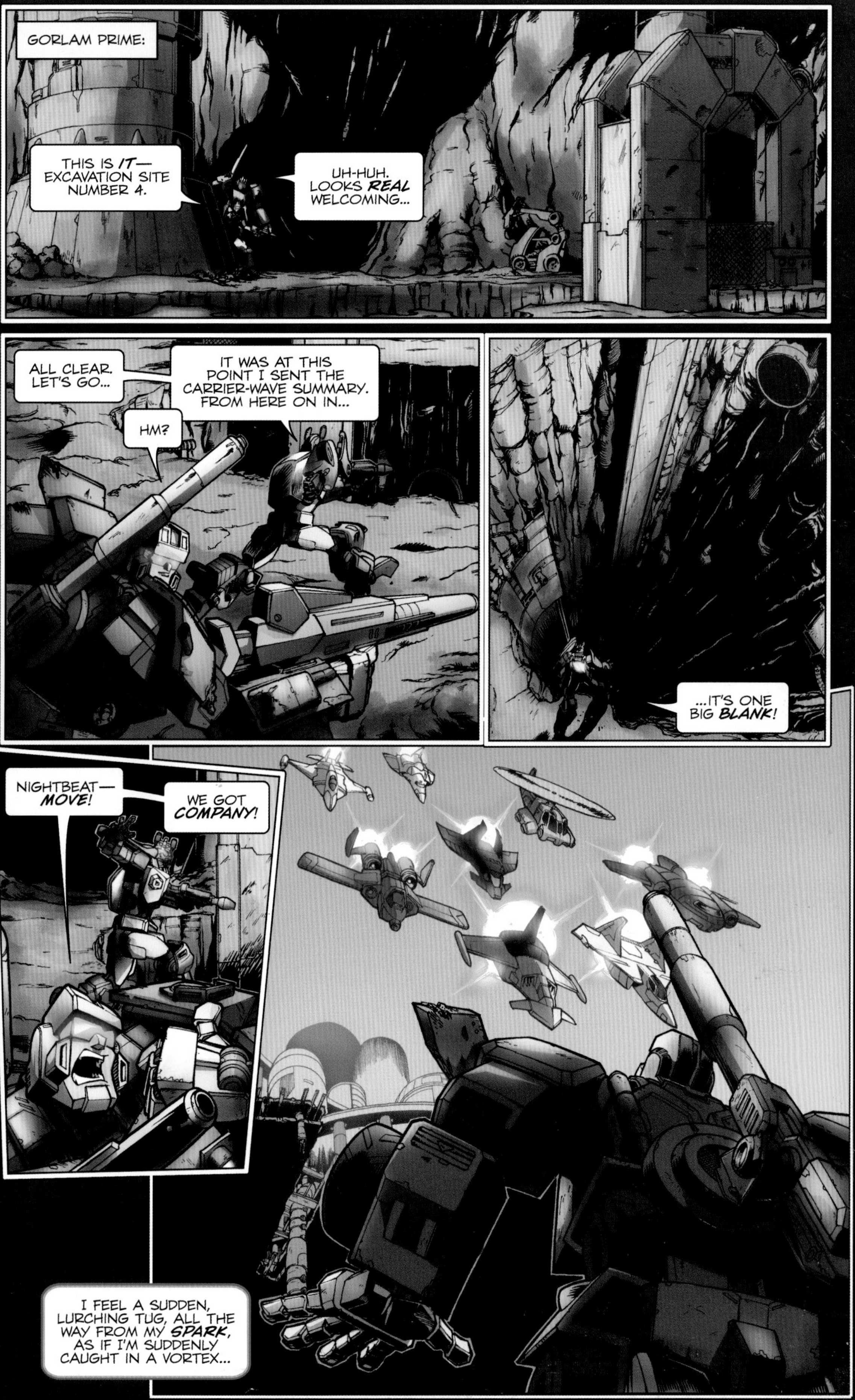
GORLAM PRIME:
THIS IS *IT*—EXCAVATION SITE NUMBER 4.
UH-HUH. LOOKS ***REAL*** WELCOMING...
ALL CLEAR. LET'S GO...
IT WAS AT THIS POINT I SENT THE CARRIER-WAVE SUMMARY. FROM HERE ON IN...
HM?
...IT'S ONE BIG ***BLANK***!
NIGHTBEAT—***MOVE***!
WE GOT ***COMPANY***!
I FEEL A SUDDEN, LURCHING TUG, ALL THE WAY FROM MY ***SPARK***, AS IF I'M SUDDENLY CAUGHT IN A VORTEX...

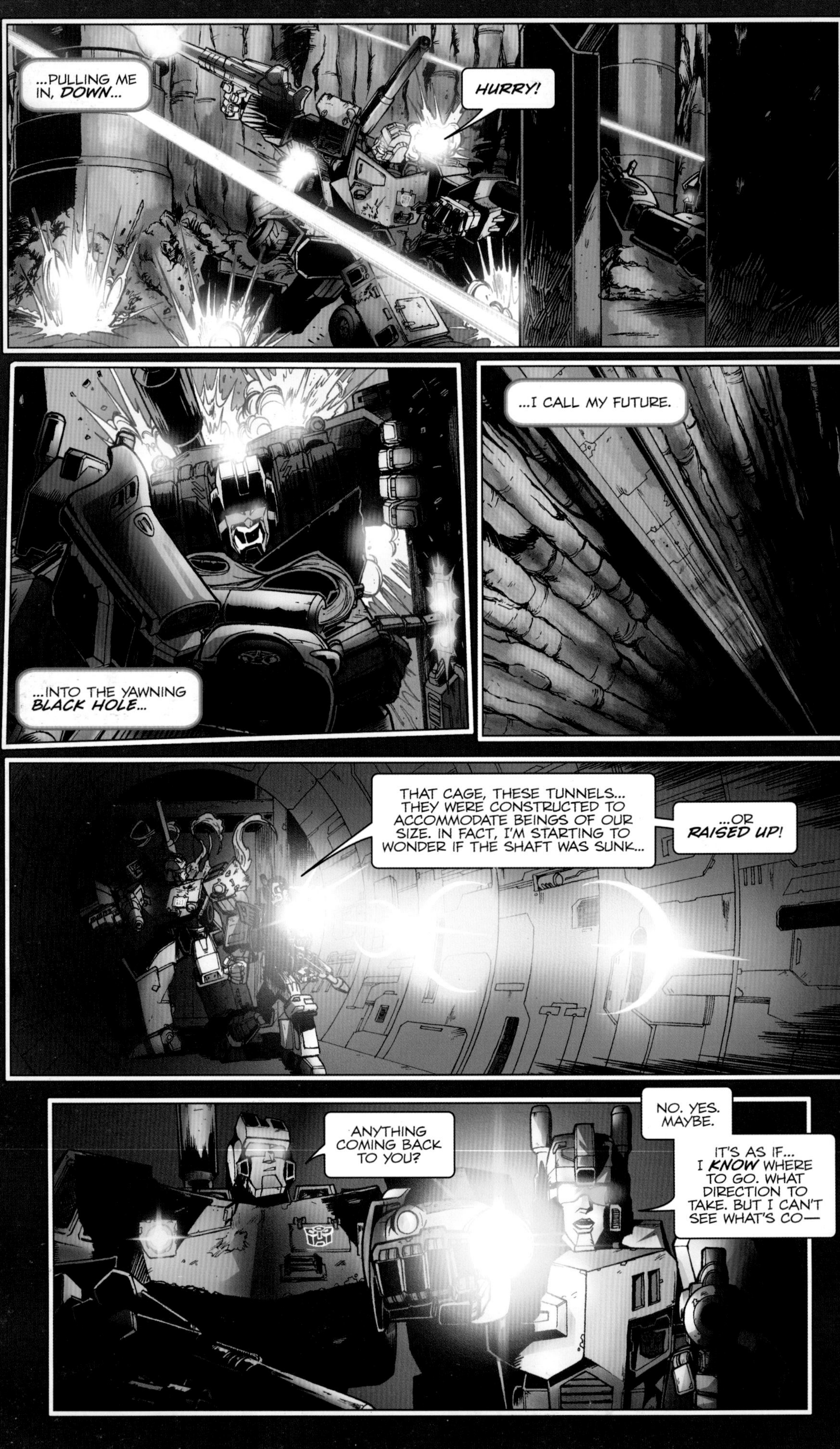
...PULLING ME IN, *DOWN*...
HURRY!
...INTO THE YAWNING *BLACK HOLE*...
...I CALL MY FUTURE.
THAT CAGE, THESE TUNNELS... THEY WERE CONSTRUCTED TO ACCOMMODATE BEINGS OF OUR SIZE. IN FACT, I'M STARTING TO WONDER IF THE SHAFT WAS SUNK...
...OR *RAISED UP!*
ANYTHING COMING BACK TO YOU?
NO. YES. MAYBE.
IT'S AS IF... I *KNOW* WHERE TO GO. WHAT DIRECTION TO TAKE. BUT I CAN'T SEE WHAT'S CO—

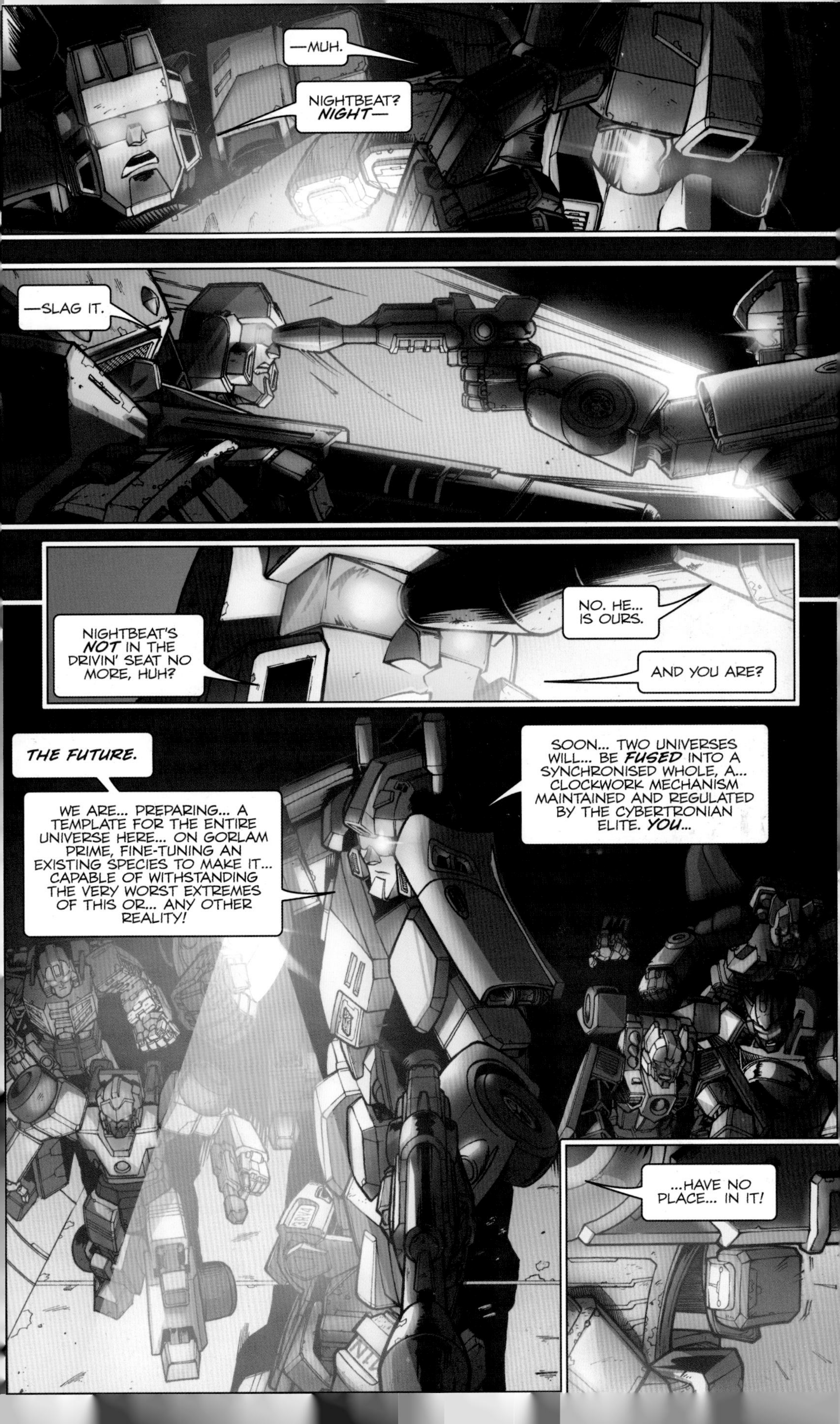
—MUH.
NIGHTBEAT? *NIGHT*—
—SLAG IT.
NIGHTBEAT'S *NOT* IN THE DRIVIN' SEAT NO MORE, HUH?
NO. HE... IS OURS.
AND YOU ARE?
THE FUTURE.
WE ARE... PREPARING... A TEMPLATE FOR THE ENTIRE UNIVERSE HERE... ON GORLAM PRIME, FINE-TUNING AN EXISTING SPECIES TO MAKE IT... CAPABLE OF WITHSTANDING THE VERY WORST EXTREMES OF THIS OR... ANY OTHER REALITY!
SOON... TWO UNIVERSES WILL... BE *FUSED* INTO A SYNCHRONISED WHOLE, A... CLOCKWORK MECHANISM MAINTAINED AND REGULATED BY THE CYBERTRONIAN ELITE. *YOU*...
...HAVE NO PLACE... IN IT!

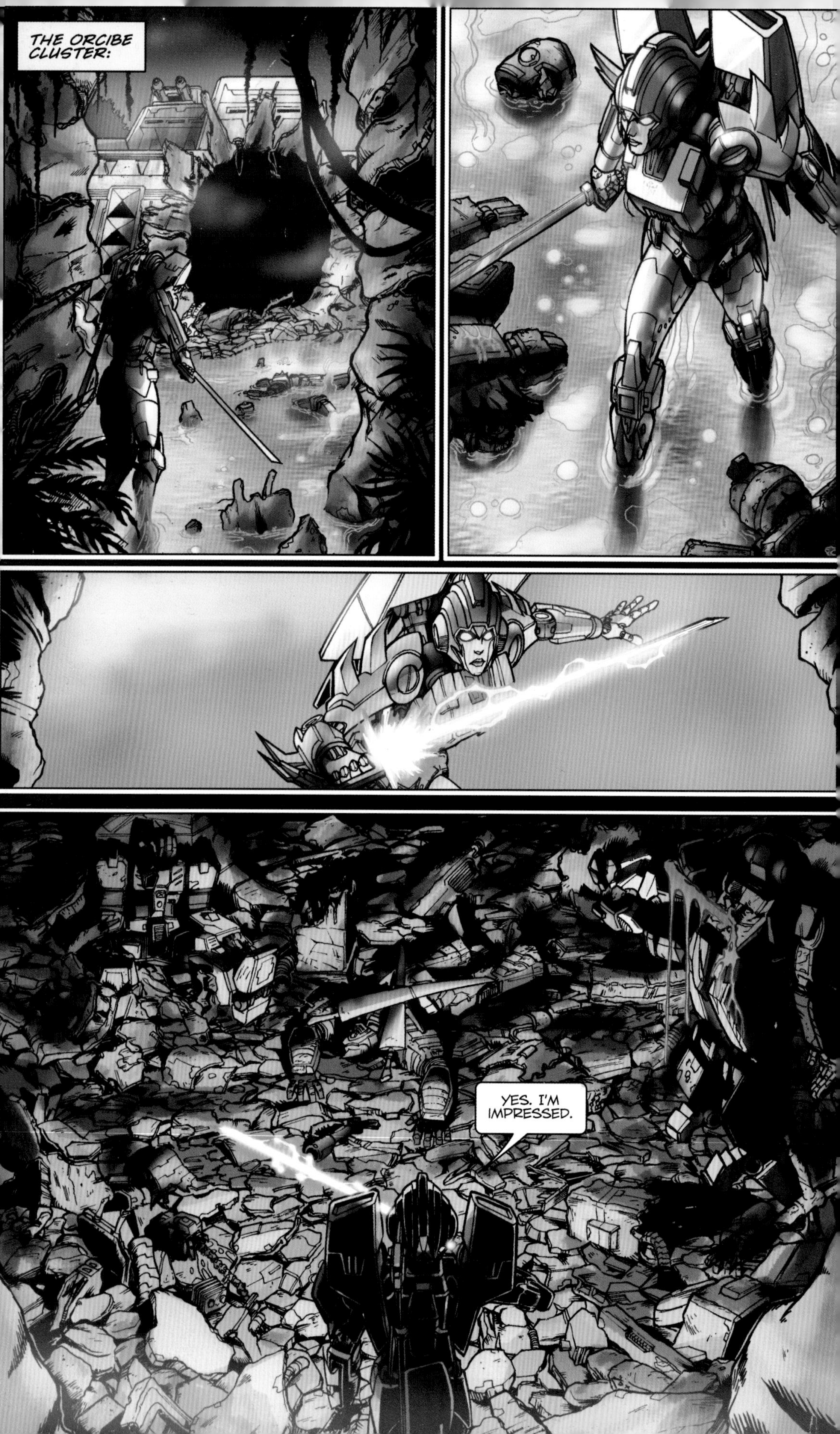
THE ORCIBE CLUSTER:
YES. I'M IMPRESSED.

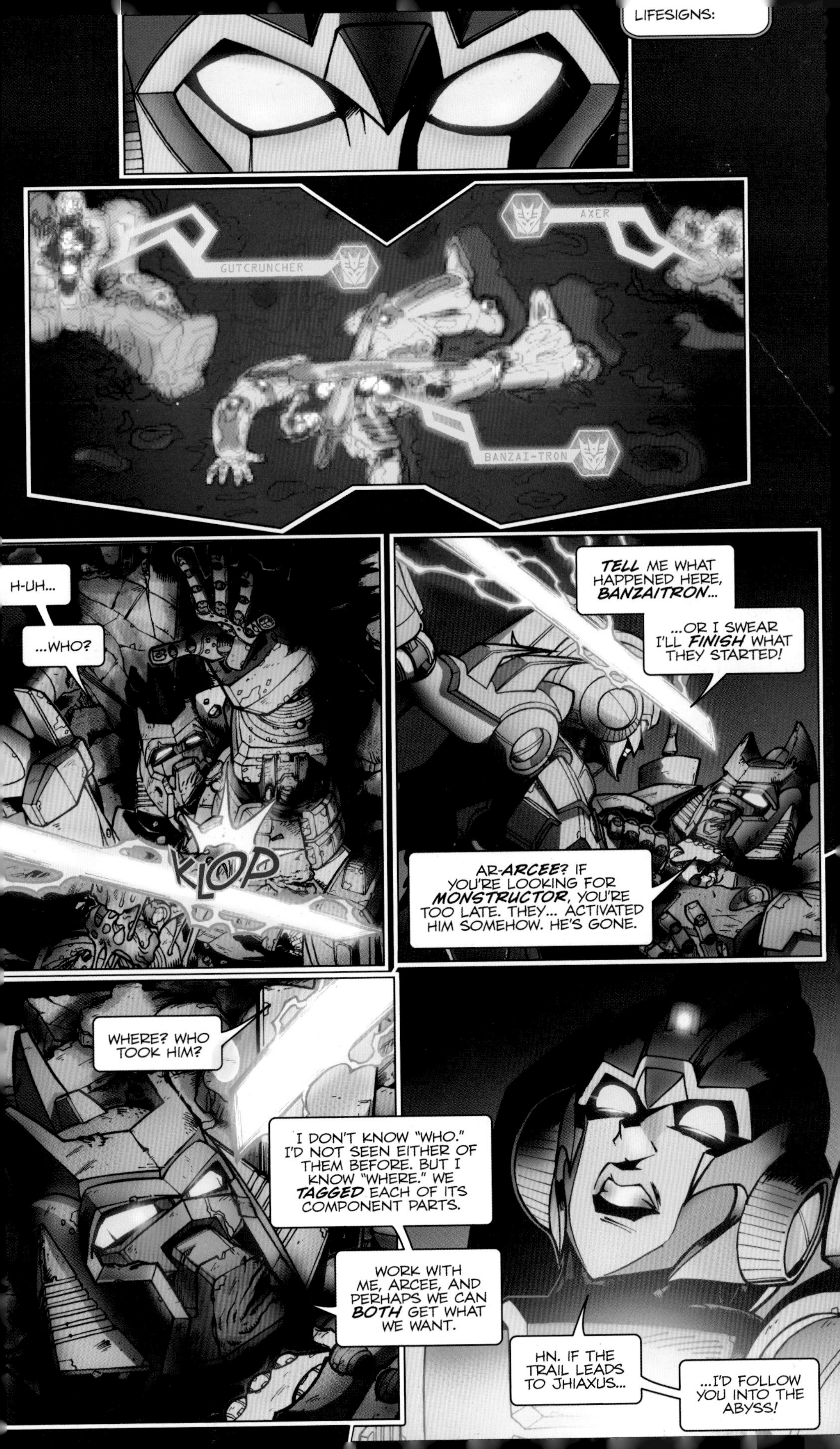
LIFESIGNS:
GUTCRUNCHER
AXER
BANZAI-TRON
H-UH...
...WHO?
KLOP
TELL ME WHAT HAPPENED HERE, BANZAITRON...
...OR I SWEAR I'LL FINISH WHAT THEY STARTED!
AR-ARCEE? IF YOU'RE LOOKING FOR MONSTRUCTOR, YOU'RE TOO LATE. THEY... ACTIVATED HIM SOMEHOW. HE'S GONE.
WHERE? WHO TOOK HIM?
I DON'T KNOW "WHO." I'D NOT SEEN EITHER OF THEM BEFORE. BUT I KNOW "WHERE." WE TAGGED EACH OF ITS COMPONENT PARTS.
WORK WITH ME, ARCEE, AND PERHAPS WE CAN BOTH GET WHAT WE WANT.
HN. IF THE TRAIL LEADS TO JHIAXUS...
...I'D FOLLOW YOU INTO THE ABYSS!

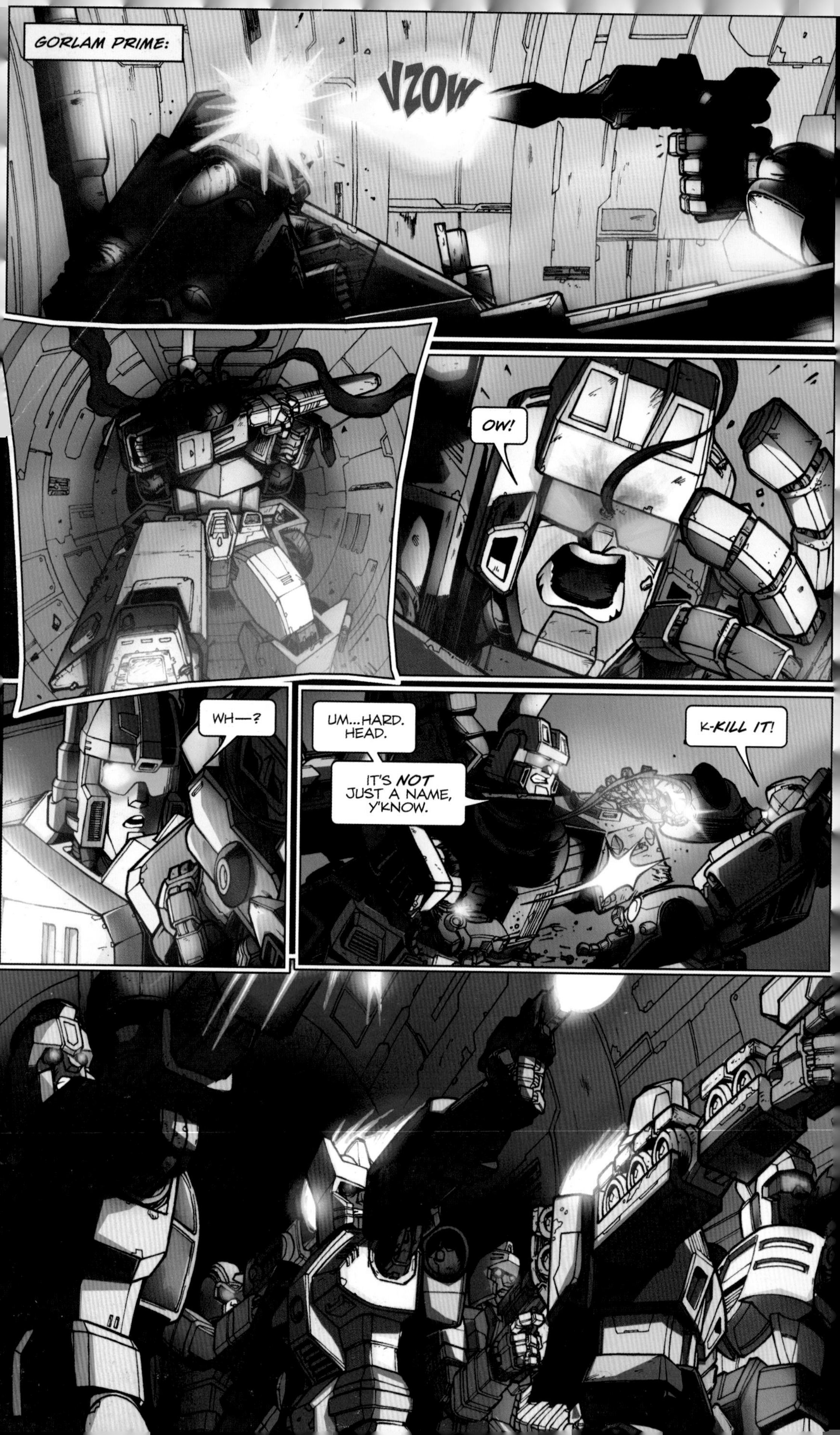
GORLAM PRIME:
VZOW
OW!
WH—?
UM...HARD. HEAD.
IT'S NOT JUST A NAME, Y'KNOW.
K-KILL IT!

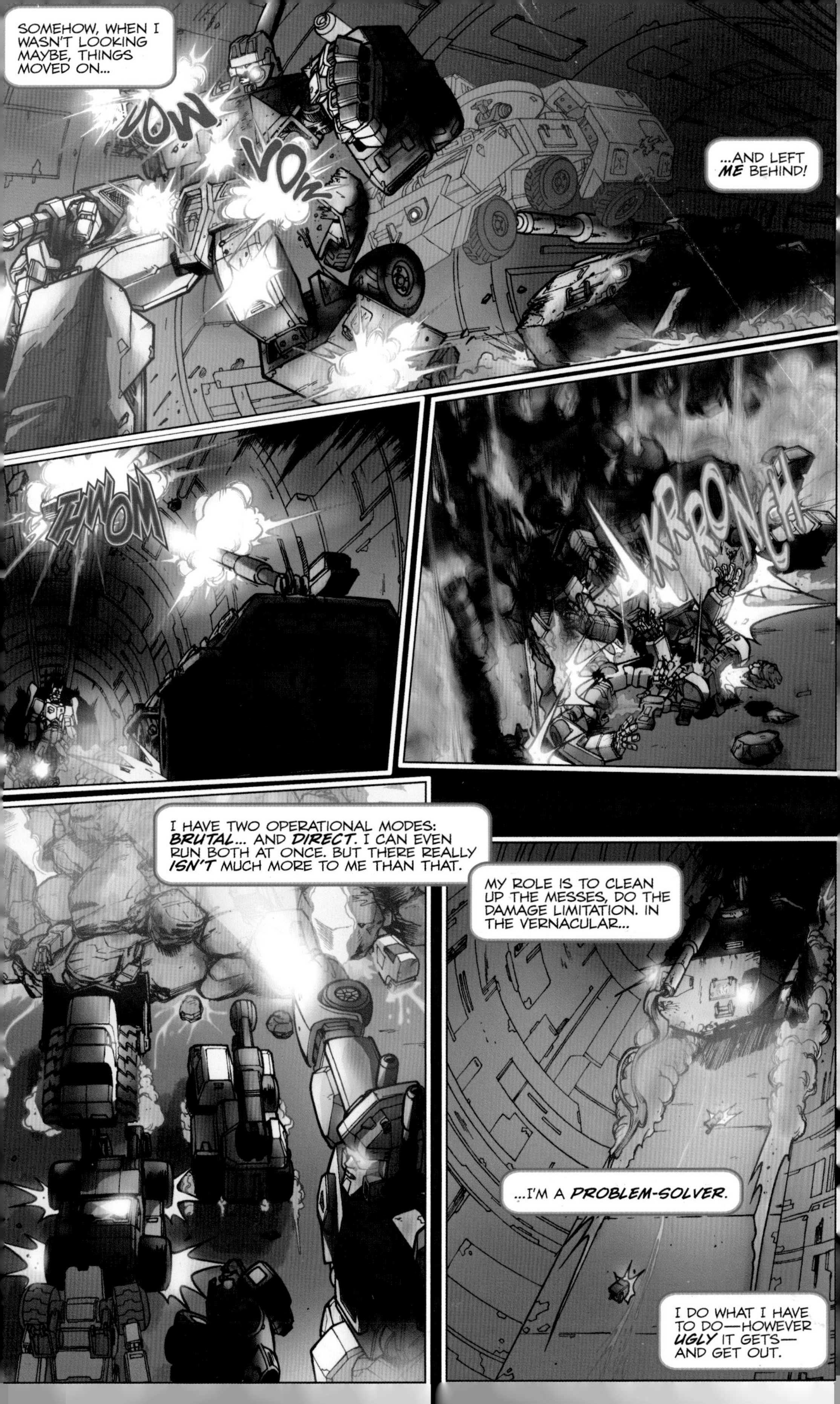
SOMEHOW, WHEN I WASN'T LOOKING MAYBE, THINGS MOVED ON...
VOW
VOW
...AND LEFT ME BEHIND!
THWOM
KRONCH
I HAVE TWO OPERATIONAL MODES: BRUTAL... AND DIRECT. I CAN EVEN RUN BOTH AT ONCE. BUT THERE REALLY ISN'T MUCH MORE TO ME THAN THAT.
MY ROLE IS TO CLEAN UP THE MESSES, DO THE DAMAGE LIMITATION. IN THE VERNACULAR...
...I'M A PROBLEM-SOLVER.
I DO WHAT I HAVE TO DO—HOWEVER UGLY IT GETS—AND GET OUT.

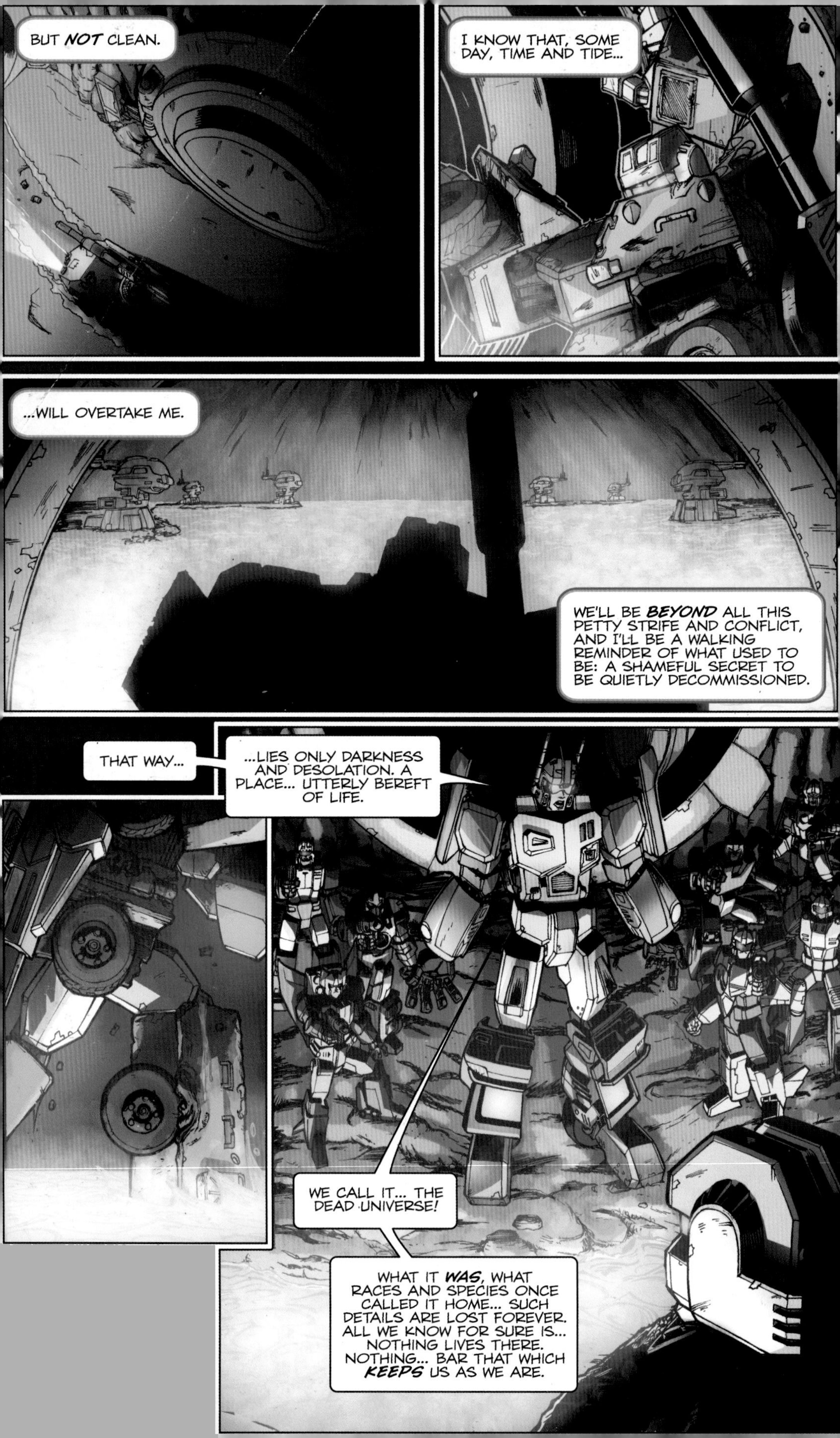

BUT NOT CLEAN.
I KNOW THAT, SOME DAY, TIME AND TIDE...
...WILL OVERTAKE ME.
WE'LL BE BEYOND ALL THIS PETTY STRIFE AND CONFLICT, AND I'LL BE A WALKING REMINDER OF WHAT USED TO BE: A SHAMEFUL SECRET TO BE QUIETLY DECOMMISSIONED.
THAT WAY...
...LIES ONLY DARKNESS AND DESOLATION. A PLACE... UTTERLY BEREFT OF LIFE.
WE CALL IT... THE DEAD UNIVERSE!
WHAT IT WAS, WHAT RACES AND SPECIES ONCE CALLED IT HOME... SUCH DETAILS ARE LOST FOREVER. ALL WE KNOW FOR SURE IS... NOTHING LIVES THERE. NOTHING... BAR THAT WHICH KEEPS US AS WE ARE.

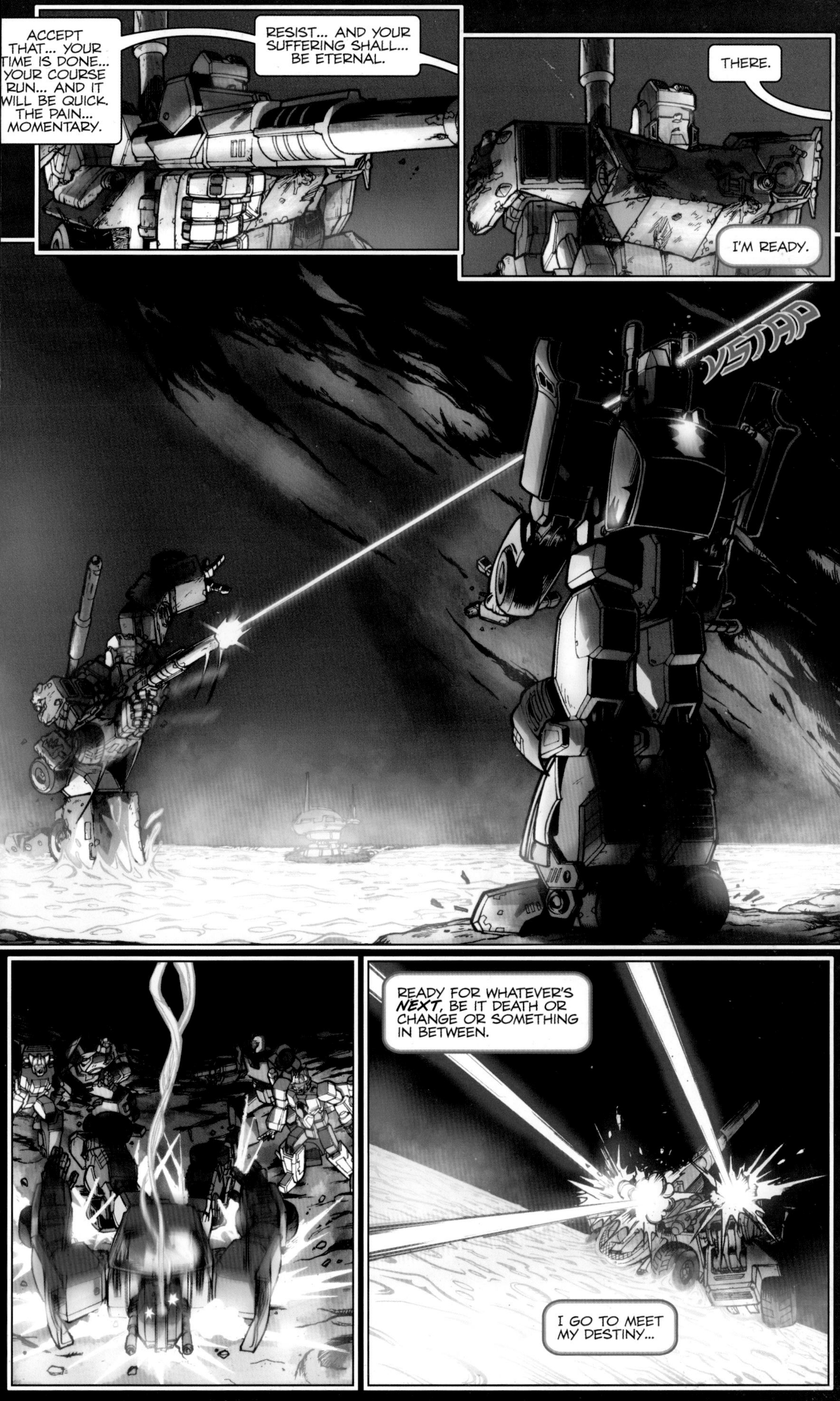

ACCEPT THAT... YOUR TIME IS DONE... YOUR COURSE RUN... AND IT WILL BE QUICK. THE PAIN... MOMENTARY.
RESIST... AND YOUR SUFFERING SHALL... BE ETERNAL.
THERE.
I'M READY.
VSTAP
READY FOR WHATEVER'S ***NEXT***, BE IT DEATH OR CHANGE OR SOMETHING IN BETWEEN.
I GO TO MEET MY DESTINY...

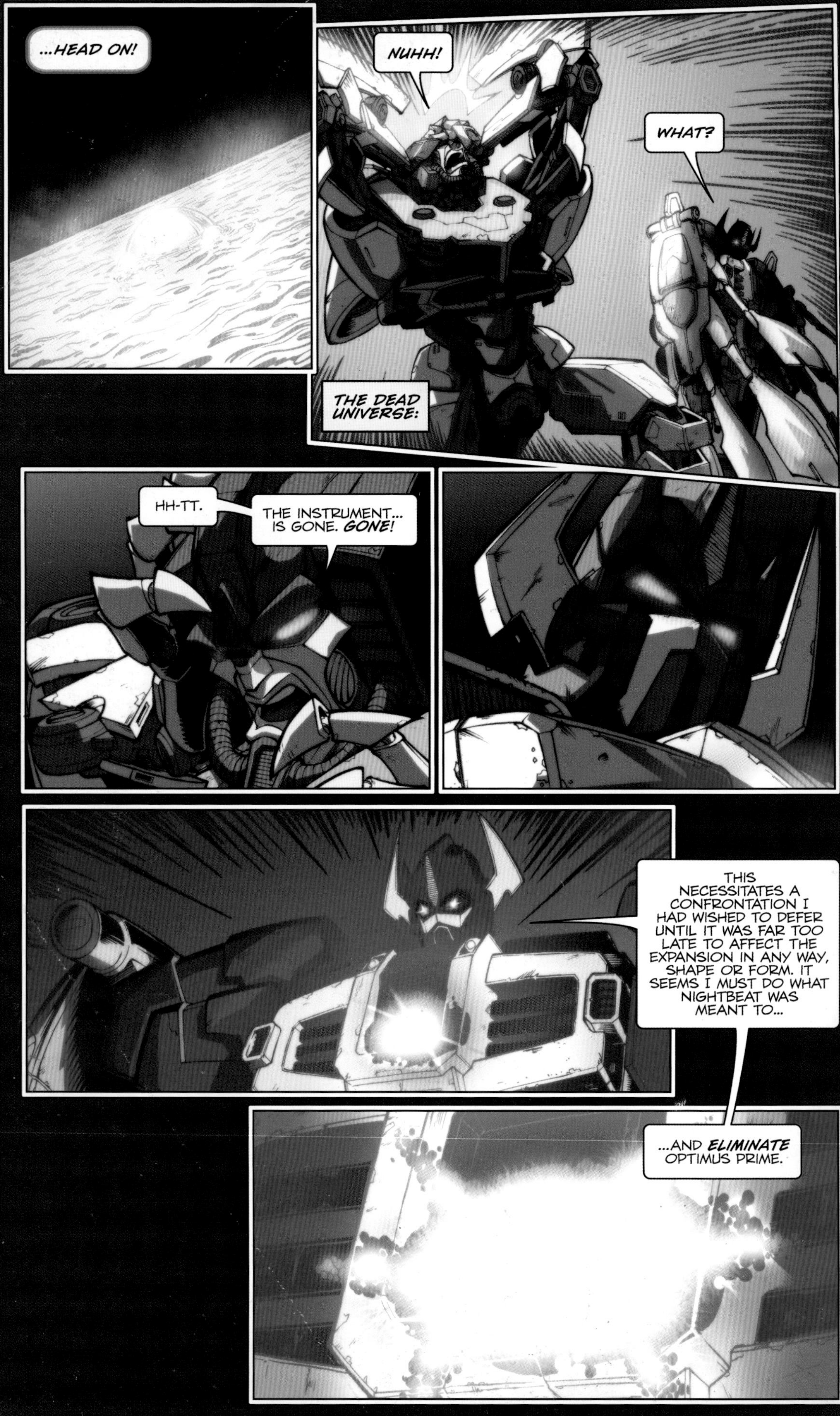
...HEAD ON!
NUHH!
WHAT?
THE DEAD UNIVERSE:
HH-TT.
THE INSTRUMENT... IS GONE. GONE!
THIS NECESSITATES A CONFRONTATION I HAD WISHED TO DEFER UNTIL IT WAS FAR TOO LATE TO AFFECT THE EXPANSION IN ANY WAY, SHAPE OR FORM. IT SEEMS I MUST DO WHAT NIGHTBEAT WAS MEANT TO...
...AND ELIMINATE OPTIMUS PRIME.

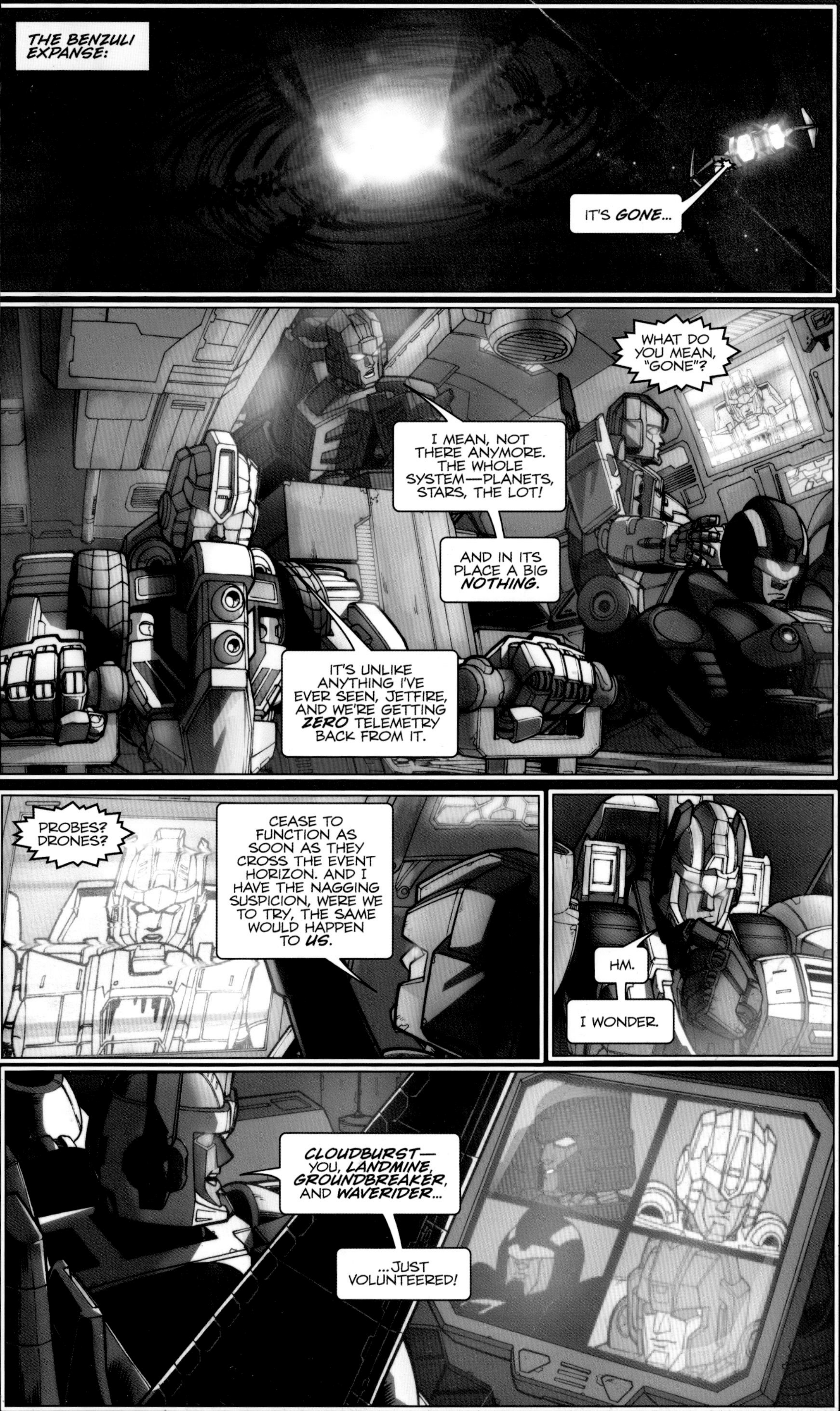

THE BENZULI EXPANSE:
IT'S GONE...
WHAT DO YOU MEAN, "GONE"?
I MEAN, NOT THERE ANYMORE. THE WHOLE SYSTEM—PLANETS, STARS, THE LOT!
AND IN ITS PLACE A BIG NOTHING.
IT'S UNLIKE ANYTHING I'VE EVER SEEN, JETFIRE, AND WE'RE GETTING ZERO TELEMETRY BACK FROM IT.
PROBES? DRONES?
CEASE TO FUNCTION AS SOON AS THEY CROSS THE EVENT HORIZON. AND I HAVE THE NAGGING SUSPICION, WERE WE TO TRY, THE SAME WOULD HAPPEN TO US.
HM.
I WONDER.
CLOUDBURST— YOU, LANDMINE, GROUNDBREAKER, AND WAVERIDER...
...JUST VOLUNTEERED!

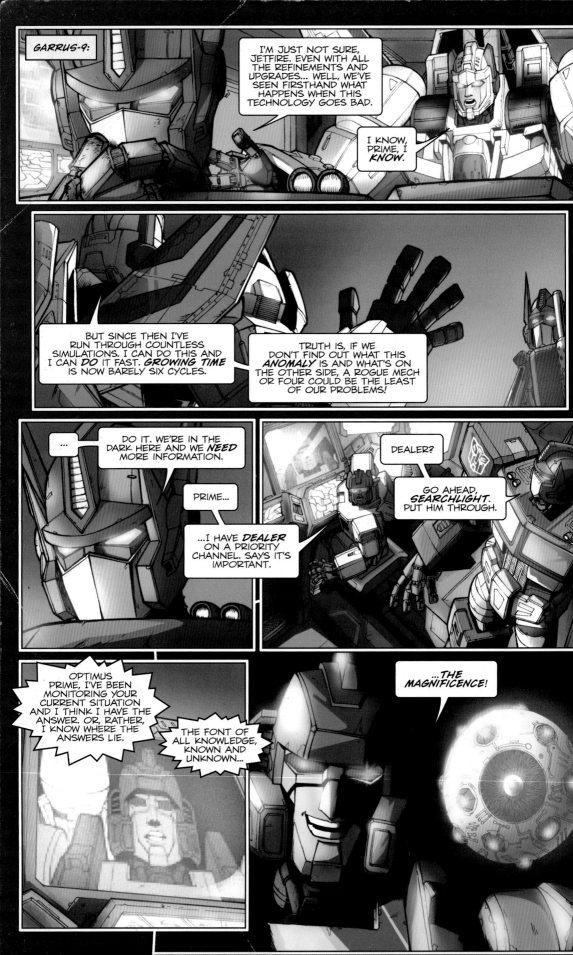

GARRUS-9:

I'M JUST NOT SURE, JETFIRE. EVEN WITH ALL THE REFINEMENTS AND UPGRADES... WELL, WE'VE SEEN FIRSTHAND WHAT HAPPENS WHEN THIS TECHNOLOGY GOES BAD.

I KNOW, PRIME, I **KNOW**.

BUT SINCE THEN I'VE RUN THROUGH COUNTLESS SIMULATIONS. I CAN DO THIS AND I CAN **DO** IT FAST. **GROWING TIME** IS NOW BARELY SIX CYCLES.

TRUTH IS, IF WE DON'T FIND OUT WHAT THIS **ANOMALY** IS AND WHAT'S ON THE OTHER SIDE, A ROGUE MECH OR FOUR COULD BE THE LEAST OF OUR PROBLEMS!

...

DO IT. WE'RE IN THE DARK HERE AND WE **NEED** MORE INFORMATION.

PRIME...

...I HAVE **DEALER** ON A PRIORITY CHANNEL. SAYS IT'S IMPORTANT.

DEALER?

GO AHEAD, **SEARCHLIGHT**. PUT HIM THROUGH.

OPTIMUS PRIME, I'VE BEEN MONITORING YOUR CURRENT SITUATION AND I THINK I HAVE THE ANSWER. OR, RATHER, I KNOW WHERE THE ANSWERS LIE.

THE FONT OF ALL KNOWLEDGE, KNOWN AND UNKNOWN...

...THE MAGNIFICENCE!

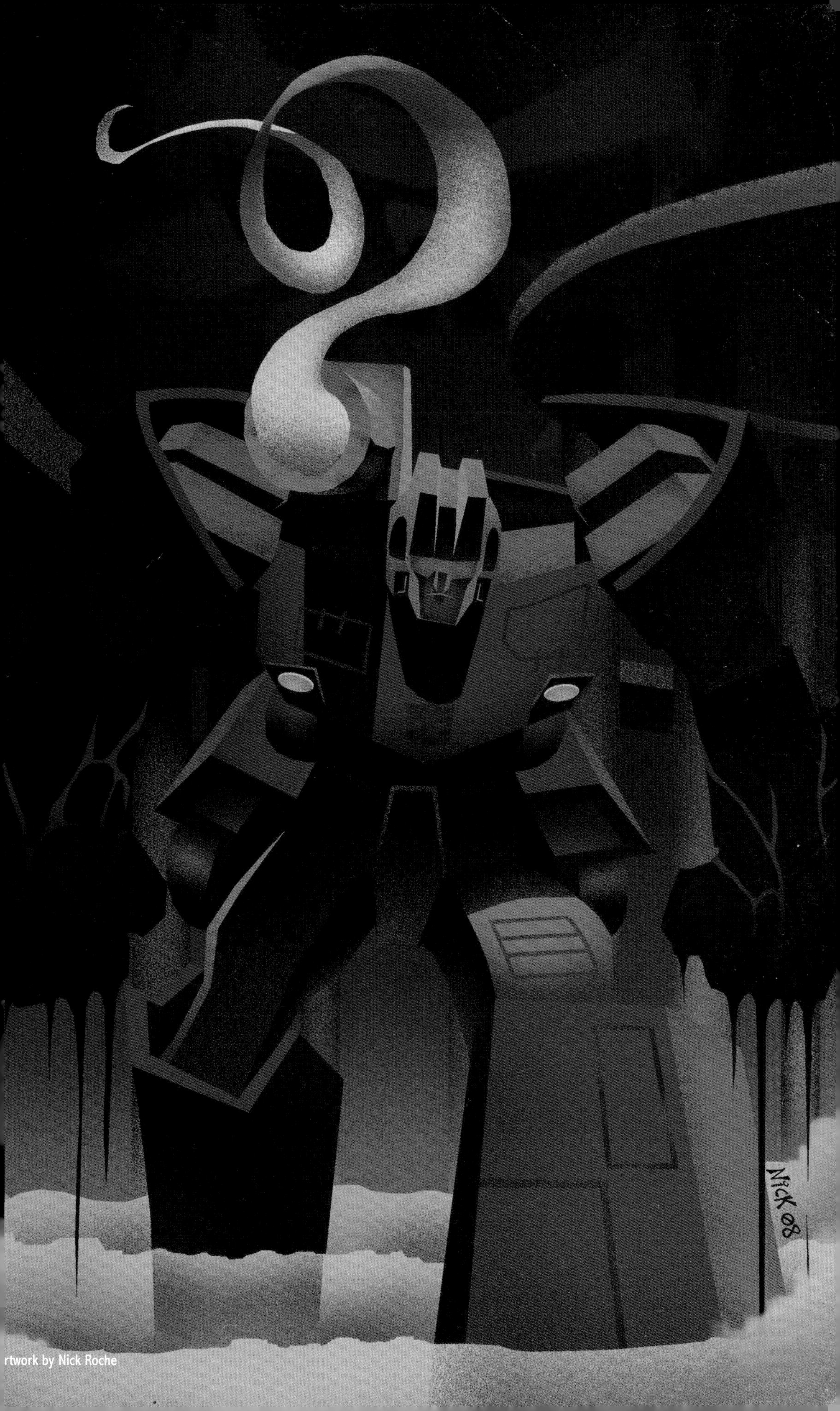
NicK 08

rtwork by Nick Roche

DOUBLEDEALER

DEALER is all inner and outer self: show one face to the world and hide the true one. Let no one in. Be an island, self-supportive, and insular. Incredibly clever and manipulative (Double) DEALER will smile at your face and stab you in the back. Often for self-advancement or material rewards but sometimes just because he can. It reinforces the belief that he is utterly superior to those around him, better, smarter, more cunning. The war is a means to an end, faction for fools, friendship artifice. But sometimes a deception can be so good… you can even fool yourself.

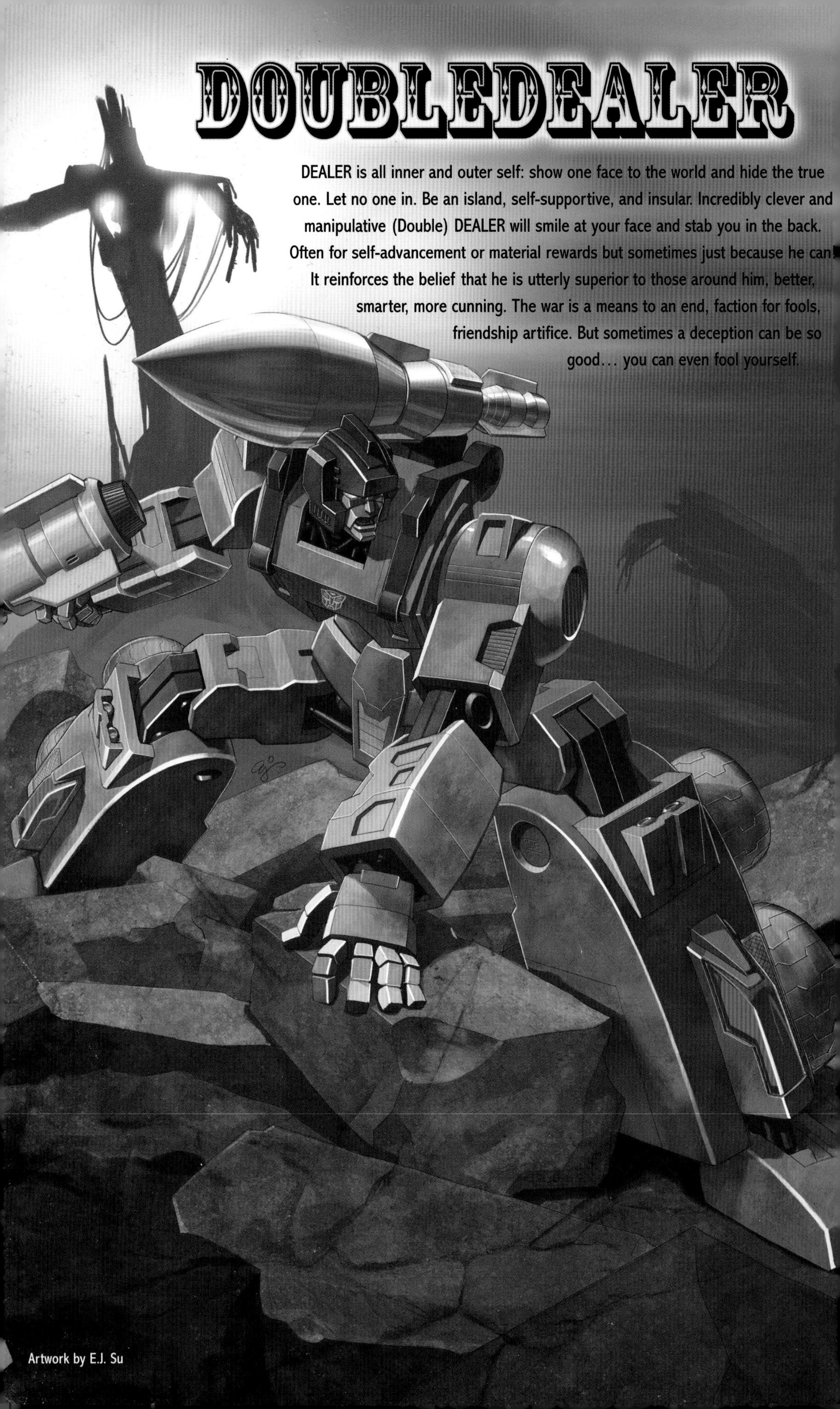

Artwork by E.J. Su

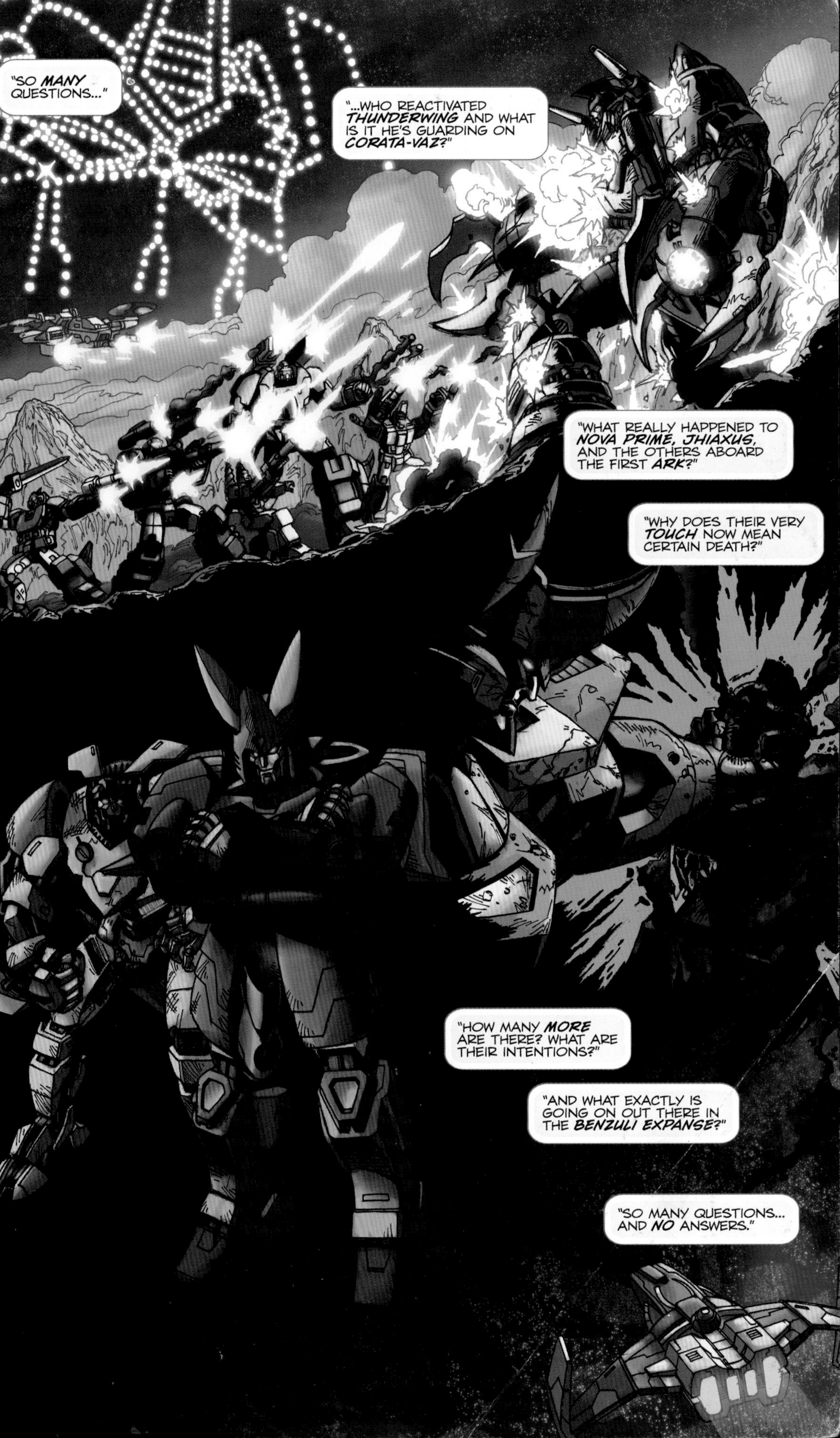
"SO *MANY* QUESTIONS..."
"...WHO REACTIVATED *THUNDERWING* AND WHAT IS IT HE'S GUARDING ON *CORATA-VAZ?*"
"WHAT REALLY HAPPENED TO *NOVA PRIME, JHIAXUS,* AND THE OTHERS ABOARD THE FIRST *ARK?*"
"WHY DOES THEIR VERY *TOUCH* NOW MEAN CERTAIN DEATH?"
"HOW MANY *MORE* ARE THERE? WHAT ARE THEIR INTENTIONS?"
"AND WHAT EXACTLY IS GOING ON OUT THERE IN THE *BENZULI EXPANSE?*"
"SO MANY QUESTIONS... AND *NO* ANSWERS."

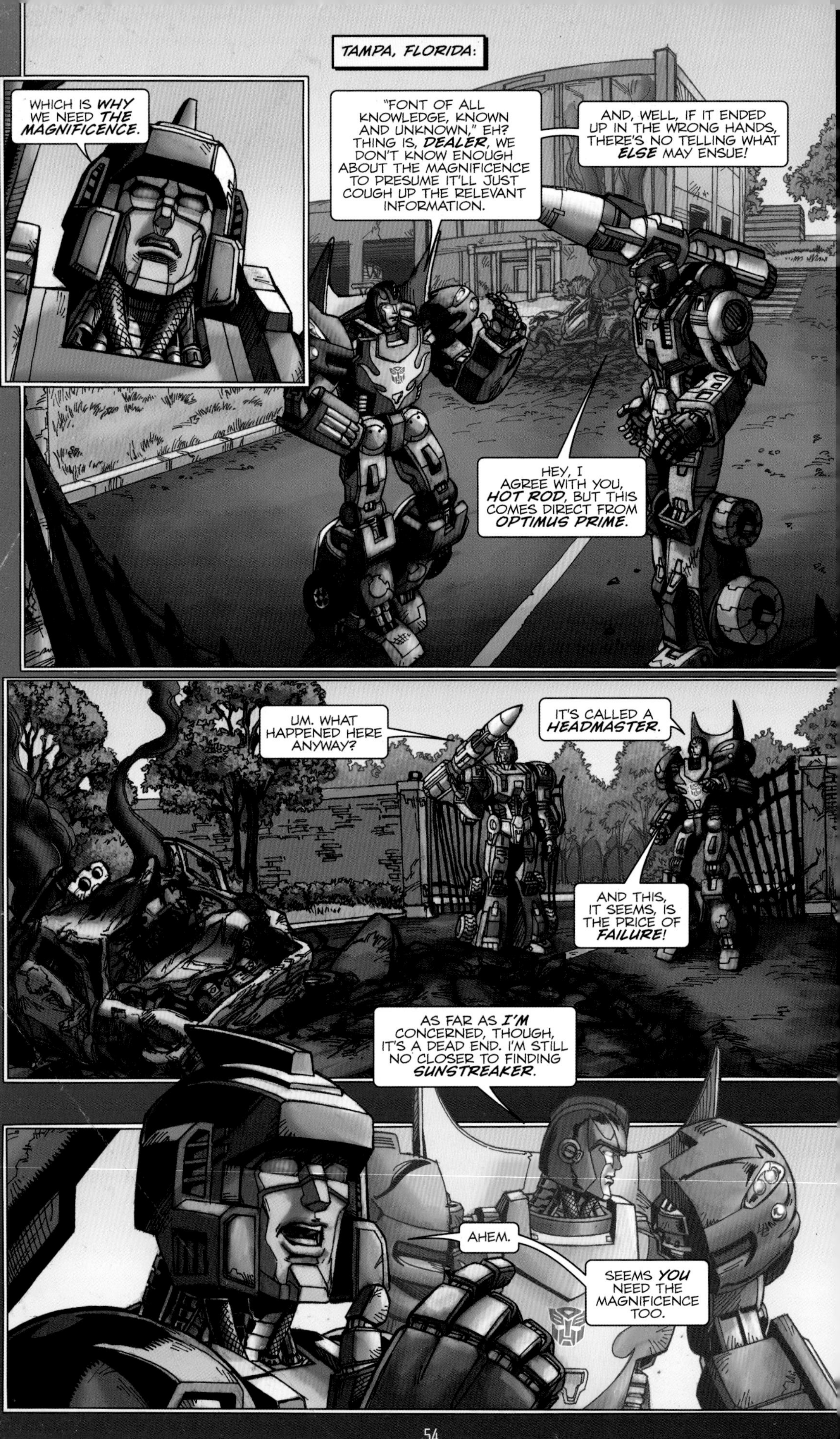
TAMPA, FLORIDA:
WHICH IS WHY WE NEED THE MAGNIFICENCE.
"FONT OF ALL KNOWLEDGE, KNOWN AND UNKNOWN," EH? THING IS, DEALER, WE DON'T KNOW ENOUGH ABOUT THE MAGNIFICENCE TO PRESUME IT'LL JUST COUGH UP THE RELEVANT INFORMATION.
AND, WELL, IF IT ENDED UP IN THE WRONG HANDS, THERE'S NO TELLING WHAT ELSE MAY ENSUE!
HEY, I AGREE WITH YOU, HOT ROD, BUT THIS COMES DIRECT FROM OPTIMUS PRIME.
UM. WHAT HAPPENED HERE ANYWAY?
IT'S CALLED A HEADMASTER.
AND THIS, IT SEEMS, IS THE PRICE OF FAILURE!
AS FAR AS I'M CONCERNED, THOUGH, IT'S A DEAD END. I'M STILL NO CLOSER TO FINDING SUNSTREAKER.
AHEM.
SEEMS YOU NEED THE MAGNIFICENCE TOO.

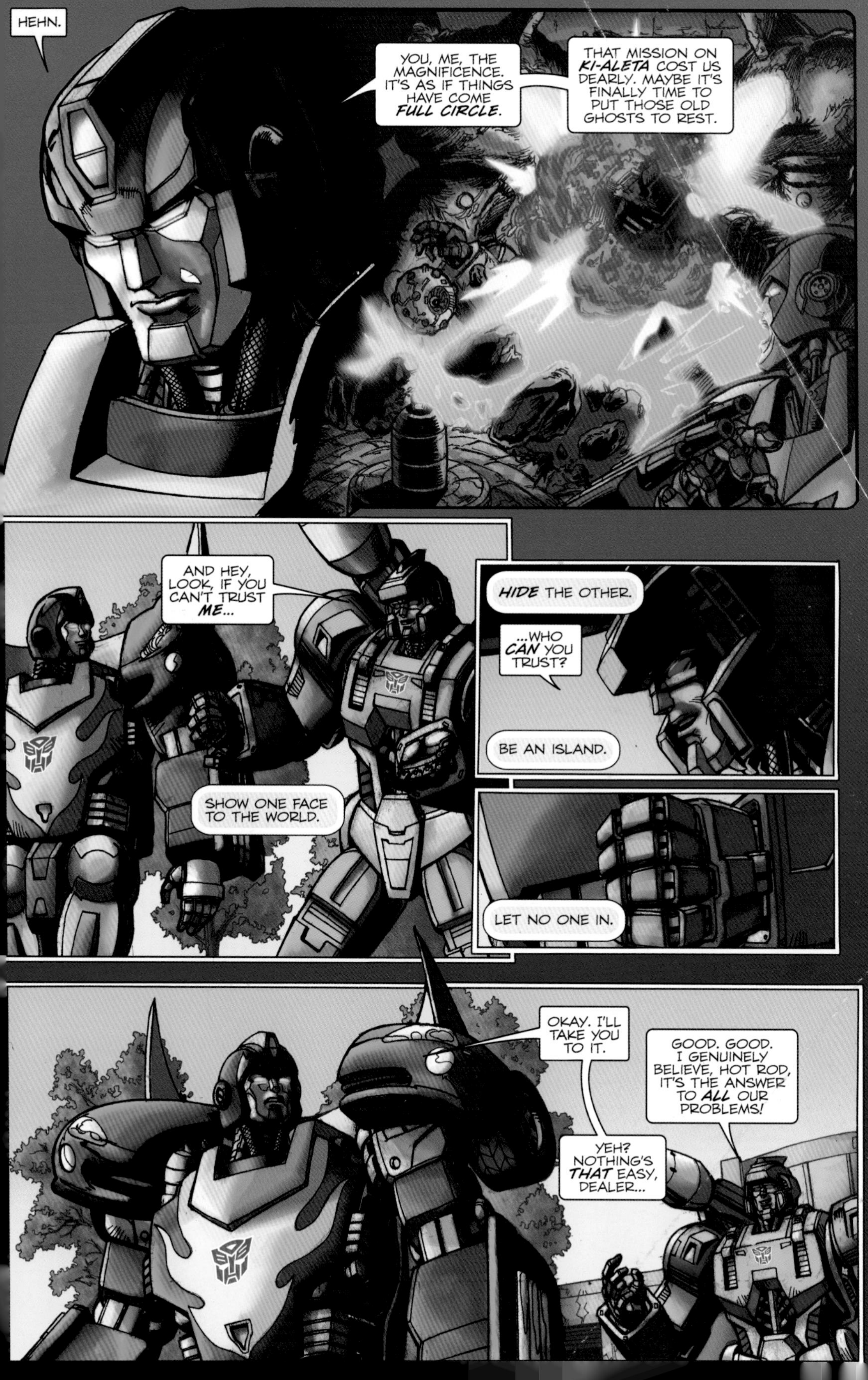
HEHN.
YOU, ME, THE MAGNIFICENCE. IT'S AS IF THINGS HAVE COME FULL CIRCLE.
THAT MISSION ON KI-ALETA COST US DEARLY. MAYBE IT'S FINALLY TIME TO PUT THOSE OLD GHOSTS TO REST.
AND HEY, LOOK, IF YOU CAN'T TRUST ME...
SHOW ONE FACE TO THE WORLD.
HIDE THE OTHER.
...WHO CAN YOU TRUST?
BE AN ISLAND.
LET NO ONE IN.
OKAY. I'LL TAKE YOU TO IT.
YEH? NOTHING'S THAT EASY, DEALER...
GOOD. GOOD. I GENUINELY BELIEVE, HOT ROD, IT'S THE ANSWER TO ALL OUR PROBLEMS!

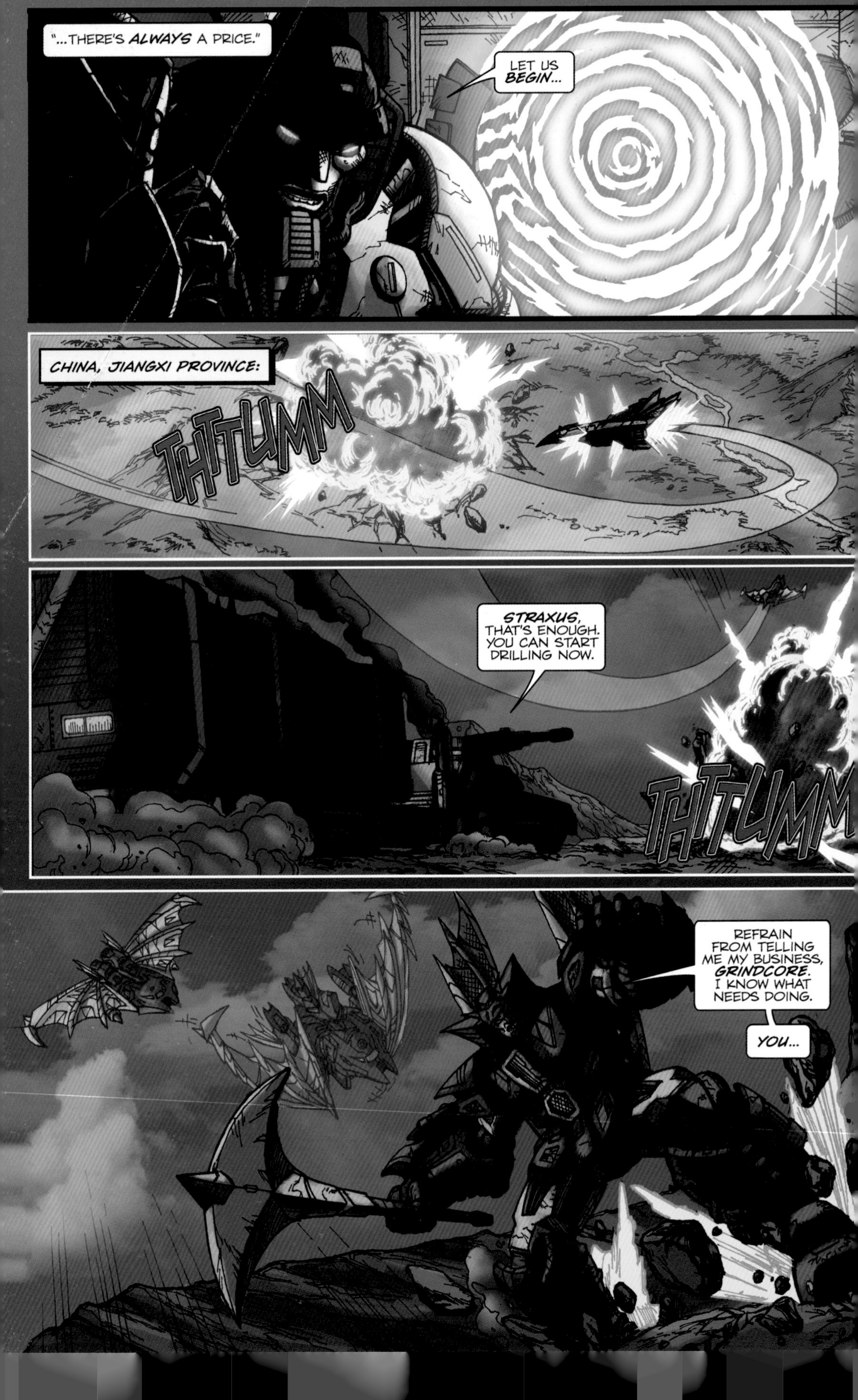
"...THERE'S ALWAYS A PRICE."
LET US BEGIN...
CHINA, JIANGXI PROVINCE:
THTUMM
STRAXUS, THAT'S ENOUGH. YOU CAN START DRILLING NOW.
THTUMM
REFRAIN FROM TELLING ME MY BUSINESS, GRINDCORE. I KNOW WHAT NEEDS DOING.
YOU...

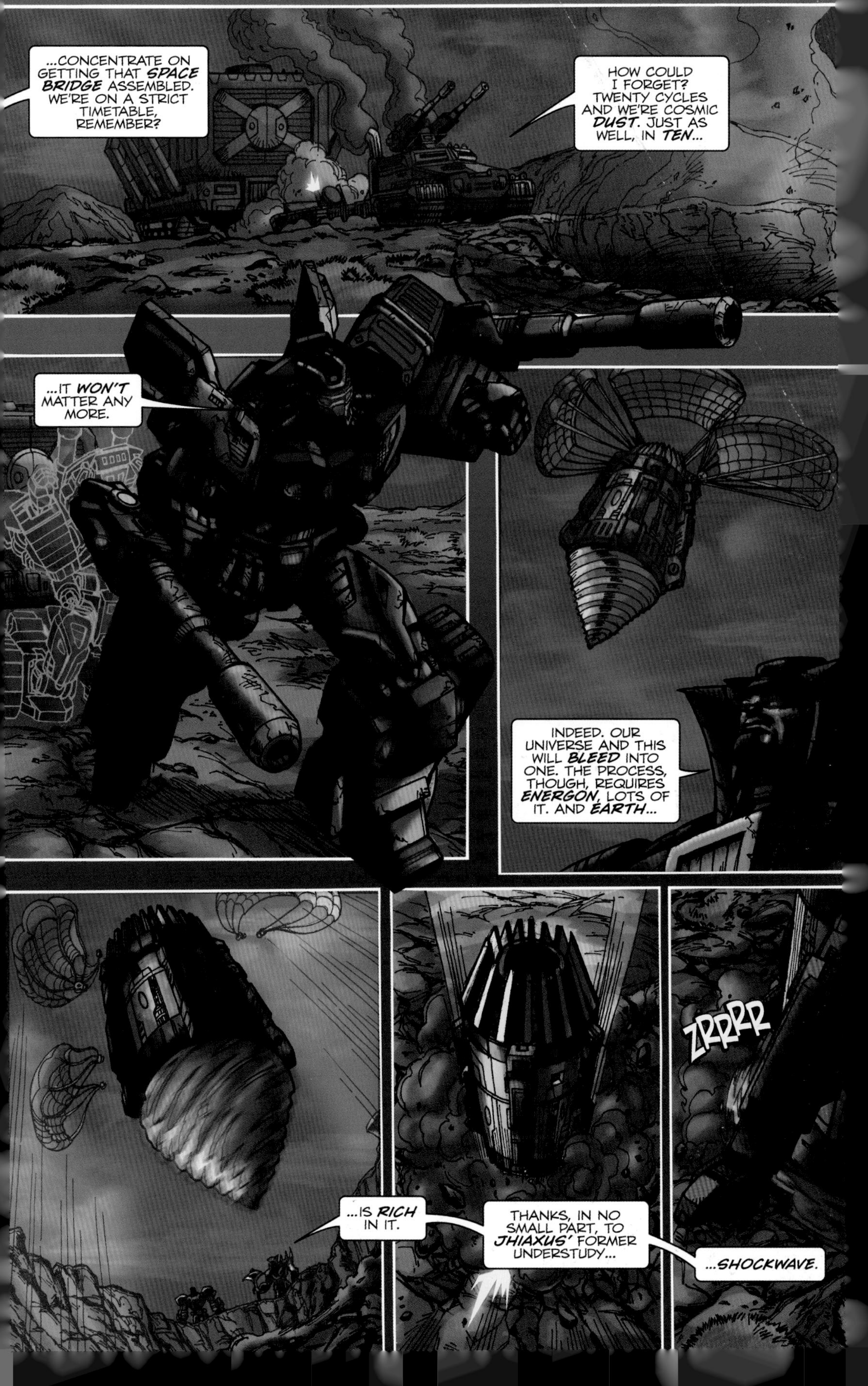
...CONCENTRATE ON GETTING THAT SPACE BRIDGE ASSEMBLED. WE'RE ON A STRICT TIMETABLE, REMEMBER?
HOW COULD I FORGET? TWENTY CYCLES AND WE'RE COSMIC DUST. JUST AS WELL, IN TEN...
...IT WON'T MATTER ANY MORE.
INDEED. OUR UNIVERSE AND THIS WILL BLEED INTO ONE. THE PROCESS, THOUGH, REQUIRES ENERGON, LOTS OF IT. AND EARTH...
ZRRRR
...IS RICH IN IT.
THANKS, IN NO SMALL PART, TO JHIAXUS' FORMER UNDERSTUDY...
...SHOCKWAVE.

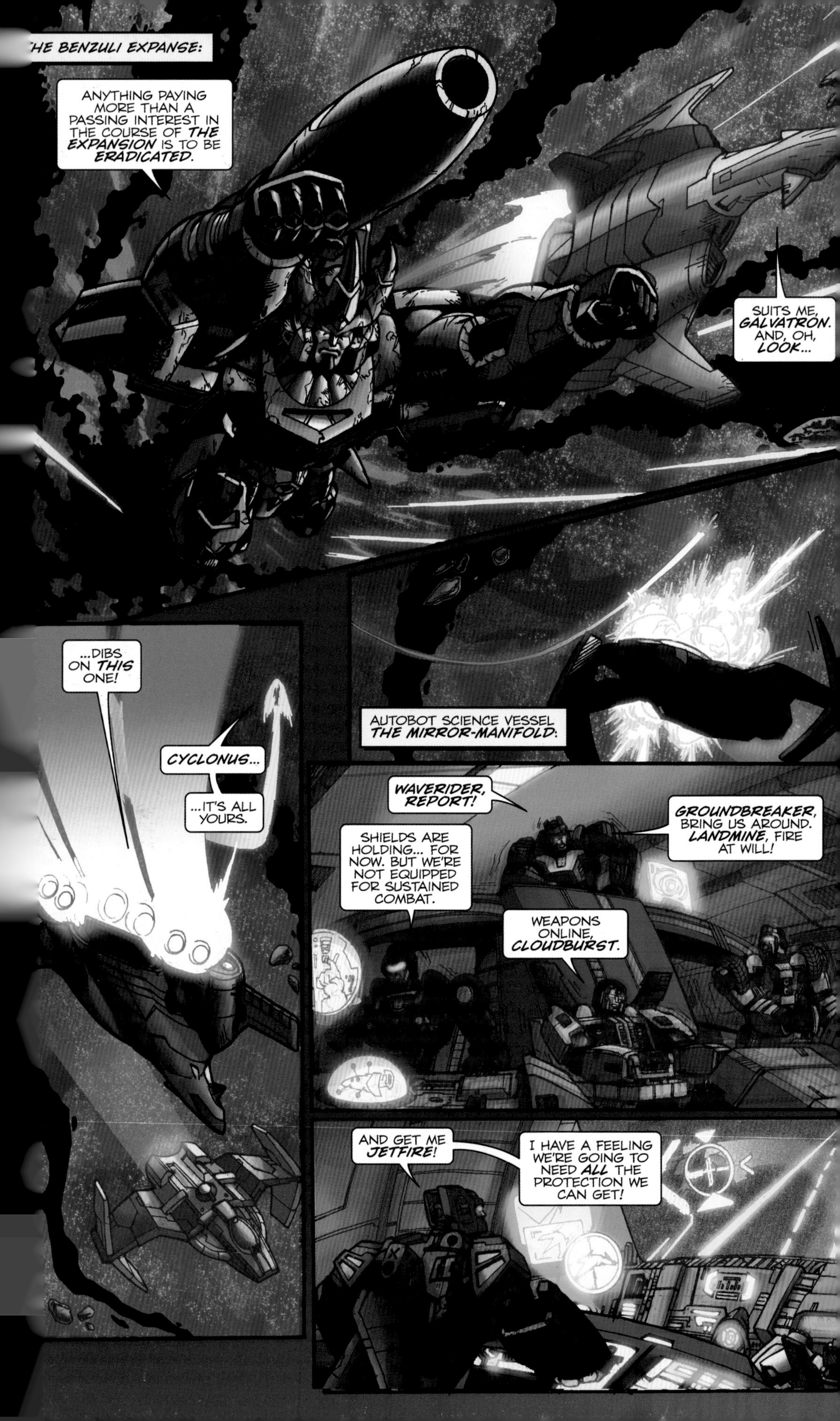

THE BENZULI EXPANSE:
ANYTHING PAYING MORE THAN A PASSING INTEREST IN THE COURSE OF THE EXPANSION IS TO BE ERADICATED.
SUITS ME, GALVATRON. AND, OH, LOOK...
...DIBS ON THIS ONE!
CYCLONUS...
...IT'S ALL YOURS.
AUTOBOT SCIENCE VESSEL THE MIRROR-MANIFOLD:
WAVERIDER, REPORT!
SHIELDS ARE HOLDING... FOR NOW. BUT WE'RE NOT EQUIPPED FOR SUSTAINED COMBAT.
GROUNDBREAKER, BRING US AROUND. LANDMINE, FIRE AT WILL!
WEAPONS ONLINE, CLOUDBURST.
AND GET ME JETFIRE!
I HAVE A FEELING WE'RE GOING TO NEED ALL THE PROTECTION WE CAN GET!

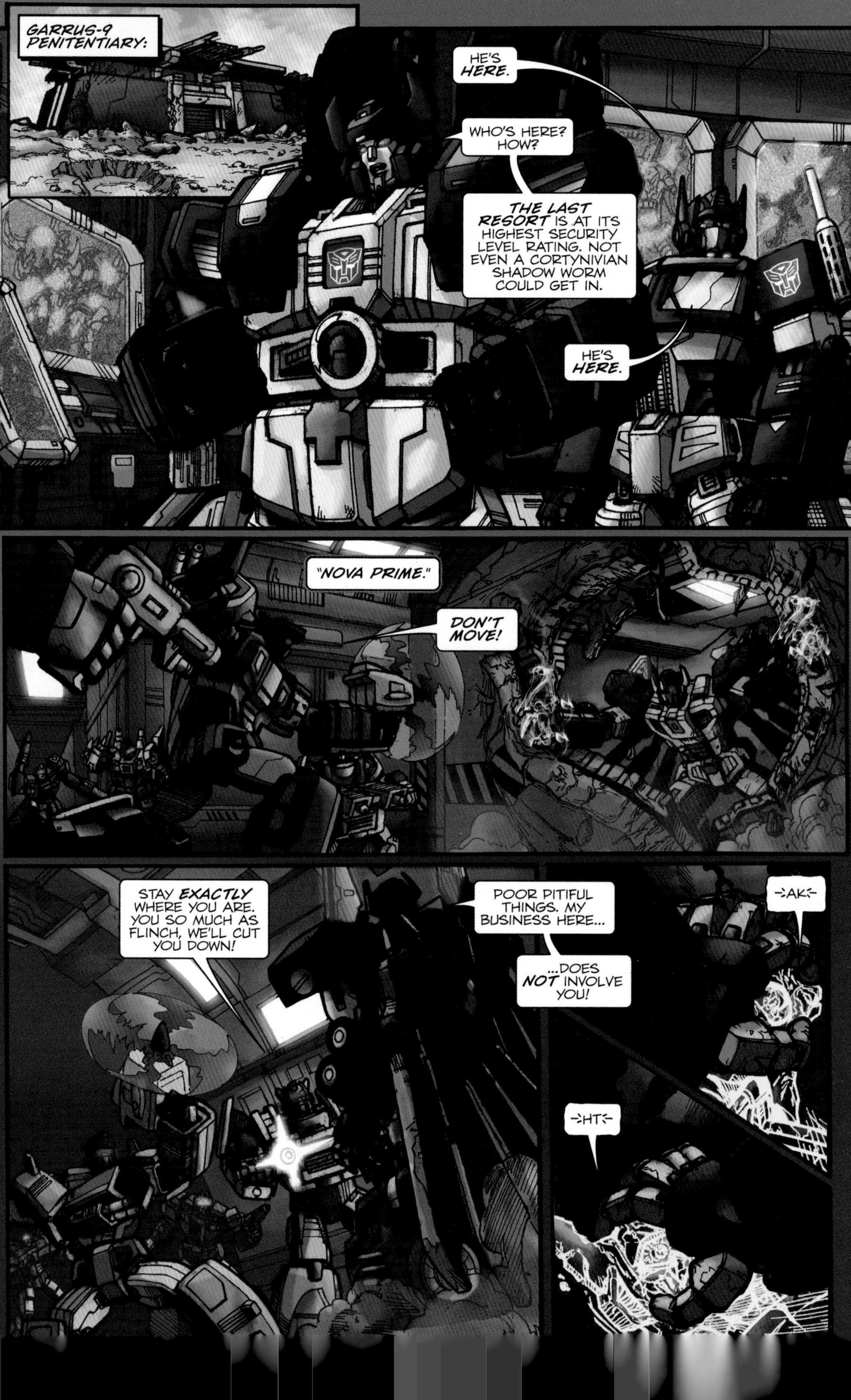

GARRUS-9 PENITENTIARY:
HE'S HERE.
WHO'S HERE? HOW?
THE LAST RESORT IS AT ITS HIGHEST SECURITY LEVEL RATING. NOT EVEN A CORTYNIVIAN SHADOW WORM COULD GET IN.
HE'S HERE.
"NOVA PRIME."
DON'T MOVE!
STAY EXACTLY WHERE YOU ARE. YOU SO MUCH AS FLINCH, WE'LL CUT YOU DOWN!
POOR PITIFUL THINGS. MY BUSINESS HERE...
...DOES NOT INVOLVE YOU!
-AK-
-HT-

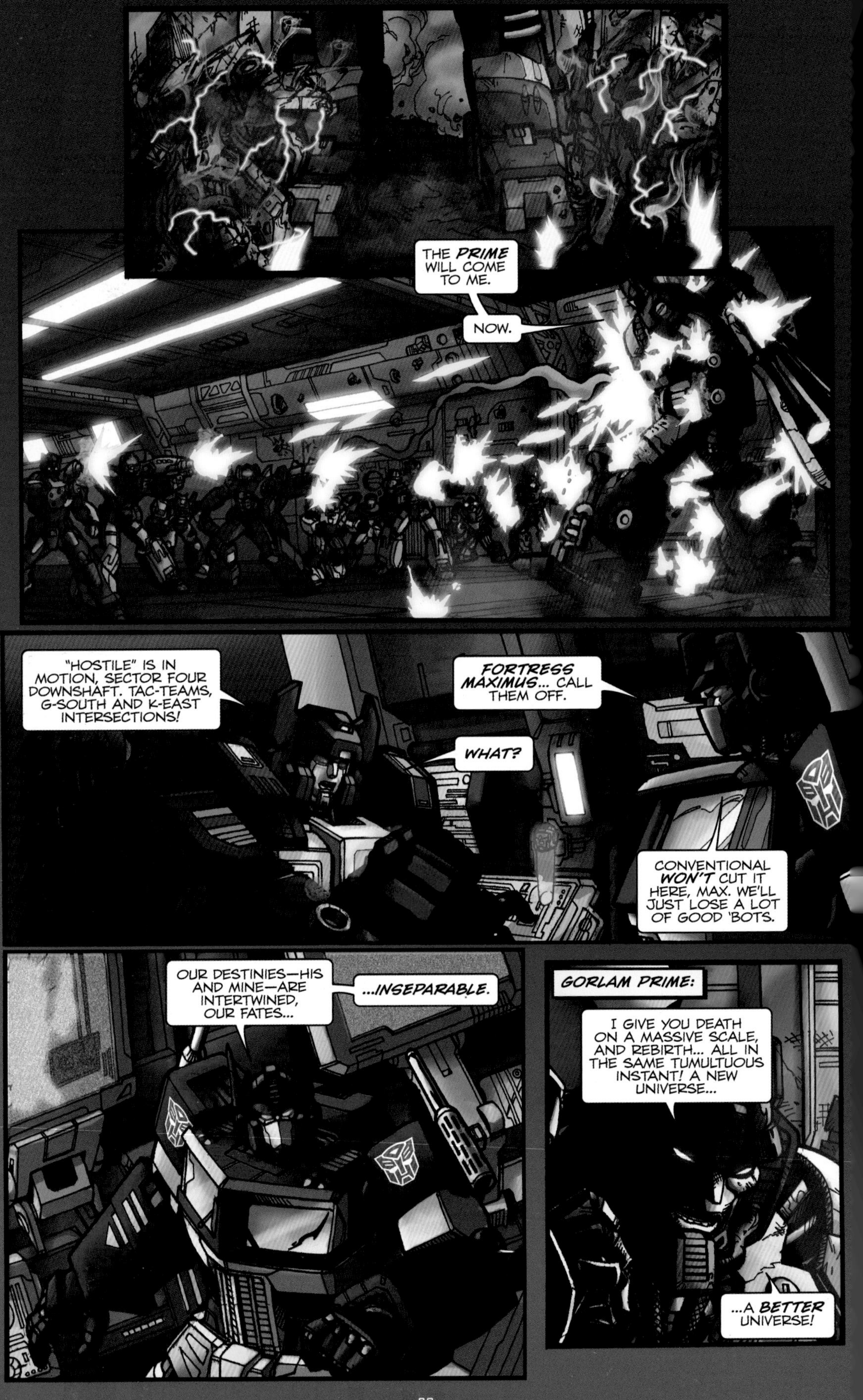
THE PRIME WILL COME TO ME.
NOW.
"HOSTILE" IS IN MOTION, SECTOR FOUR DOWNSHAFT. TAC-TEAMS, G-SOUTH AND K-EAST INTERSECTIONS!
FORTRESS MAXIMUS... CALL THEM OFF.
WHAT?
CONVENTIONAL WON'T CUT IT HERE, MAX. WE'LL JUST LOSE A LOT OF GOOD 'BOTS.
OUR DESTINIES—HIS AND MINE—ARE INTERTWINED, OUR FATES...
...INSEPARABLE.
GORLAM PRIME:
I GIVE YOU DEATH ON A MASSIVE SCALE, AND REBIRTH... ALL IN THE SAME TUMULTUOUS INSTANT! A NEW UNIVERSE...
...A BETTER UNIVERSE!

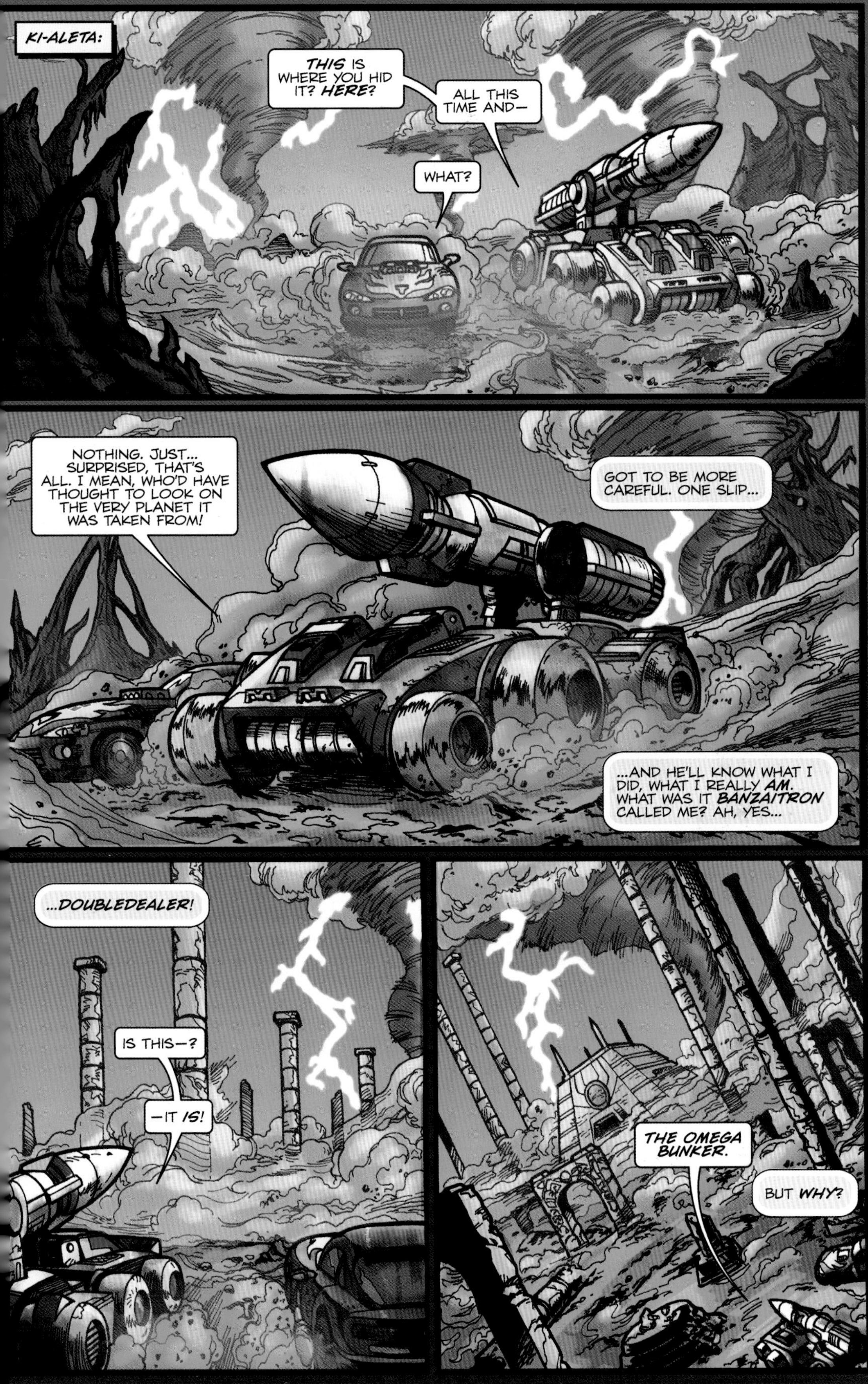
KI-ALETA:
THIS IS WHERE YOU HID IT? HERE?
ALL THIS TIME AND—
WHAT?
NOTHING. JUST... SURPRISED, THAT'S ALL. I MEAN, WHO'D HAVE THOUGHT TO LOOK ON THE VERY PLANET IT WAS TAKEN FROM!
GOT TO BE MORE CAREFUL. ONE SLIP...
...AND HE'LL KNOW WHAT I DID, WHAT I REALLY AM. WHAT WAS IT BANZAITRON CALLED ME? AH, YES...
...DOUBLEDEALER!
IS THIS—?
—IT IS!
THE OMEGA BUNKER.
BUT WHY?

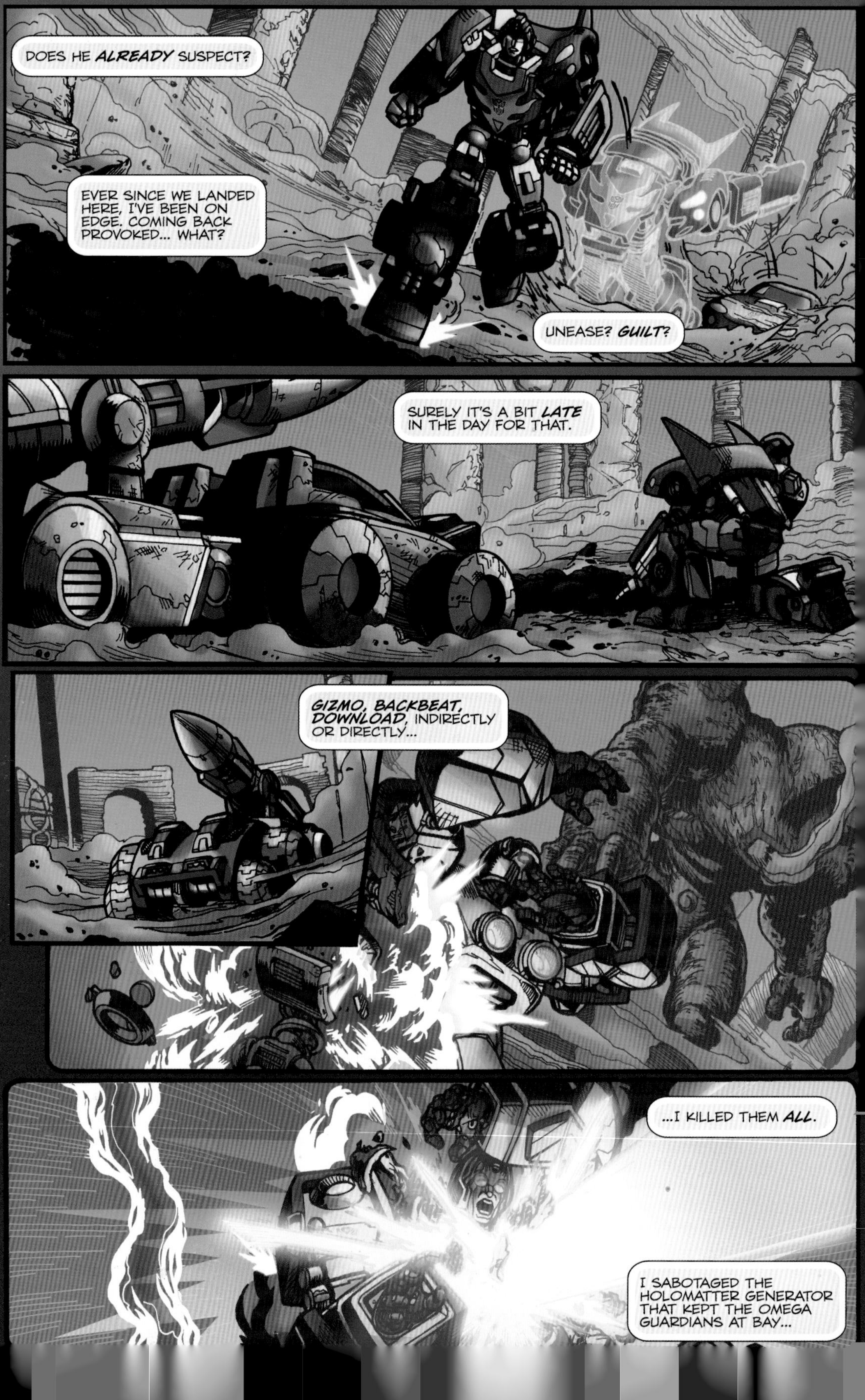
DOES HE ALREADY SUSPECT?
EVER SINCE WE LANDED HERE, I'VE BEEN ON EDGE. COMING BACK PROVOKED... WHAT?
UNEASE? GUILT?
SURELY IT'S A BIT LATE IN THE DAY FOR THAT.
GIZMO, BACKBEAT, DOWNLOAD, INDIRECTLY OR DIRECTLY...
...I KILLED THEM ALL.
I SABOTAGED THE HOLOMATTER GENERATOR THAT KEPT THE OMEGA GUARDIANS AT BAY...

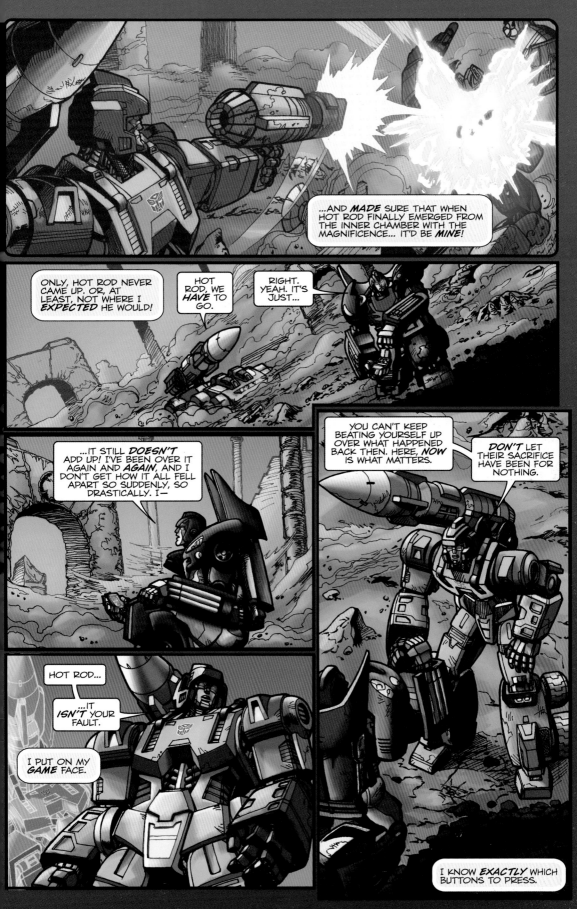

...AND **MADE** SURE THAT WHEN HOT ROD FINALLY EMERGED FROM THE INNER CHAMBER WITH THE MAGNIFICENCE... IT'D BE **MINE**!

ONLY, HOT ROD NEVER CAME UP. OR, AT LEAST, NOT WHERE I **EXPECTED** HE WOULD!

HOT ROD, WE **HAVE** TO GO.

RIGHT. YEAH. IT'S JUST...

YOU CAN'T KEEP BEATING YOURSELF UP OVER WHAT HAPPENED BACK THEN. HERE, **NOW** IS WHAT MATTERS.

DON'T LET THEIR SACRIFICE HAVE BEEN FOR NOTHING.

...IT STILL **DOESN'T** ADD UP! I'VE BEEN OVER IT AGAIN AND **AGAIN**, AND I DON'T GET HOW IT ALL FELL APART SO SUDDENLY, SO DRASTICALLY. I—

HOT ROD...

...IT **ISN'T** YOUR FAULT.

I PUT ON MY **GAME** FACE.

I KNOW **EXACTLY** WHICH BUTTONS TO PRESS.

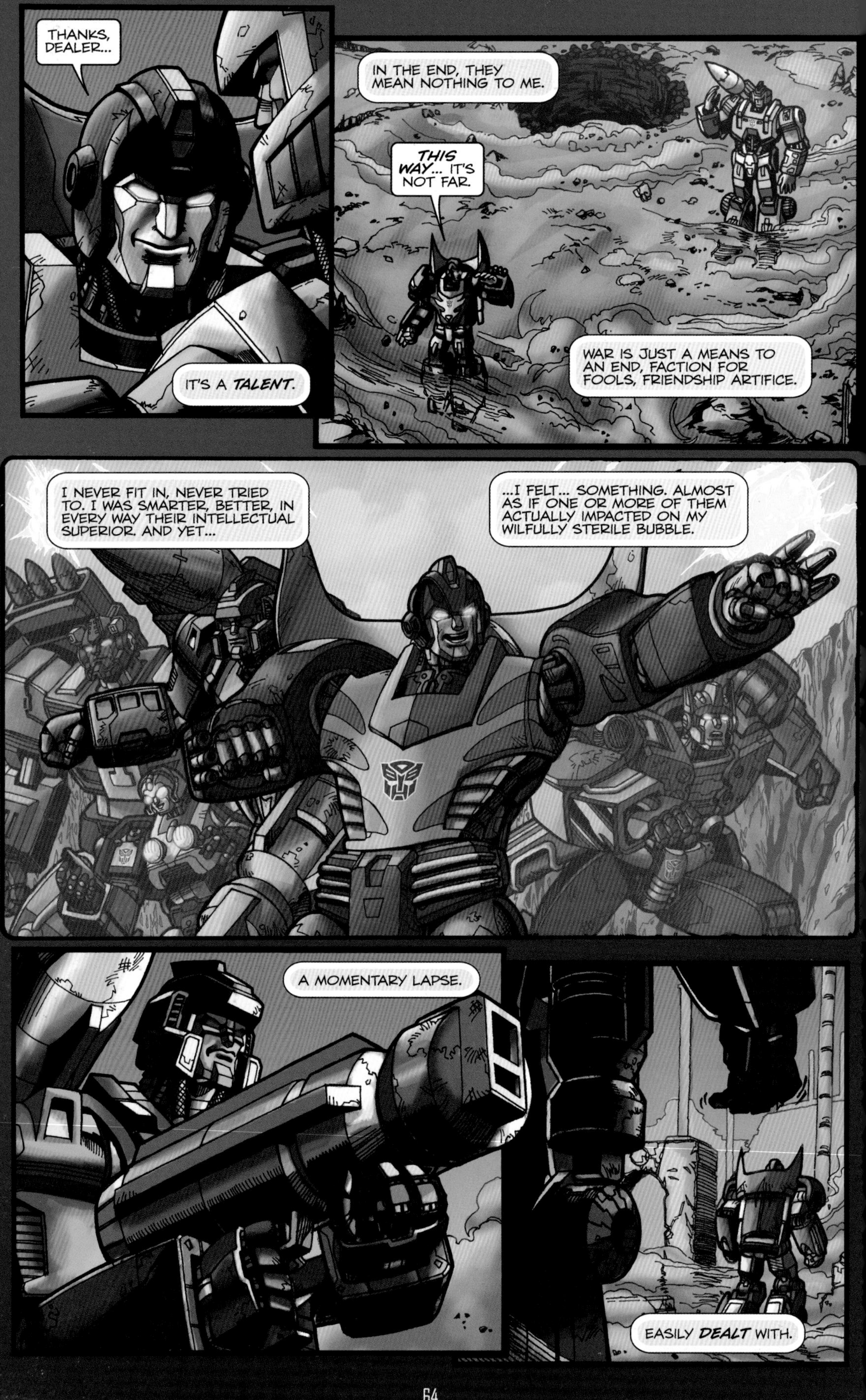
THANKS, DEALER...
IT'S A TALENT.
IN THE END, THEY MEAN NOTHING TO ME.
THIS WAY... IT'S NOT FAR.
WAR IS JUST A MEANS TO AN END, FACTION FOR FOOLS, FRIENDSHIP ARTIFICE.
I NEVER FIT IN, NEVER TRIED TO. I WAS SMARTER, BETTER, IN EVERY WAY THEIR INTELLECTUAL SUPERIOR. AND YET...
...I FELT... SOMETHING. ALMOST AS IF ONE OR MORE OF THEM ACTUALLY IMPACTED ON MY WILFULLY STERILE BUBBLE.
A MOMENTARY LAPSE.
EASILY DEALT WITH.

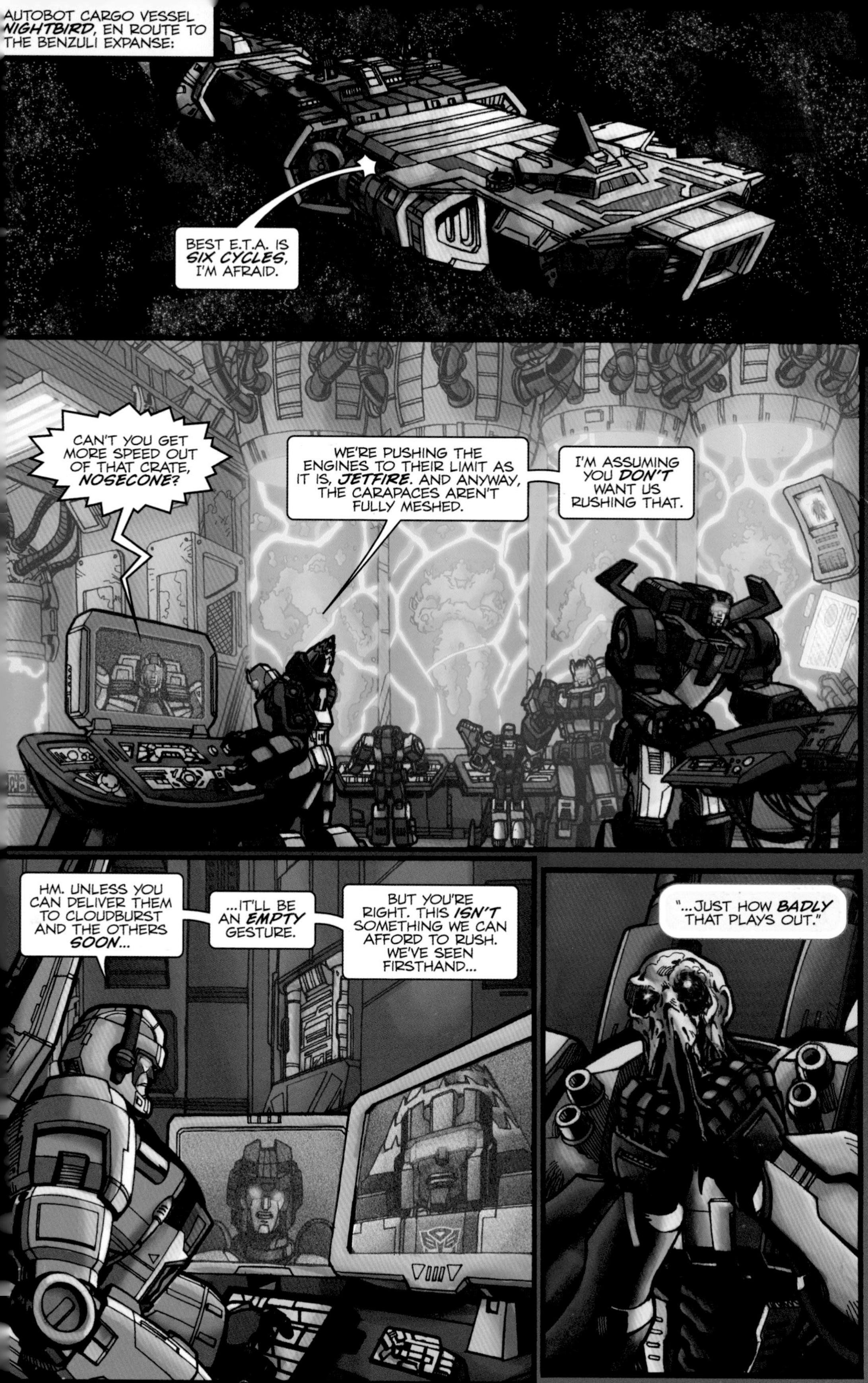
AUTOBOT CARGO VESSEL NIGHTBIRD, EN ROUTE TO THE BENZULI EXPANSE:
BEST E.T.A. IS SIX CYCLES, I'M AFRAID.
CAN'T YOU GET MORE SPEED OUT OF THAT CRATE, NOSECONE?
WE'RE PUSHING THE ENGINES TO THEIR LIMIT AS IT IS, JETFIRE. AND ANYWAY, THE CARAPACES AREN'T FULLY MESHED.
I'M ASSUMING YOU DON'T WANT US RUSHING THAT.
HM. UNLESS YOU CAN DELIVER THEM TO CLOUDBURST AND THE OTHERS SOON...
...IT'LL BE AN EMPTY GESTURE.
BUT YOU'RE RIGHT. THIS ISN'T SOMETHING WE CAN AFFORD TO RUSH. WE'VE SEEN FIRSTHAND...
"...JUST HOW BADLY THAT PLAYS OUT."

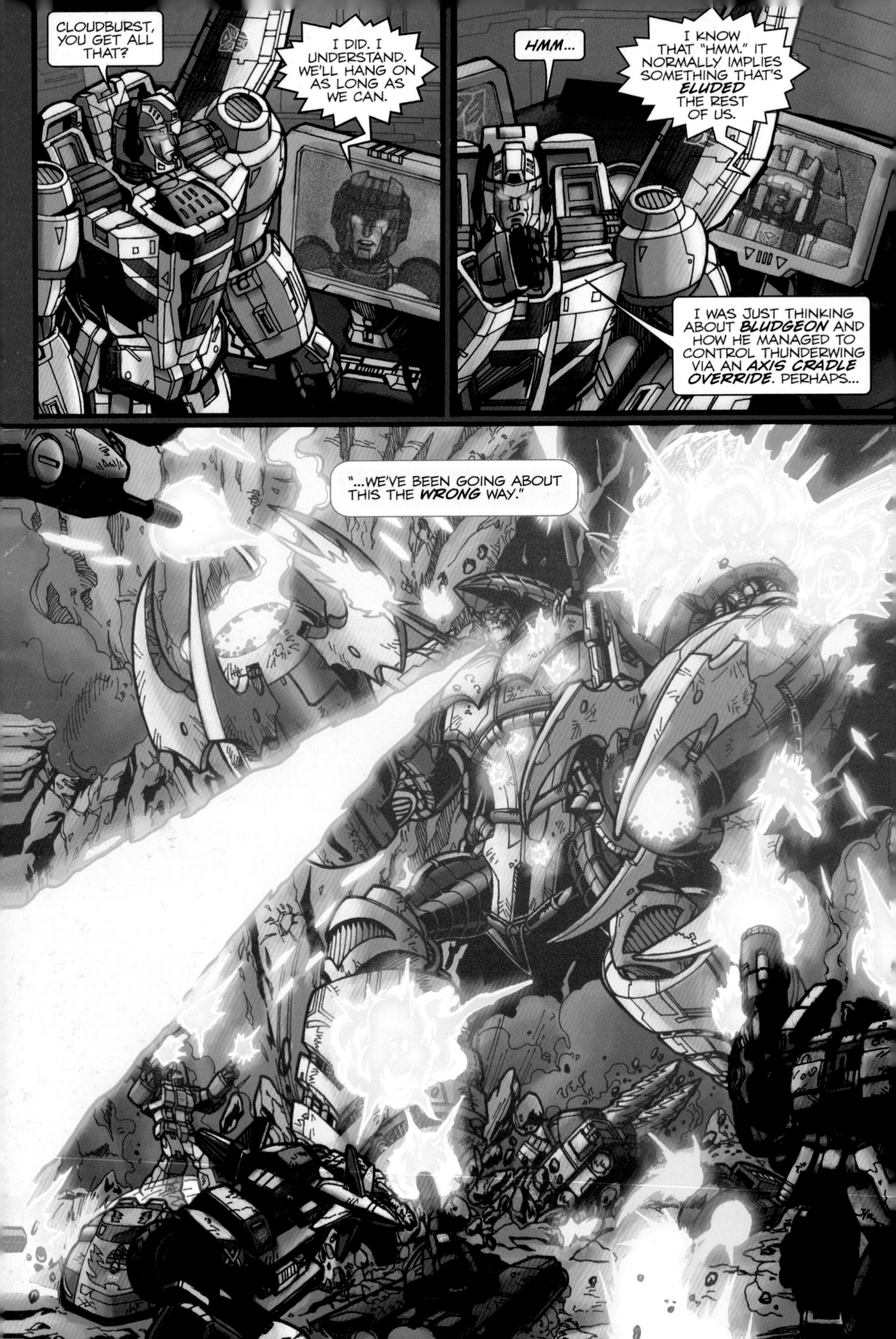
CLOUDBURST, YOU GET ALL THAT?
I DID. I UNDERSTAND. WE'LL HANG ON AS LONG AS WE CAN.
HMM...
I KNOW THAT "HMM." IT NORMALLY IMPLIES SOMETHING THAT'S ELUDED THE REST OF US.
I WAS JUST THINKING ABOUT BLUDGEON AND HOW HE MANAGED TO CONTROL THUNDERWING VIA AN AXIS CRADLE OVERRIDE. PERHAPS...
"...WE'VE BEEN GOING ABOUT THIS THE WRONG WAY."

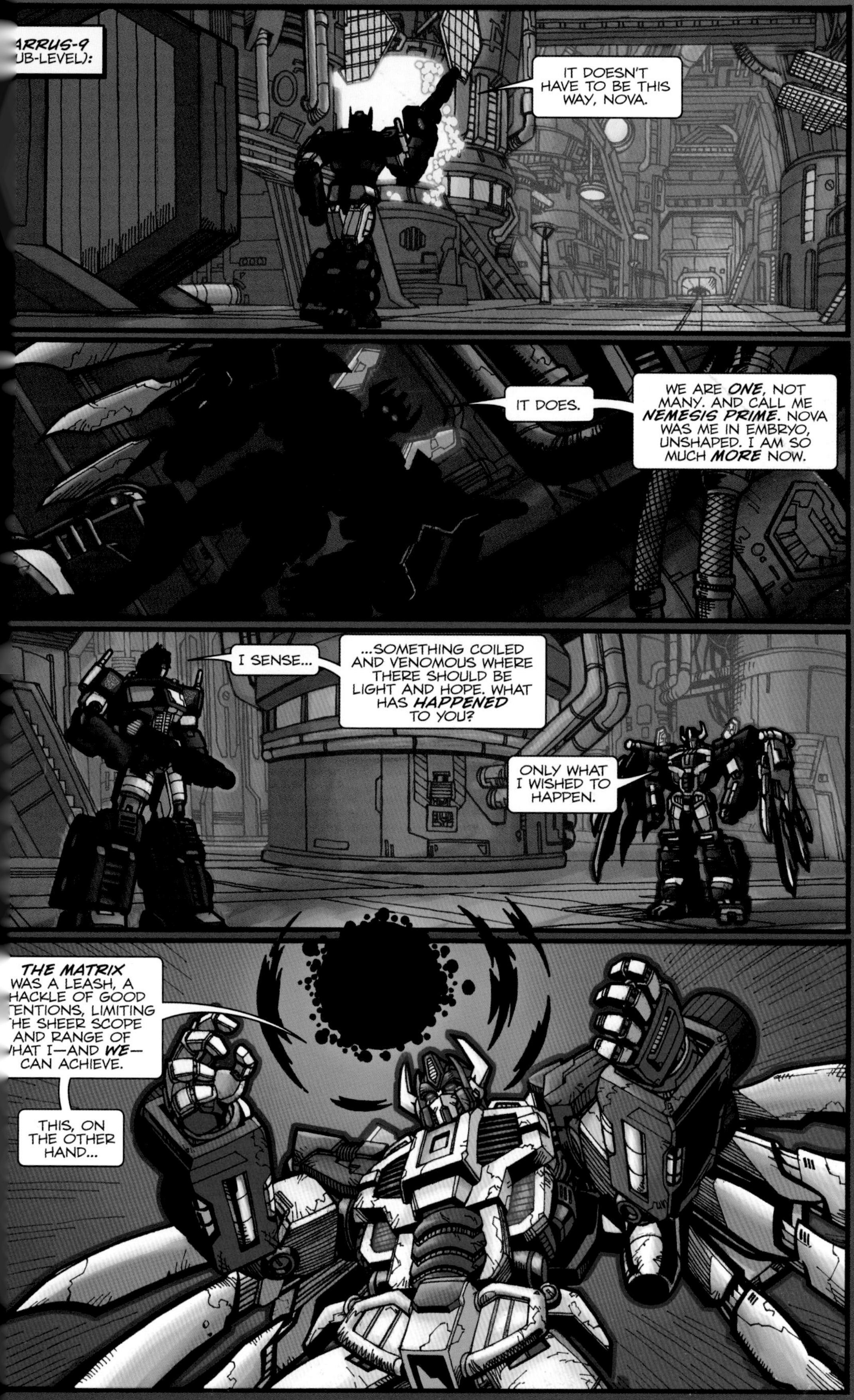

ARRUS-9
(UB-LEVEL):
IT DOESN'T HAVE TO BE THIS WAY, NOVA.
IT DOES.
WE ARE ONE, NOT MANY. AND CALL ME NEMESIS PRIME. NOVA WAS ME IN EMBRYO, UNSHAPED. I AM SO MUCH MORE NOW.
I SENSE...
...SOMETHING COILED AND VENOMOUS WHERE THERE SHOULD BE LIGHT AND HOPE. WHAT HAS HAPPENED TO YOU?
ONLY WHAT I WISHED TO HAPPEN.
THE MATRIX WAS A LEASH, A HACKLE OF GOOD TENTIONS, LIMITING HE SHEER SCOPE AND RANGE OF HAT I—AND WE— CAN ACHIEVE.
THIS, ON THE OTHER HAND...

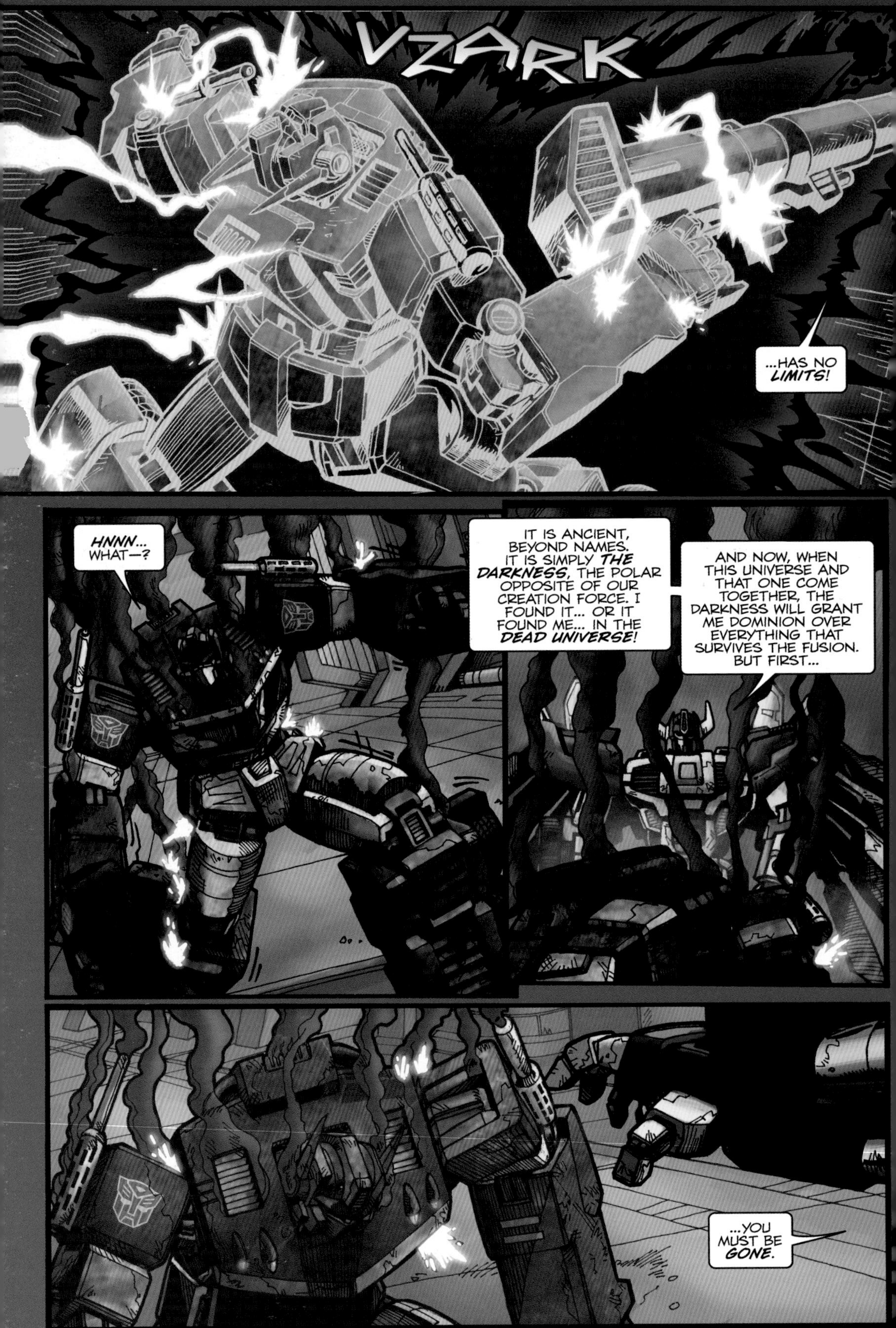
VZARK
...HAS NO LIMITS!
HNNN... WHAT—?
IT IS ANCIENT, BEYOND NAMES. IT IS SIMPLY THE DARKNESS, THE POLAR OPPOSITE OF OUR CREATION FORCE. I FOUND IT... OR IT FOUND ME... IN THE DEAD UNIVERSE!
AND NOW, WHEN THIS UNIVERSE AND THAT ONE COME TOGETHER, THE DARKNESS WILL GRANT ME DOMINION OVER EVERYTHING THAT SURVIVES THE FUSION. BUT FIRST...
...YOU MUST BE GONE.

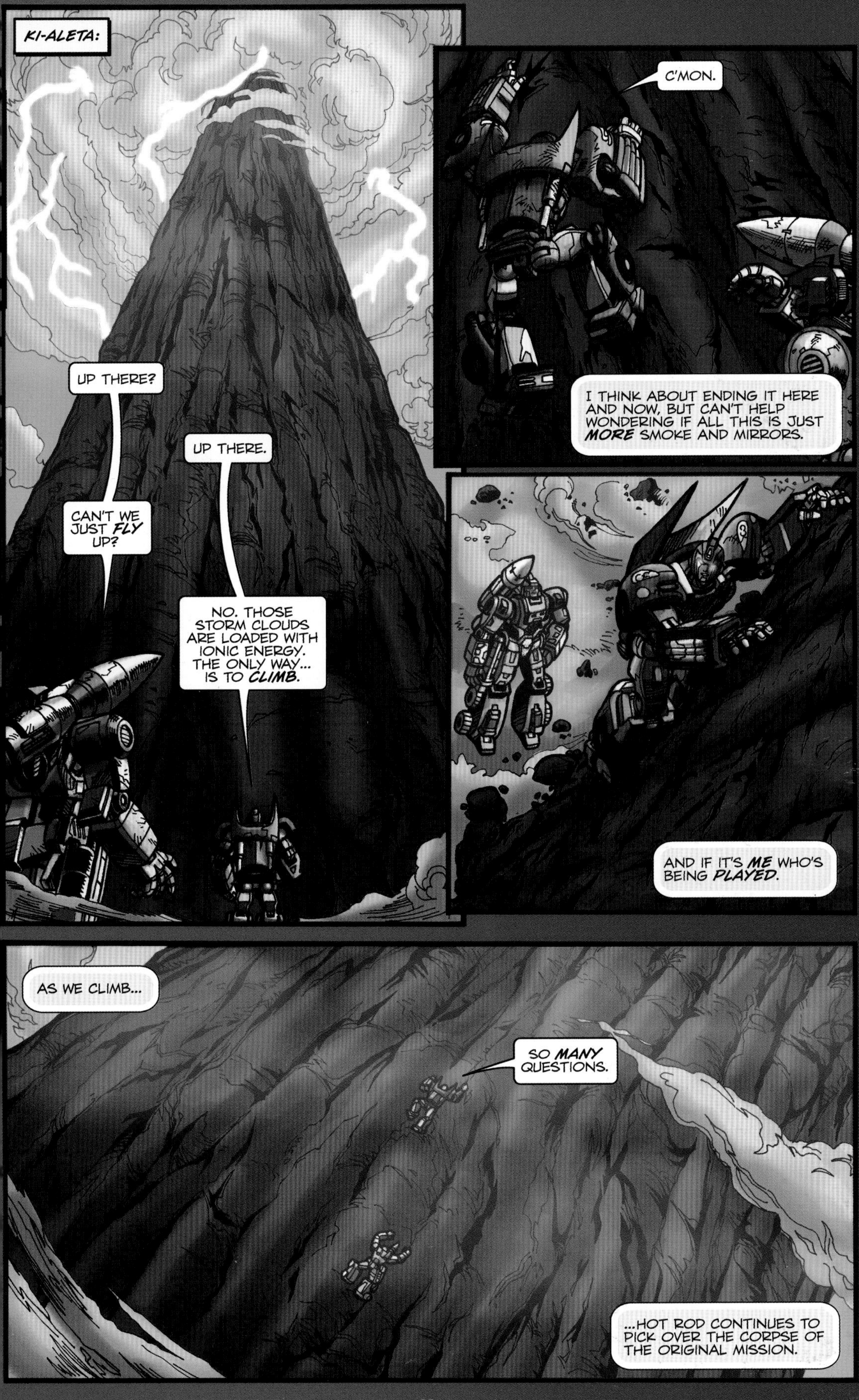
KI-ALETA:
UP THERE?
UP THERE.
CAN'T WE JUST FLY UP?
NO. THOSE STORM CLOUDS ARE LOADED WITH IONIC ENERGY. THE ONLY WAY... IS TO CLIMB.
C'MON.
I THINK ABOUT ENDING IT HERE AND NOW, BUT CAN'T HELP WONDERING IF ALL THIS IS JUST MORE SMOKE AND MIRRORS.
AND IF IT'S ME WHO'S BEING PLAYED.
AS WE CLIMB...
SO MANY QUESTIONS.
...HOT ROD CONTINUES TO PICK OVER THE CORPSE OF THE ORIGINAL MISSION.

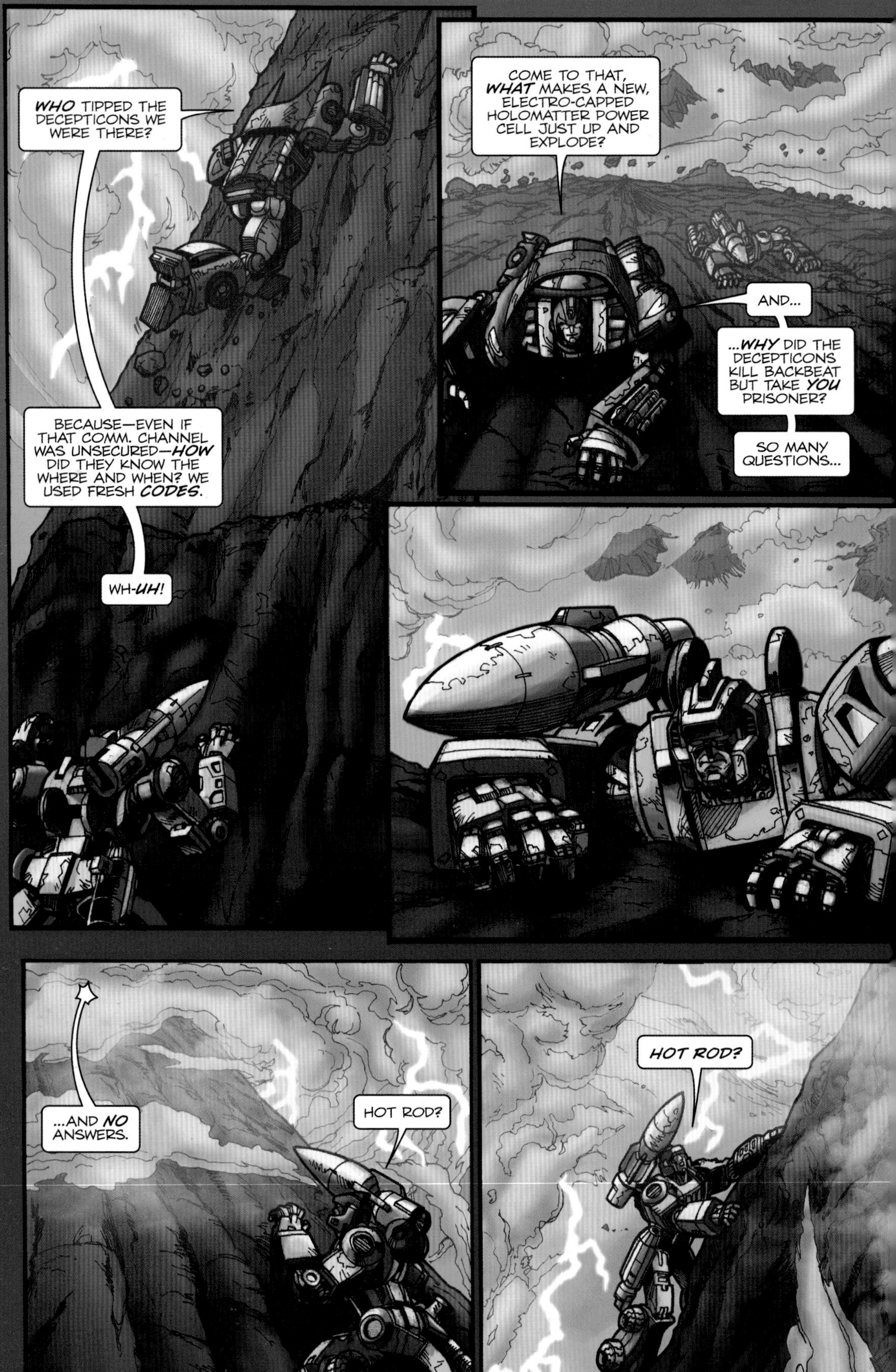
WHO TIPPED THE DECEPTICONS WE WERE THERE?
BECAUSE—EVEN IF THAT COMM. CHANNEL WAS UNSECURED—HOW DID THEY KNOW THE WHERE AND WHEN? WE USED FRESH CODES.
WH-UH!
COME TO THAT, WHAT MAKES A NEW, ELECTRO-CAPPED HOLOMATTER POWER CELL JUST UP AND EXPLODE?
AND...
...WHY DID THE DECEPTICONS KILL BACKBEAT BUT TAKE YOU PRISONER?
SO MANY QUESTIONS...
...AND NO ANSWERS.
HOT ROD?
HOT ROD?

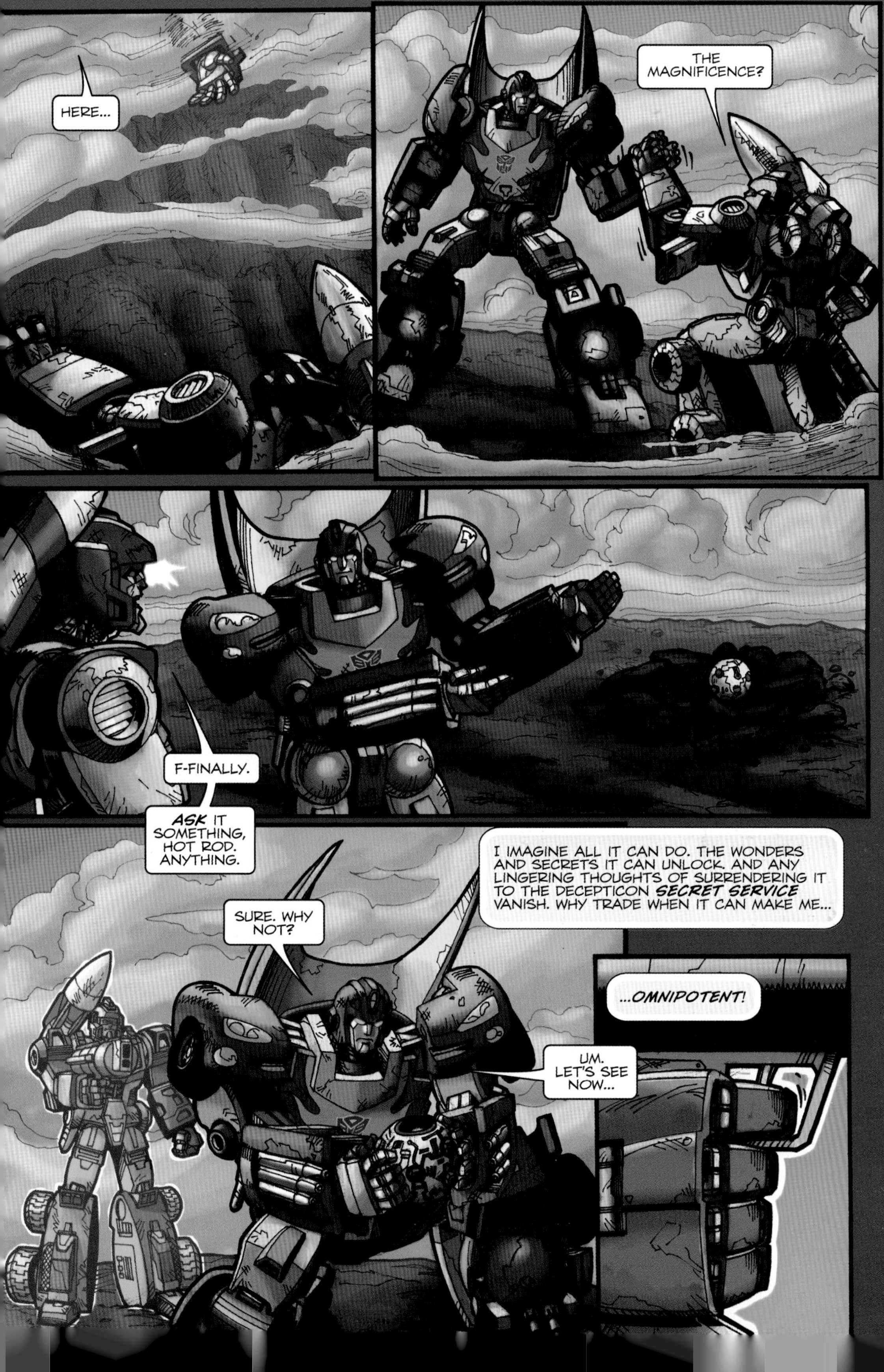
HERE...
THE MAGNIFICENCE?
F-FINALLY.
ASK IT SOMETHING, HOT ROD. ANYTHING.
SURE. WHY NOT?
I IMAGINE ALL IT CAN DO. THE WONDERS AND SECRETS IT CAN UNLOCK. AND ANY LINGERING THOUGHTS OF SURRENDERING IT TO THE DECEPTICON SECRET SERVICE VANISH. WHY TRADE WHEN IT CAN MAKE ME...
...OMNIPOTENT!
UM. LET'S SEE NOW...

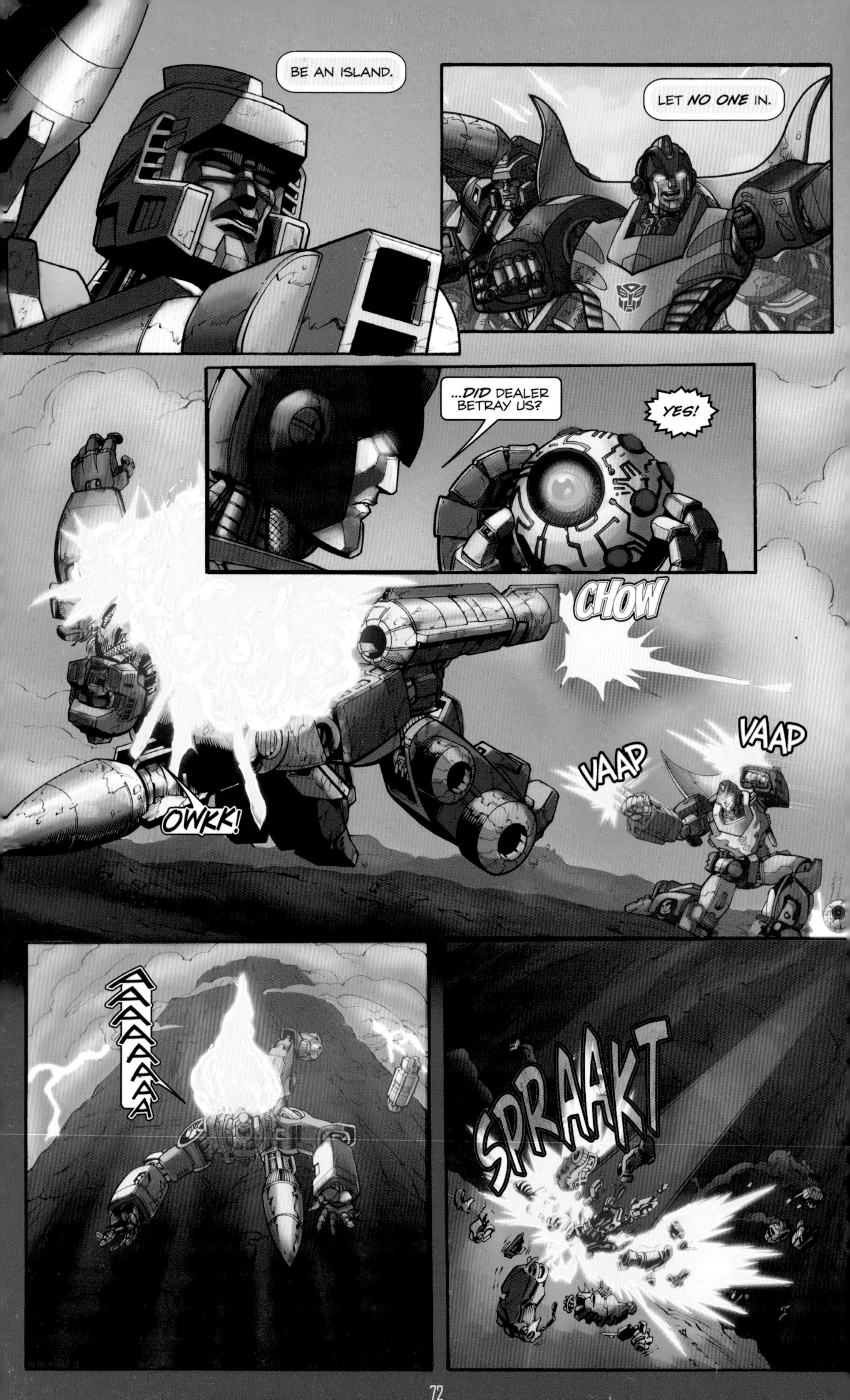
BE AN ISLAND.
LET NO ONE IN.
...DID DEALER BETRAY US?
YES!
CHOW
OWKK!
VAAP
VAAP
AAAAAAA
SPRAAKT

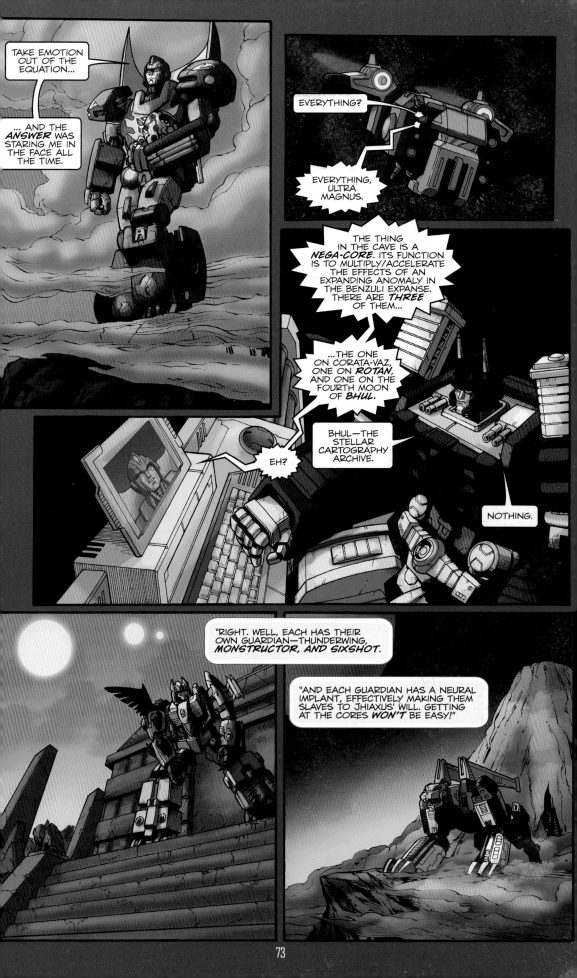

TAKE EMOTION OUT OF THE EQUATION...

... AND THE *ANSWER* WAS STARING ME IN THE FACE ALL THE TIME.

EVERYTHING?

EVERYTHING, ULTRA MAGNUS.

THE THING IN THE CAVE IS A *NEGA-CORE*. ITS FUNCTION IS TO MULTIPLY/ACCELERATE THE EFFECTS OF AN EXPANDING ANOMALY IN THE BENZULI EXPANSE. THERE ARE *THREE* OF THEM...

...THE ONE ON CORATA-VAZ, ONE ON *ROTAN*, AND ONE ON THE FOURTH MOON OF *BHUL*.

BHUL—THE STELLAR CARTOGRAPHY ARCHIVE.

EH?

NOTHING.

"RIGHT. WELL, EACH HAS THEIR OWN GUARDIAN—THUNDERWING, *MONSTRUCTOR*, AND SIXSHOT.

"AND EACH GUARDIAN HAS A NEURAL IMPLANT, EFFECTIVELY MAKING THEM SLAVES TO JHIAXUS' WILL. GETTING AT THE CORES *WON'T* BE EASY!"

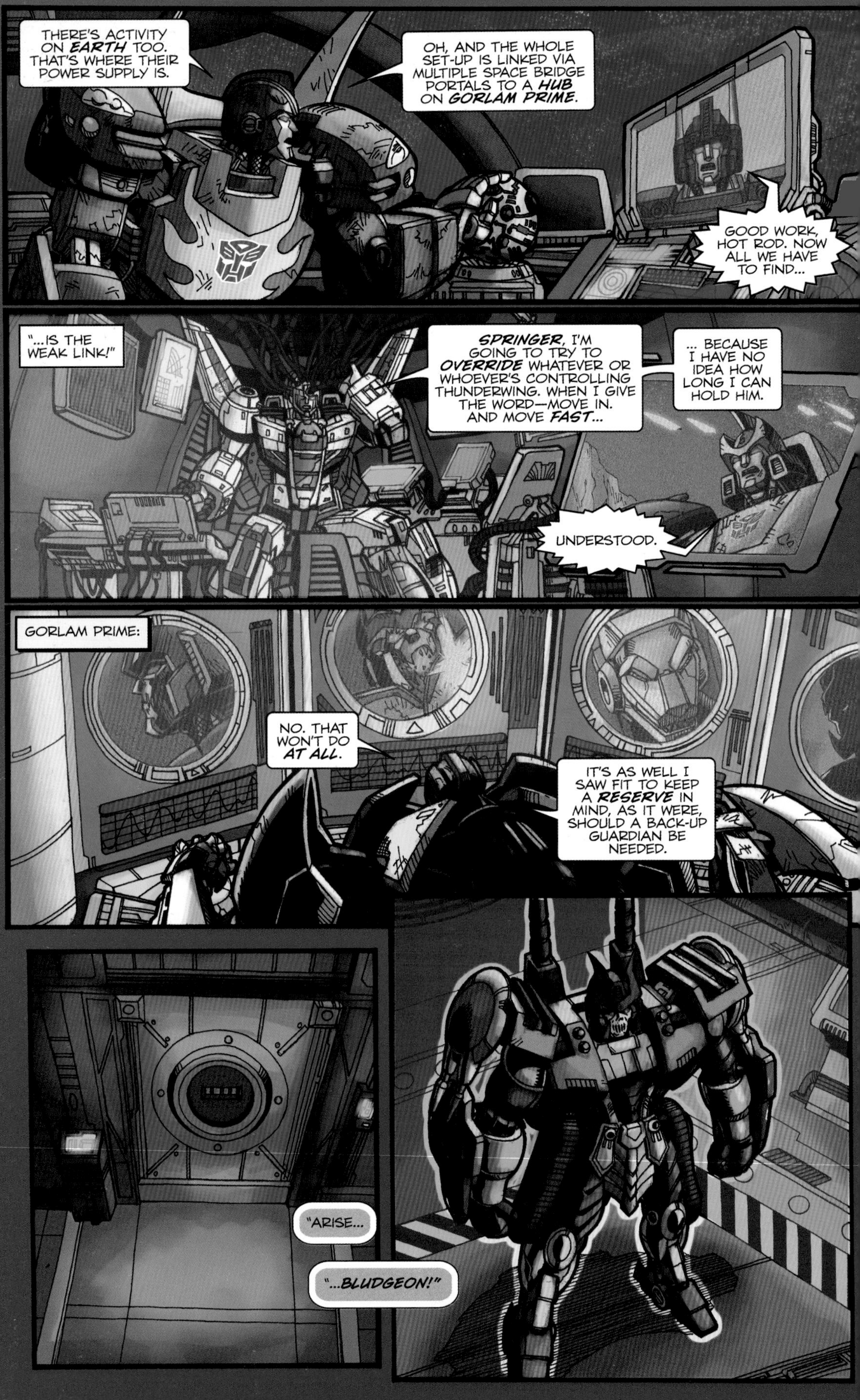
THERE'S ACTIVITY ON EARTH TOO. THAT'S WHERE THEIR POWER SUPPLY IS.
OH, AND THE WHOLE SET-UP IS LINKED VIA MULTIPLE SPACE BRIDGE PORTALS TO A HUB ON GORLAM PRIME.
GOOD WORK, HOT ROD. NOW ALL WE HAVE TO FIND...
"...IS THE WEAK LINK!"
SPRINGER, I'M GOING TO TRY TO OVERRIDE WHATEVER OR WHOEVER'S CONTROLLING THUNDERWING. WHEN I GIVE THE WORD—MOVE IN. AND MOVE FAST...
... BECAUSE I HAVE NO IDEA HOW LONG I CAN HOLD HIM.
UNDERSTOOD.
GORLAM PRIME:
NO. THAT WON'T DO AT ALL.
IT'S AS WELL I SAW FIT TO KEEP A RESERVE IN MIND, AS IT WERE, SHOULD A BACK-UP GUARDIAN BE NEEDED.
"ARISE...
"...BLUDGEON!"

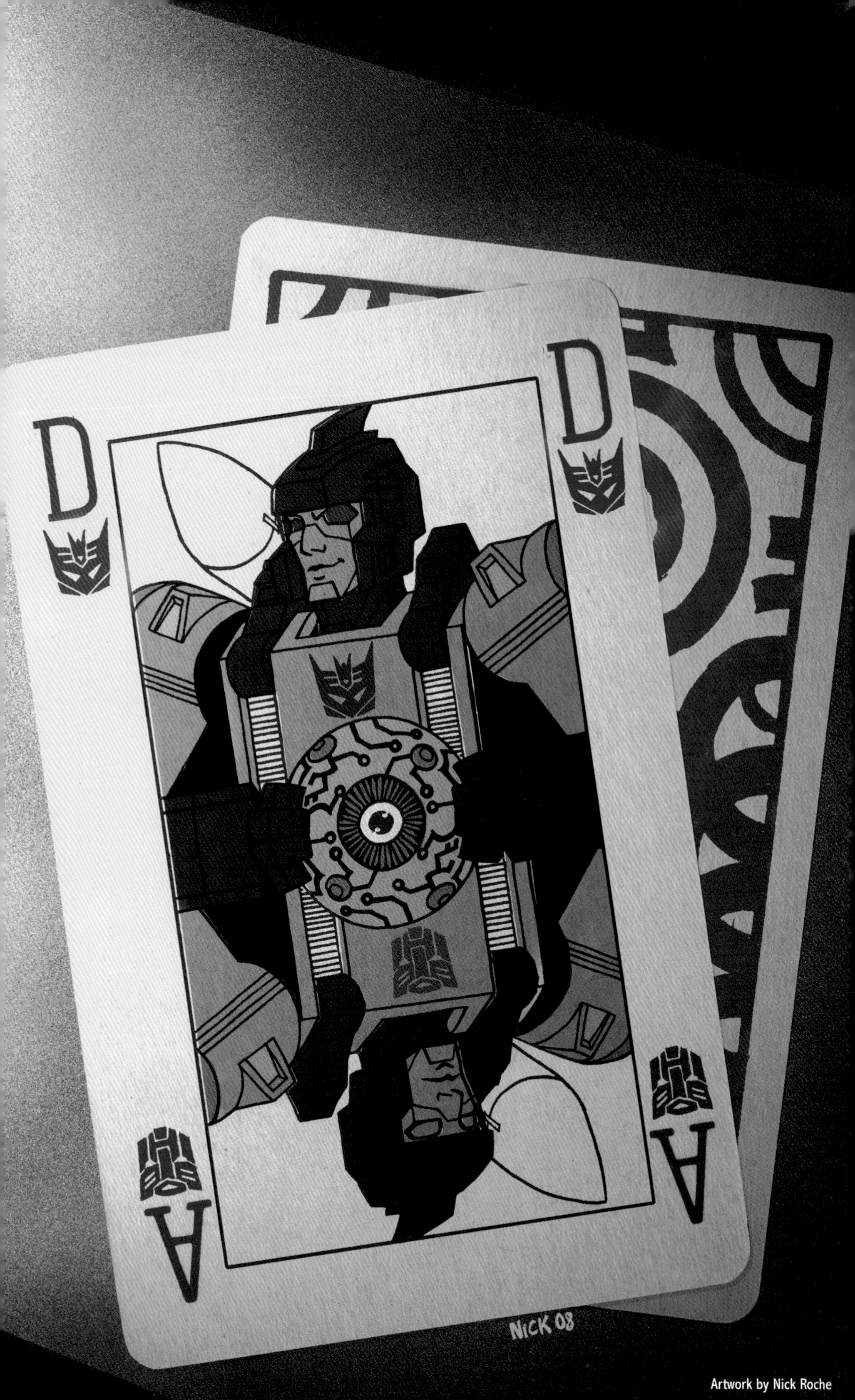
D
D
A
A
NICK 08

Artwork by Nick Roche

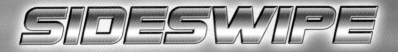

SIDESWIPE

Inaction weighs heavily on SIDESWIPE. He wants to be out there, in the thick of it, his insecurities and self-conceived shortcomings drowned out by the thunder of battle. Sullen, resentful, he carries the weight of another's dismissal and disdain, desperate—above all else—to prove himself, to be seen by others, and one in particular, as more than just the rookie trooper he once was. Bombastic, antagonistic, thorny, and the chip he carries makes him hard to like. But, perhaps, all he ever needed was the right cause...

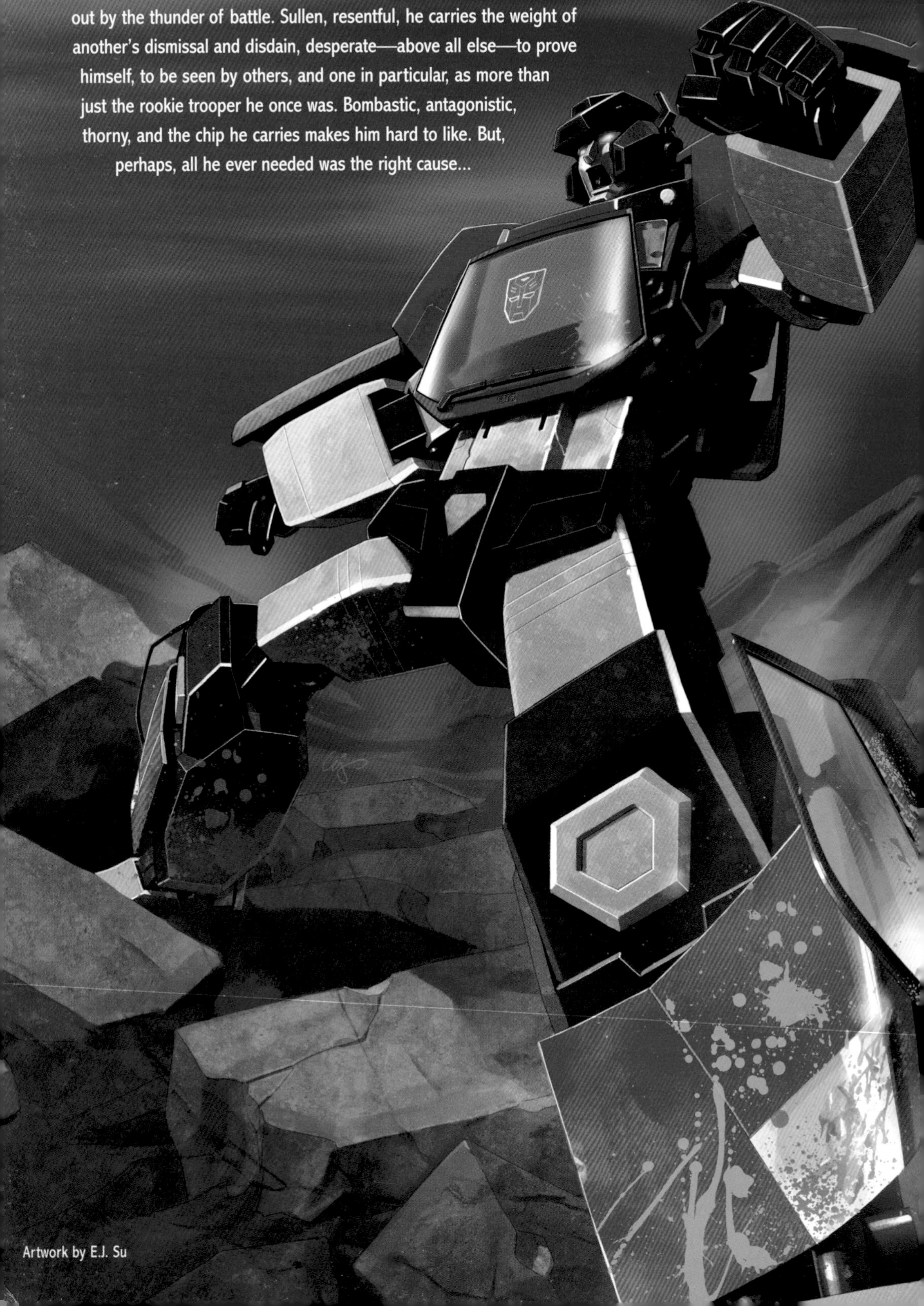

Artwork by E.J. Su

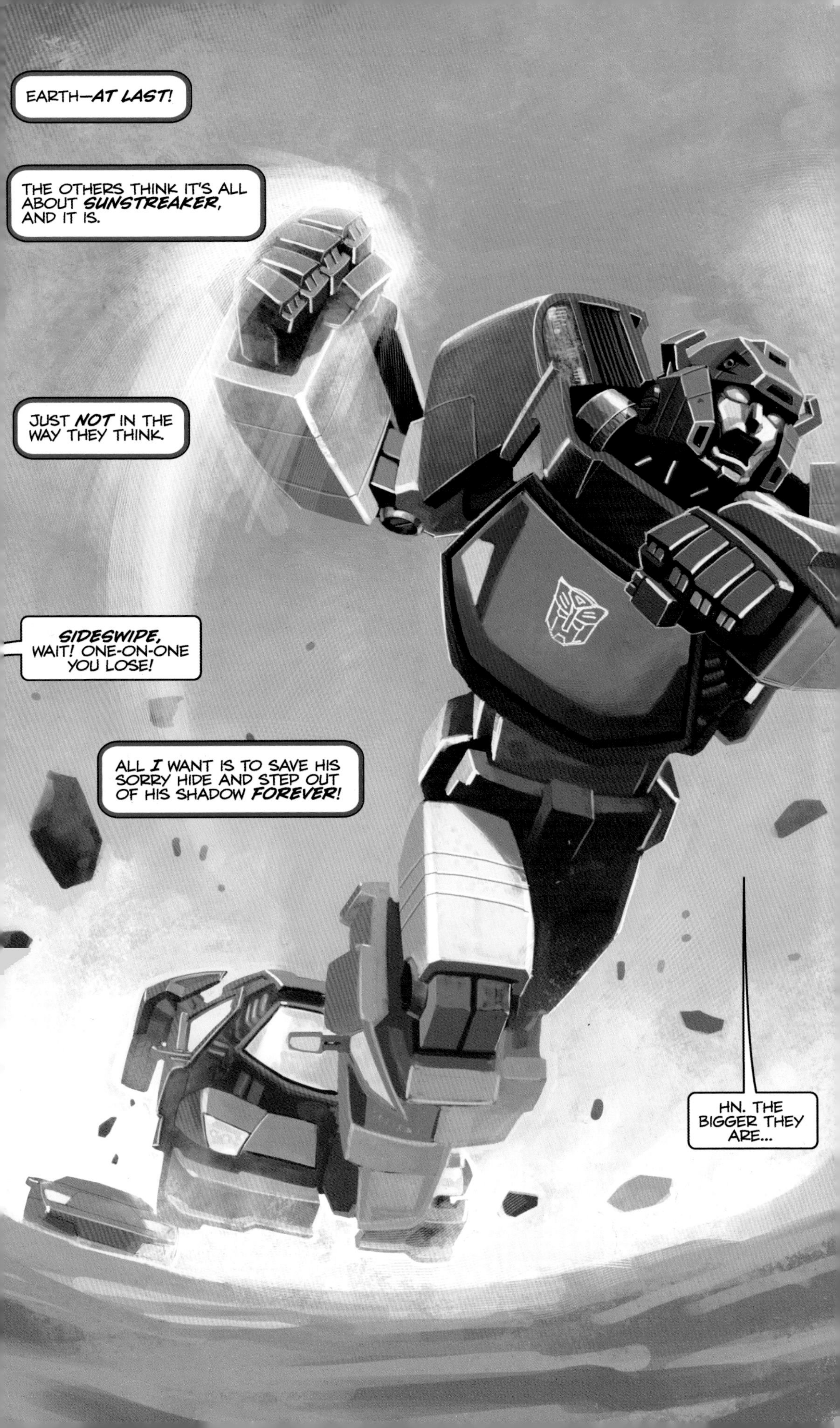
EARTH—AT LAST!
THE OTHERS THINK IT'S ALL ABOUT SUNSTREAKER, AND IT IS.
JUST NOT IN THE WAY THEY THINK.
SIDESWIPE, WAIT! ONE-ON-ONE YOU LOSE!
ALL I WANT IS TO SAVE HIS SORRY HIDE AND STEP OUT OF HIS SHADOW FOREVER!
HN. THE BIGGER THEY ARE...

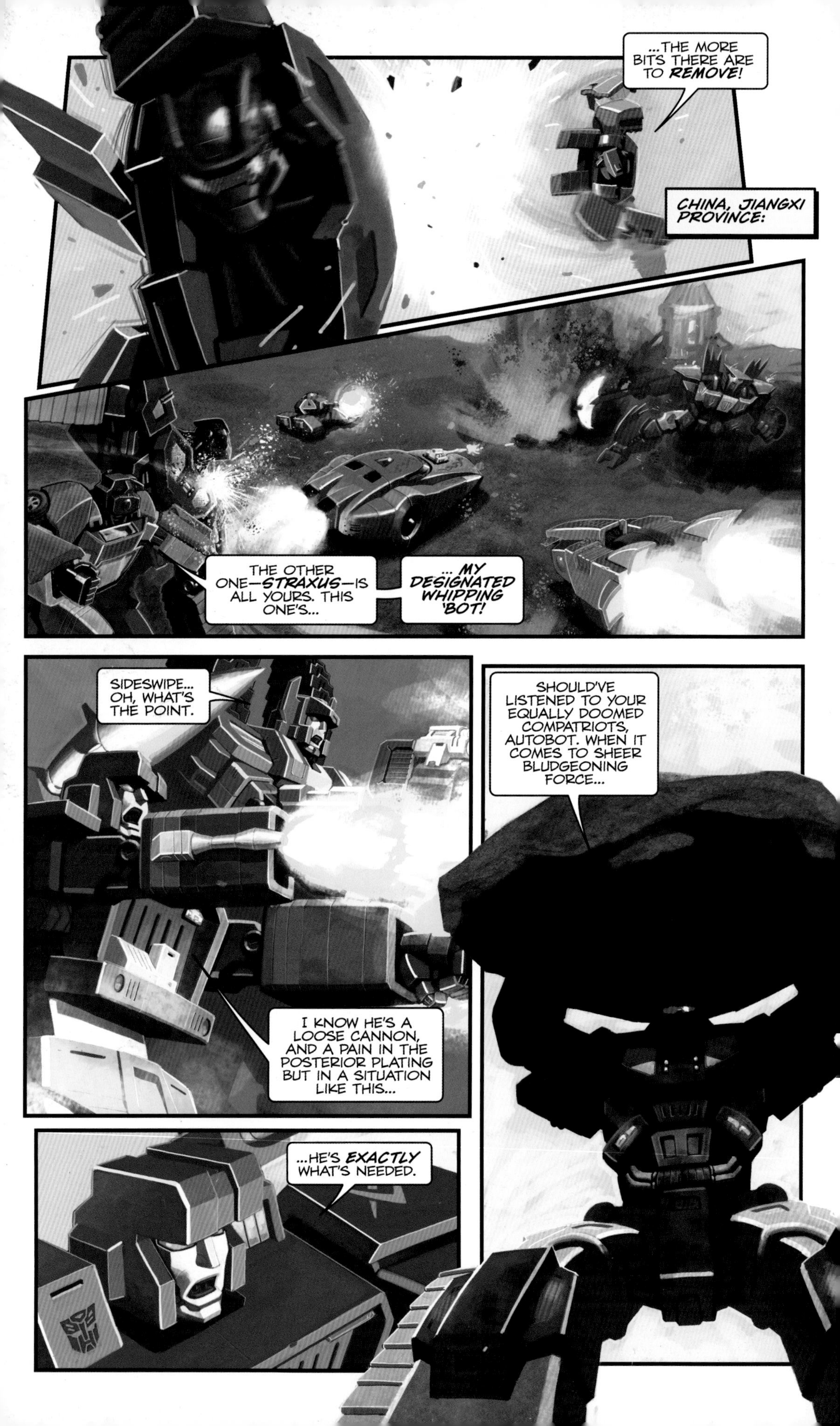
...THE MORE BITS THERE ARE TO REMOVE!
CHINA, JIANGXI PROVINCE:
THE OTHER ONE—STRAXUS—IS ALL YOURS. THIS ONE'S...
...MY DESIGNATED WHIPPING 'BOT!
SIDESWIPE... OH, WHAT'S THE POINT.
SHOULD'VE LISTENED TO YOUR EQUALLY DOOMED COMPATRIOTS, AUTOBOT. WHEN IT COMES TO SHEER BLUDGEONING FORCE...
I KNOW HE'S A LOOSE CANNON, AND A PAIN IN THE POSTERIOR PLATING BUT IN A SITUATION LIKE THIS...
...HE'S EXACTLY WHAT'S NEEDED.

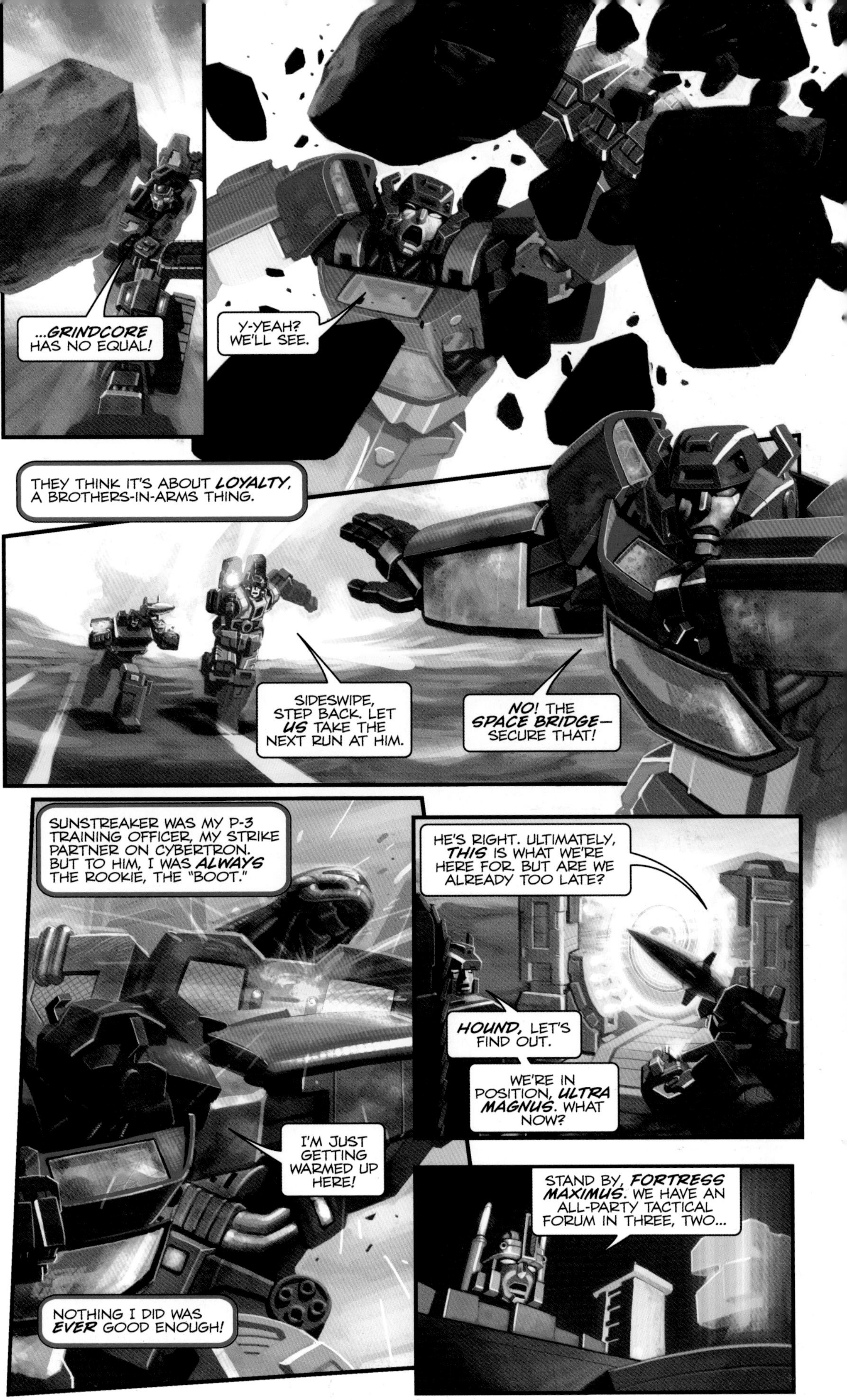
...GRINDCORE HAS NO EQUAL!
Y-YEAH? WE'LL SEE.
THEY THINK IT'S ABOUT LOYALTY, A BROTHERS-IN-ARMS THING.
SIDESWIPE, STEP BACK. LET US TAKE THE NEXT RUN AT HIM.
NO! THE SPACE BRIDGE— SECURE THAT!
SUNSTREAKER WAS MY P-3 TRAINING OFFICER, MY STRIKE PARTNER ON CYBERTRON. BUT TO HIM, I WAS ALWAYS THE ROOKIE, THE "BOOT."
I'M JUST GETTING WARMED UP HERE!
NOTHING I DID WAS EVER GOOD ENOUGH!
HE'S RIGHT. ULTIMATELY, THIS IS WHAT WE'RE HERE FOR. BUT ARE WE ALREADY TOO LATE?
HOUND, LET'S FIND OUT.
WE'RE IN POSITION, ULTRA MAGNUS. WHAT NOW?
STAND BY, FORTRESS MAXIMUS. WE HAVE AN ALL-PARTY TACTICAL FORUM IN THREE, TWO...

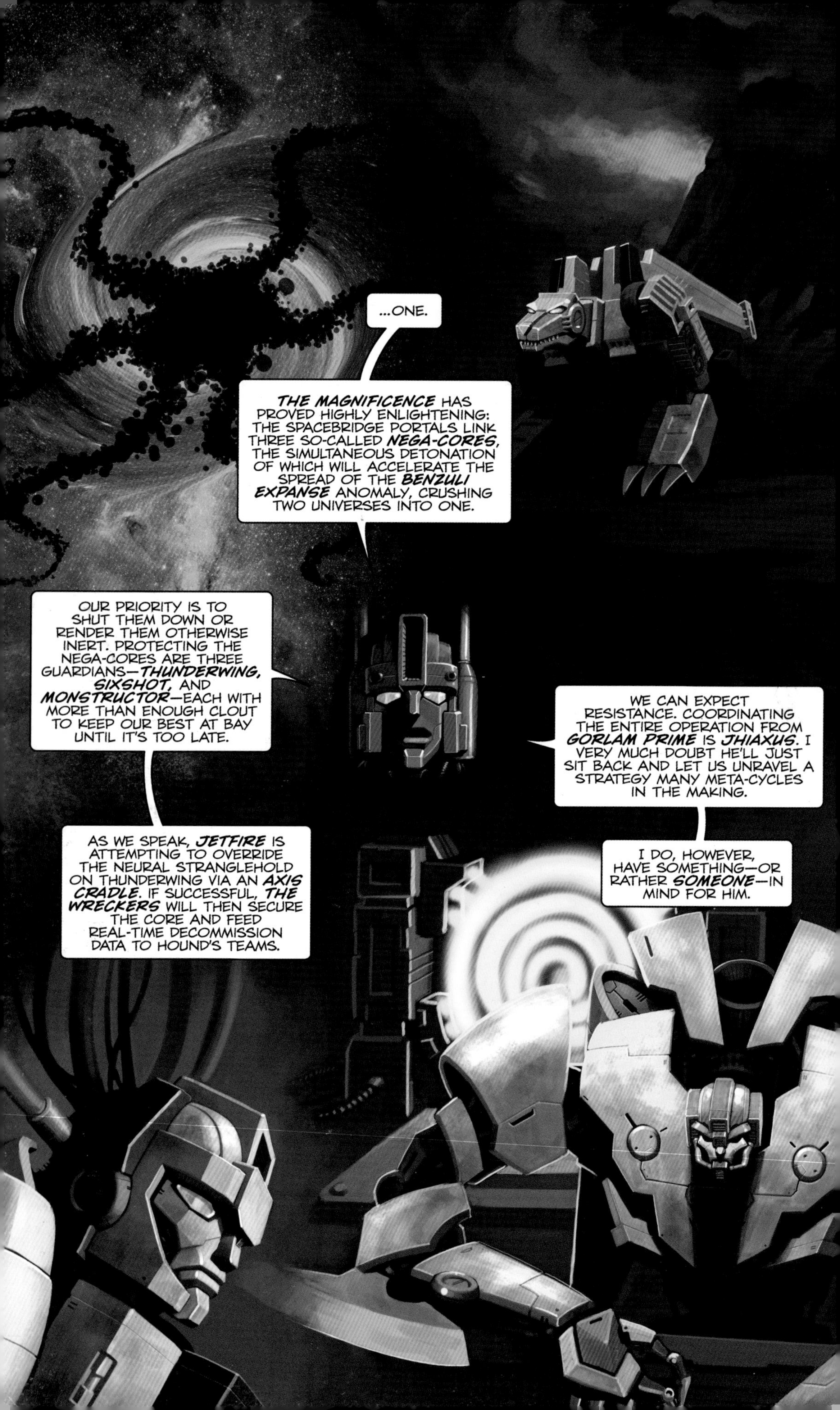

...ONE.
THE MAGNIFICENCE HAS PROVED HIGHLY ENLIGHTENING: THE SPACEBRIDGE PORTALS LINK THREE SO-CALLED NEGA-CORES, THE SIMULTANEOUS DETONATION OF WHICH WILL ACCELERATE THE SPREAD OF THE BENZULI EXPANSE ANOMALY, CRUSHING TWO UNIVERSES INTO ONE.
OUR PRIORITY IS TO SHUT THEM DOWN OR RENDER THEM OTHERWISE INERT. PROTECTING THE NEGA-CORES ARE THREE GUARDIANS—THUNDERWING, SIXSHOT, AND MONSTRUCTOR—EACH WITH MORE THAN ENOUGH CLOUT TO KEEP OUR BEST AT BAY UNTIL IT'S TOO LATE.
WE CAN EXPECT RESISTANCE. COORDINATING THE ENTIRE OPERATION FROM GORLAM PRIME IS JHIAXUS. I VERY MUCH DOUBT HE'LL JUST SIT BACK AND LET US UNRAVEL A STRATEGY MANY META-CYCLES IN THE MAKING.
AS WE SPEAK, JETFIRE IS ATTEMPTING TO OVERRIDE THE NEURAL STRANGLEHOLD ON THUNDERWING VIA AN AXIS CRADLE. IF SUCCESSFUL, THE WRECKERS WILL THEN SECURE THE CORE AND FEED REAL-TIME DECOMMISSION DATA TO HOUND'S TEAMS.
I DO, HOWEVER, HAVE SOMETHING—OR RATHER SOMEONE—IN MIND FOR HIM.

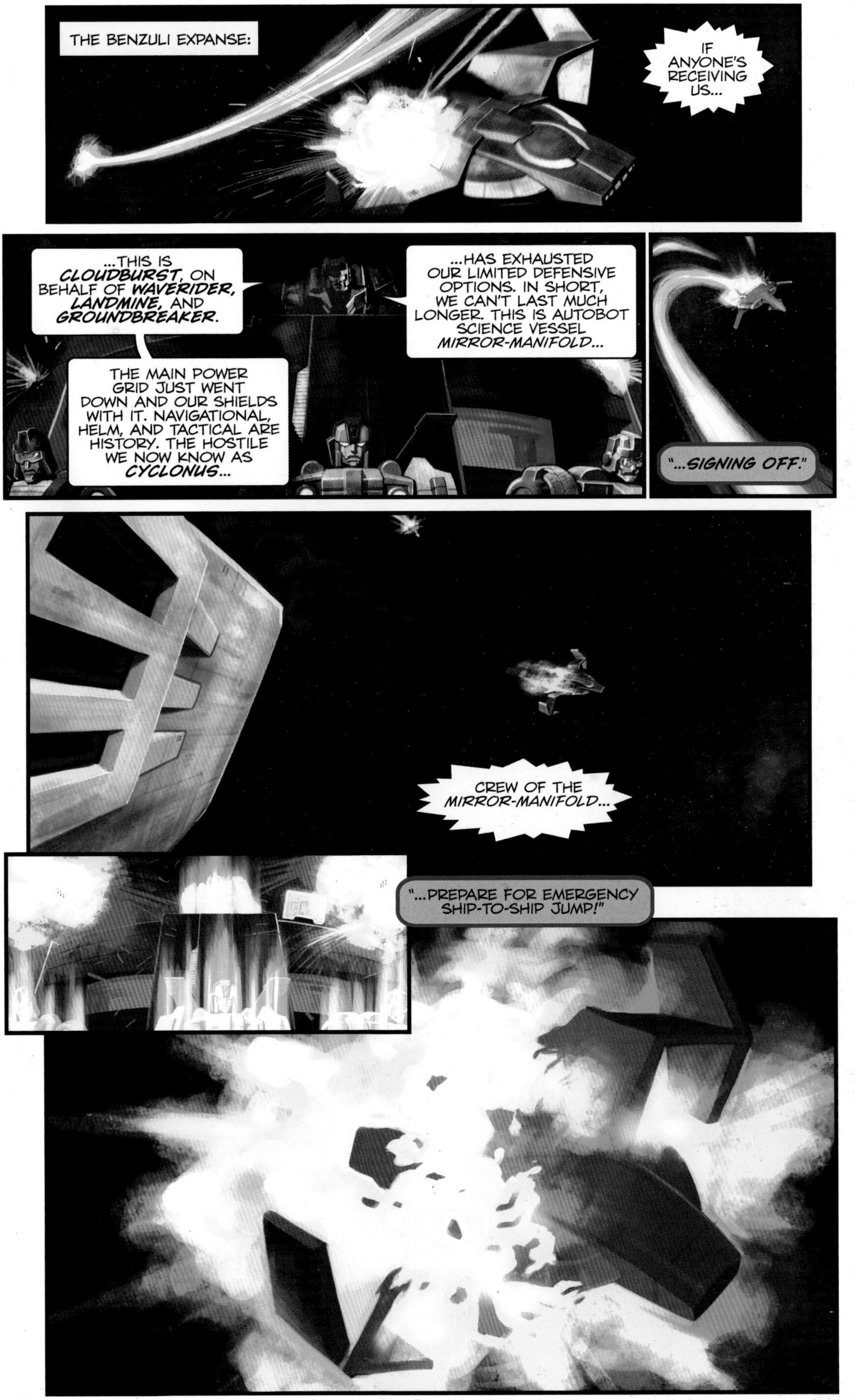
THE BENZULI EXPANSE:
IF ANYONE'S RECEIVING US...
...THIS IS CLOUDBURST, ON BEHALF OF WAVERIDER, LANDMINE, AND GROUNDBREAKER.
THE MAIN POWER GRID JUST WENT DOWN AND OUR SHIELDS WITH IT. NAVIGATIONAL, HELM, AND TACTICAL ARE HISTORY. THE HOSTILE WE NOW KNOW AS CYCLONUS...
...HAS EXHAUSTED OUR LIMITED DEFENSIVE OPTIONS. IN SHORT, WE CAN'T LAST MUCH LONGER. THIS IS AUTOBOT SCIENCE VESSEL MIRROR-MANIFOLD...
"...SIGNING OFF."
CREW OF THE MIRROR-MANIFOLD...
"...PREPARE FOR EMERGENCY SHIP-TO-SHIP JUMP!"

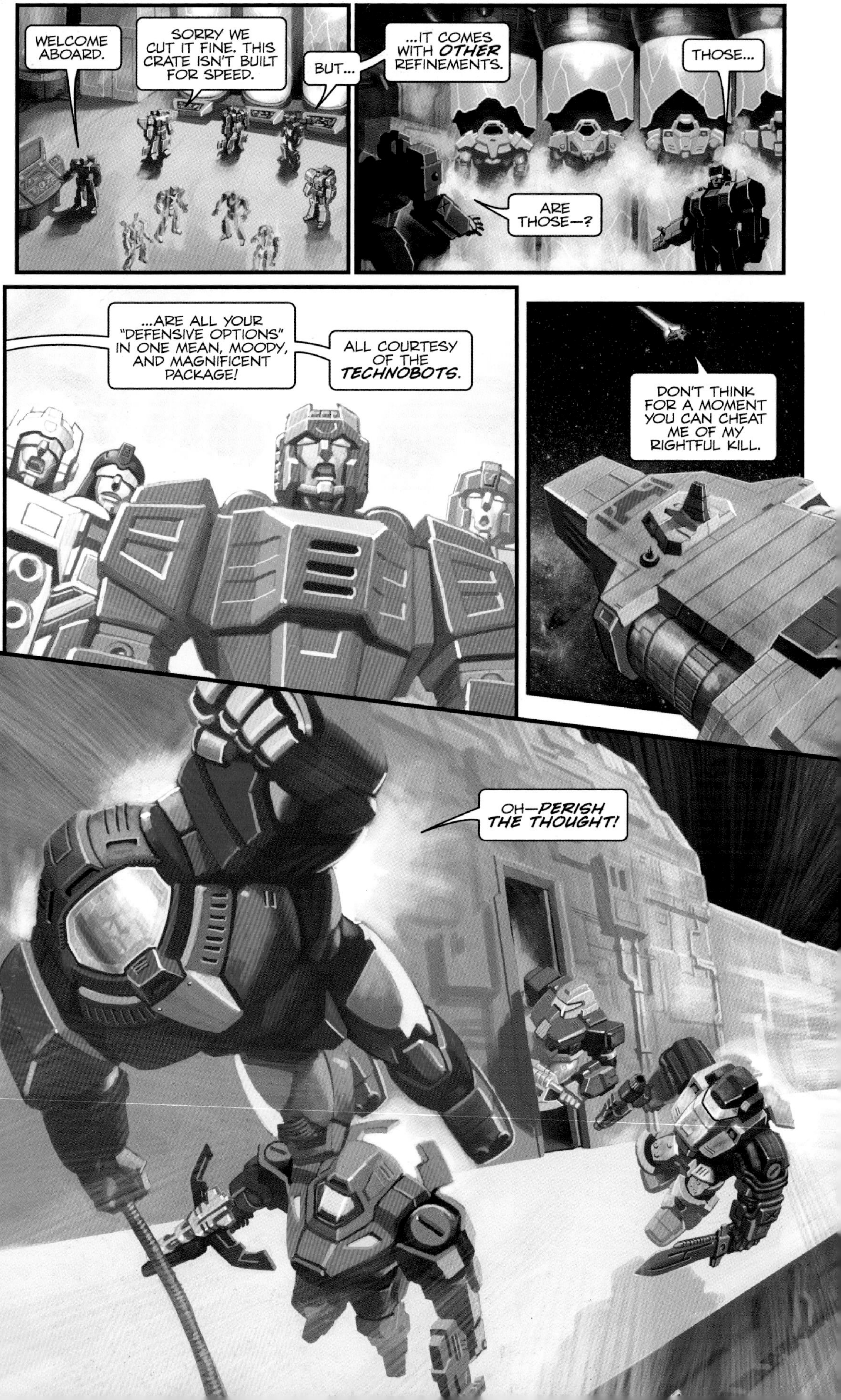
WELCOME ABOARD.
SORRY WE CUT IT FINE. THIS CRATE ISN'T BUILT FOR SPEED.
BUT...
...IT COMES WITH *OTHER* REFINEMENTS.
THOSE...
ARE THOSE--?
...ARE ALL YOUR "DEFENSIVE OPTIONS" IN ONE MEAN, MOODY, AND MAGNIFICENT PACKAGE!
ALL COURTESY OF THE *TECHNOBOTS*.
DON'T THINK FOR A MOMENT YOU CAN CHEAT ME OF MY RIGHTFUL KILL.
OH--*PERISH THE THOUGHT!*

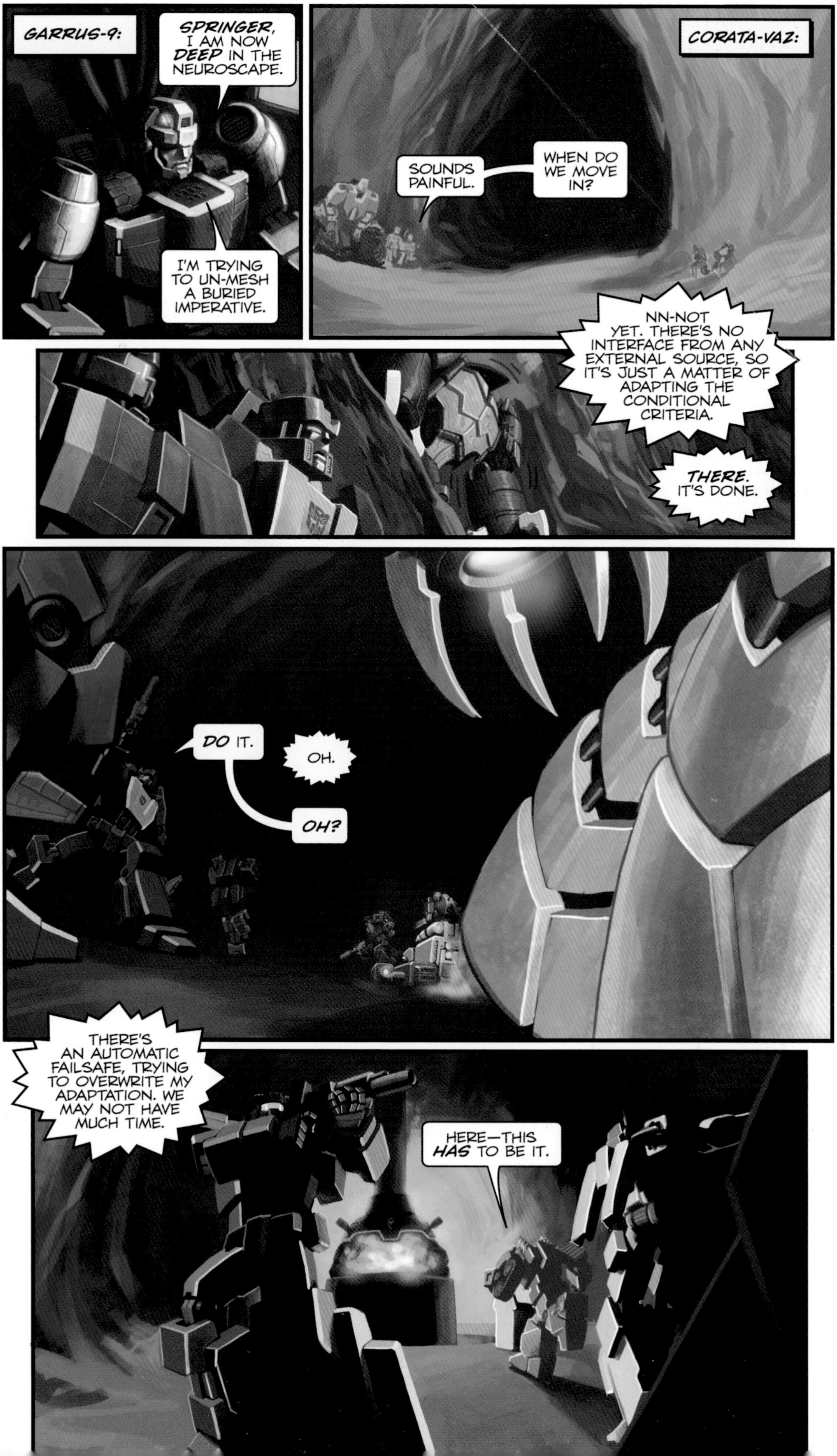
GARRUS-9:
SPRINGER, I AM NOW DEEP IN THE NEUROSCAPE.
I'M TRYING TO UN-MESH A BURIED IMPERATIVE.
CORATA-VAZ:
SOUNDS PAINFUL.
WHEN DO WE MOVE IN?
NN-NOT YET. THERE'S NO INTERFACE FROM ANY EXTERNAL SOURCE, SO IT'S JUST A MATTER OF ADAPTING THE CONDITIONAL CRITERIA.
THERE. IT'S DONE.
DO IT.
OH.
OH?
THERE'S AN AUTOMATIC FAILSAFE, TRYING TO OVERWRITE MY ADAPTATION. WE MAY NOT HAVE MUCH TIME.
HERE—THIS HAS TO BE IT.

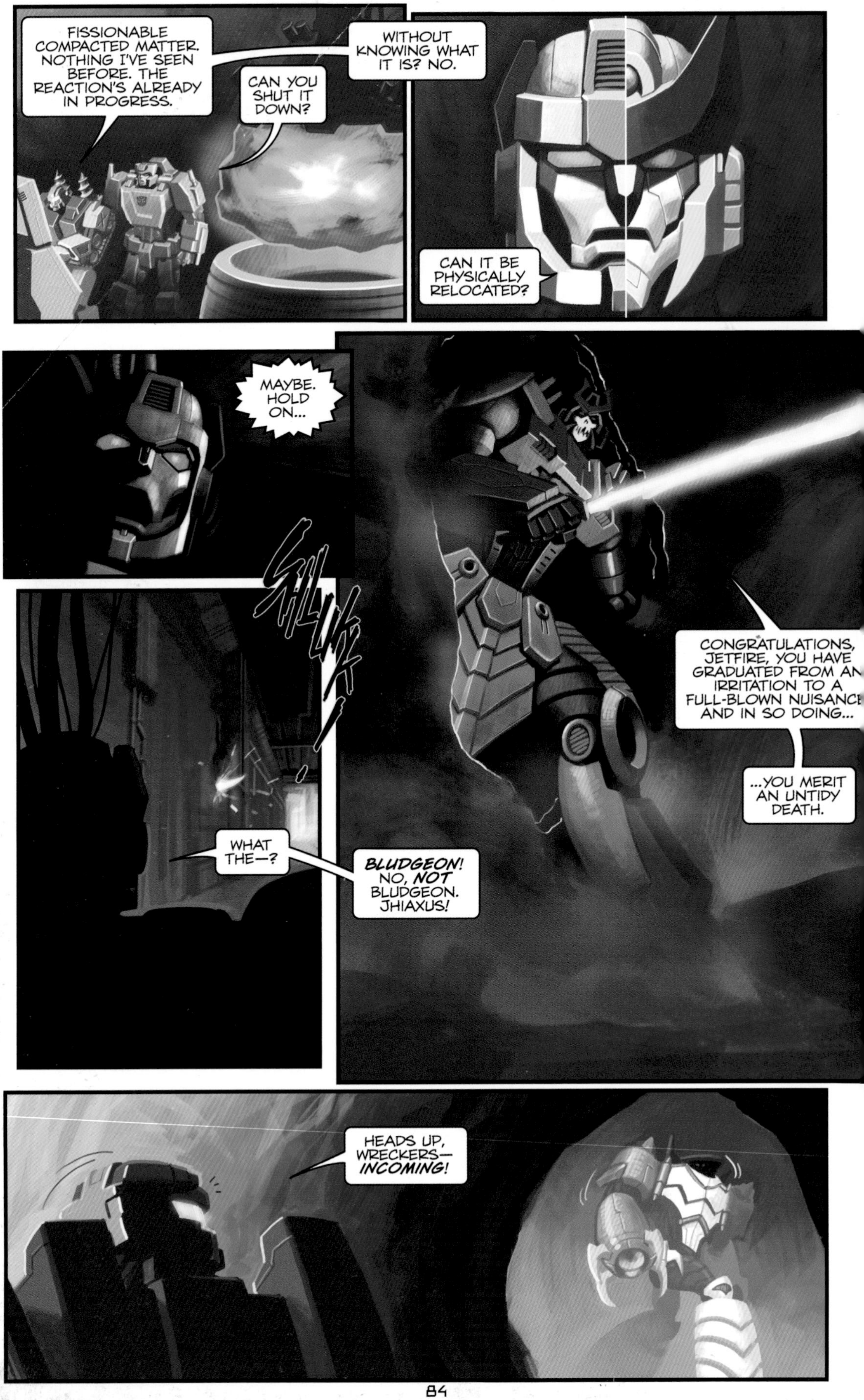
FISSIONABLE COMPACTED MATTER. NOTHING I'VE SEEN BEFORE. THE REACTION'S ALREADY IN PROGRESS.
CAN YOU SHUT IT DOWN?
WITHOUT KNOWING WHAT IT IS? NO.
CAN IT BE PHYSICALLY RELOCATED?
MAYBE. HOLD ON...
SHLUK
WHAT THE—?
BLUDGEON! NO, NOT BLUDGEON. JHIAXUS!
CONGRATULATIONS, JETFIRE, YOU HAVE GRADUATED FROM AN IRRITATION TO A FULL-BLOWN NUISANCE AND IN SO DOING...
...YOU MERIT AN UNTIDY DEATH.
HEADS UP, WRECKERS—INCOMING!

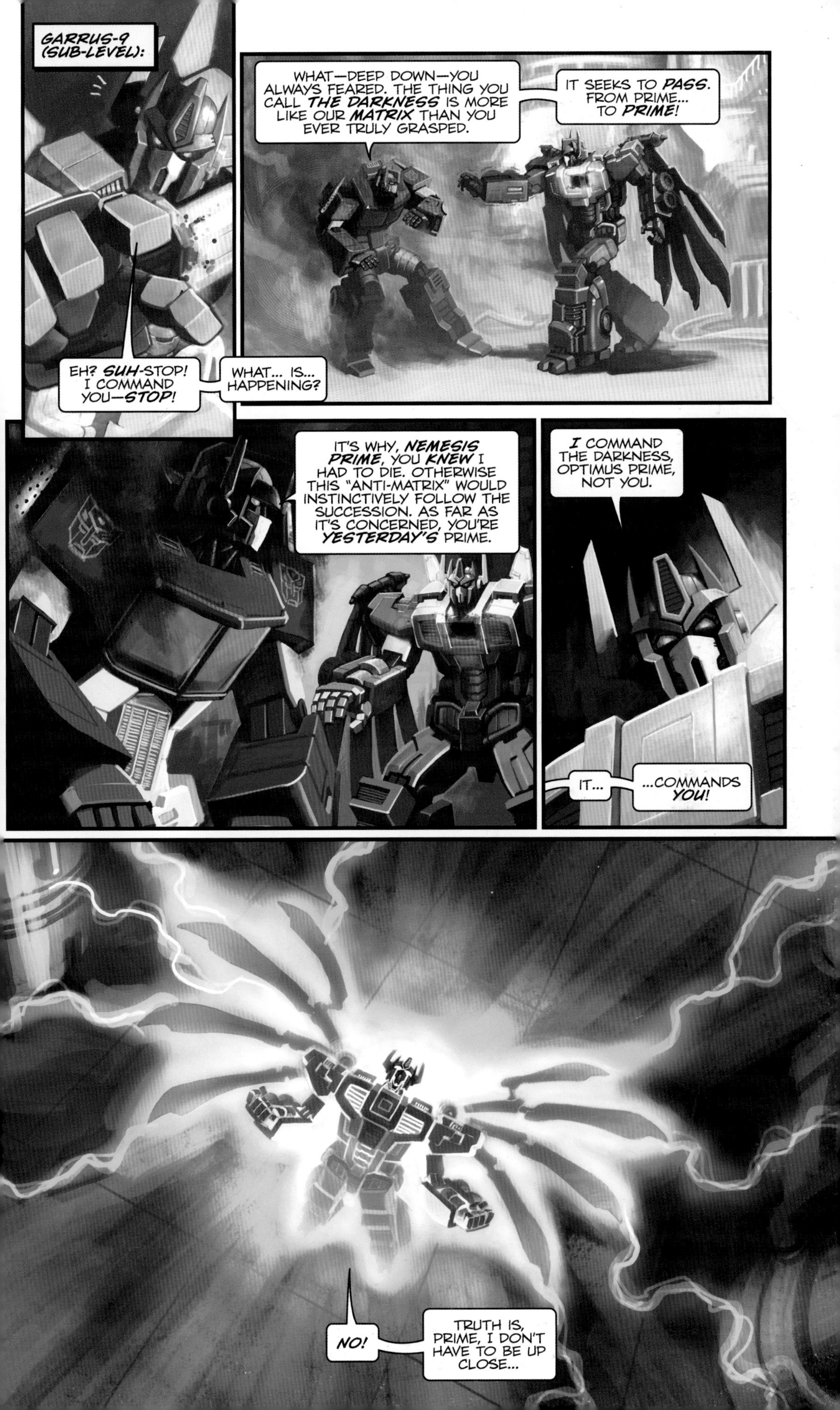
GARRUS-9 (SUB-LEVEL):
WHAT—DEEP DOWN—YOU ALWAYS FEARED. THE THING YOU CALL THE DARKNESS IS MORE LIKE OUR MATRIX THAN YOU EVER TRULY GRASPED.
IT SEEKS TO PASS. FROM PRIME... TO PRIME!
EH? SUH-STOP! I COMMAND YOU—STOP!
WHAT... IS... HAPPENING?
IT'S WHY, NEMESIS PRIME, YOU KNEW I HAD TO DIE. OTHERWISE THIS "ANTI-MATRIX" WOULD INSTINCTIVELY FOLLOW THE SUCCESSION. AS FAR AS IT'S CONCERNED, YOU'RE YESTERDAY'S PRIME.
I COMMAND THE DARKNESS, OPTIMUS PRIME, NOT YOU.
IT...
...COMMANDS YOU!
NO!
TRUTH IS, PRIME, I DON'T HAVE TO BE UP CLOSE...

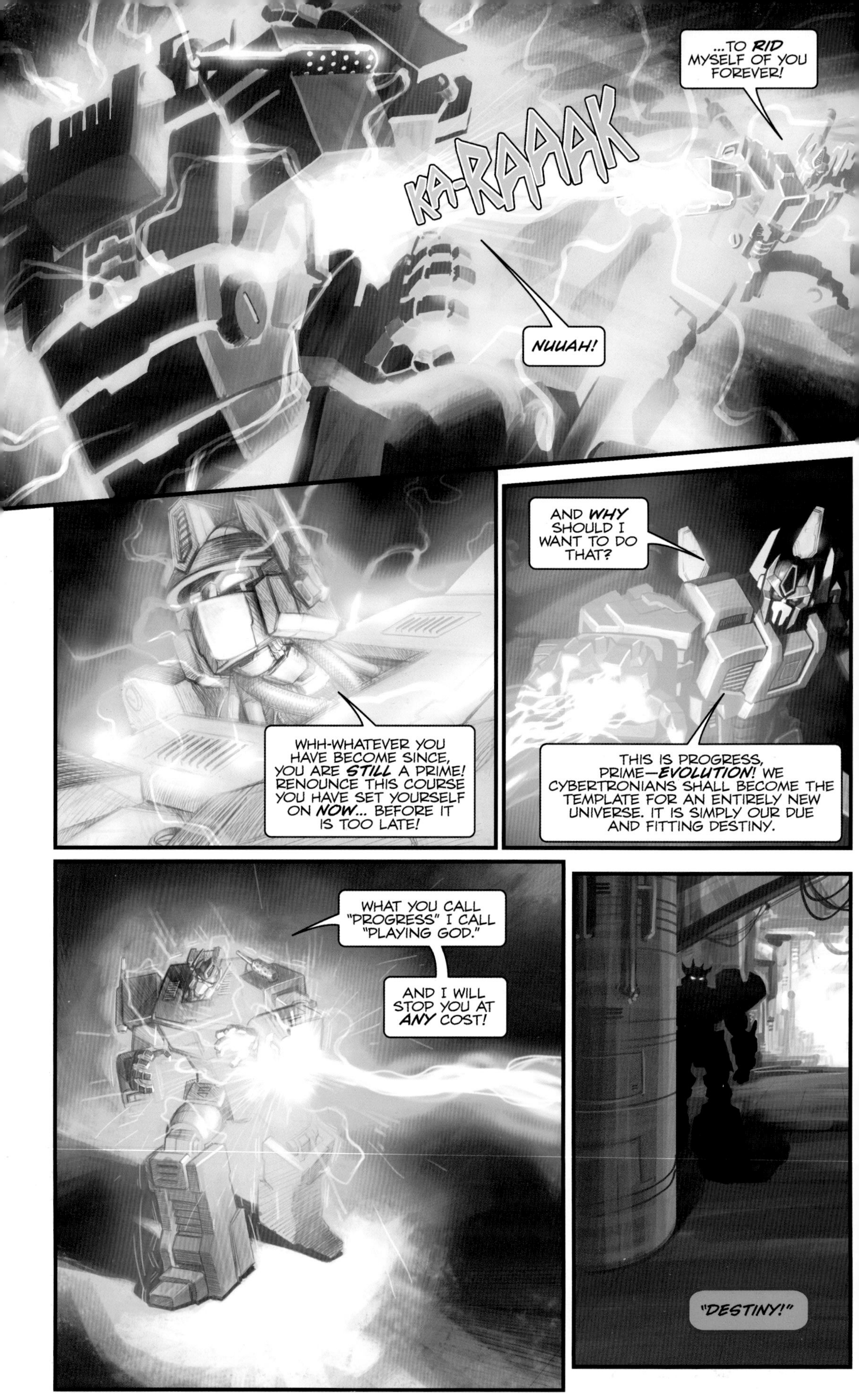
...TO RID MYSELF OF YOU FOREVER!
KA-RAAAK
NUUAH!
WHH-WHATEVER YOU HAVE BECOME SINCE, YOU ARE STILL A PRIME! RENOUNCE THIS COURSE YOU HAVE SET YOURSELF ON NOW... BEFORE IT IS TOO LATE!
AND WHY SHOULD I WANT TO DO THAT?
THIS IS PROGRESS, PRIME—EVOLUTION! WE CYBERTRONIANS SHALL BECOME THE TEMPLATE FOR AN ENTIRELY NEW UNIVERSE. IT IS SIMPLY OUR DUE AND FITTING DESTINY.
WHAT YOU CALL "PROGRESS" I CALL "PLAYING GOD."
AND I WILL STOP YOU AT ANY COST!
"DESTINY!"

EARTH:

FOR THE LAST TIME, JUST...

...GO!

I CAN DO THIS. I *HAVE* TO DO THIS. DON'T YOU SEE?

FLANG

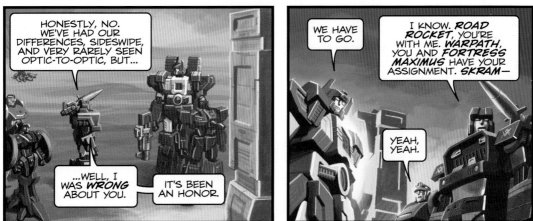

HONESTLY, NO. WE'VE HAD OUR DIFFERENCES, SIDESWIPE, AND VERY RARELY SEEN OPTIC-TO-OPTIC, BUT...

...WELL, I WAS *WRONG* ABOUT YOU.

IT'S BEEN AN HONOR.

WE HAVE TO GO.

I KNOW. *ROAD ROCKET*, YOU'RE WITH ME. *WARPATH*, YOU AND *FORTRESS MAXIMUS* HAVE YOUR ASSIGNMENT. *SKRAM—*

YEAH, YEAH.

"GO GET THE *PSYCHO*."

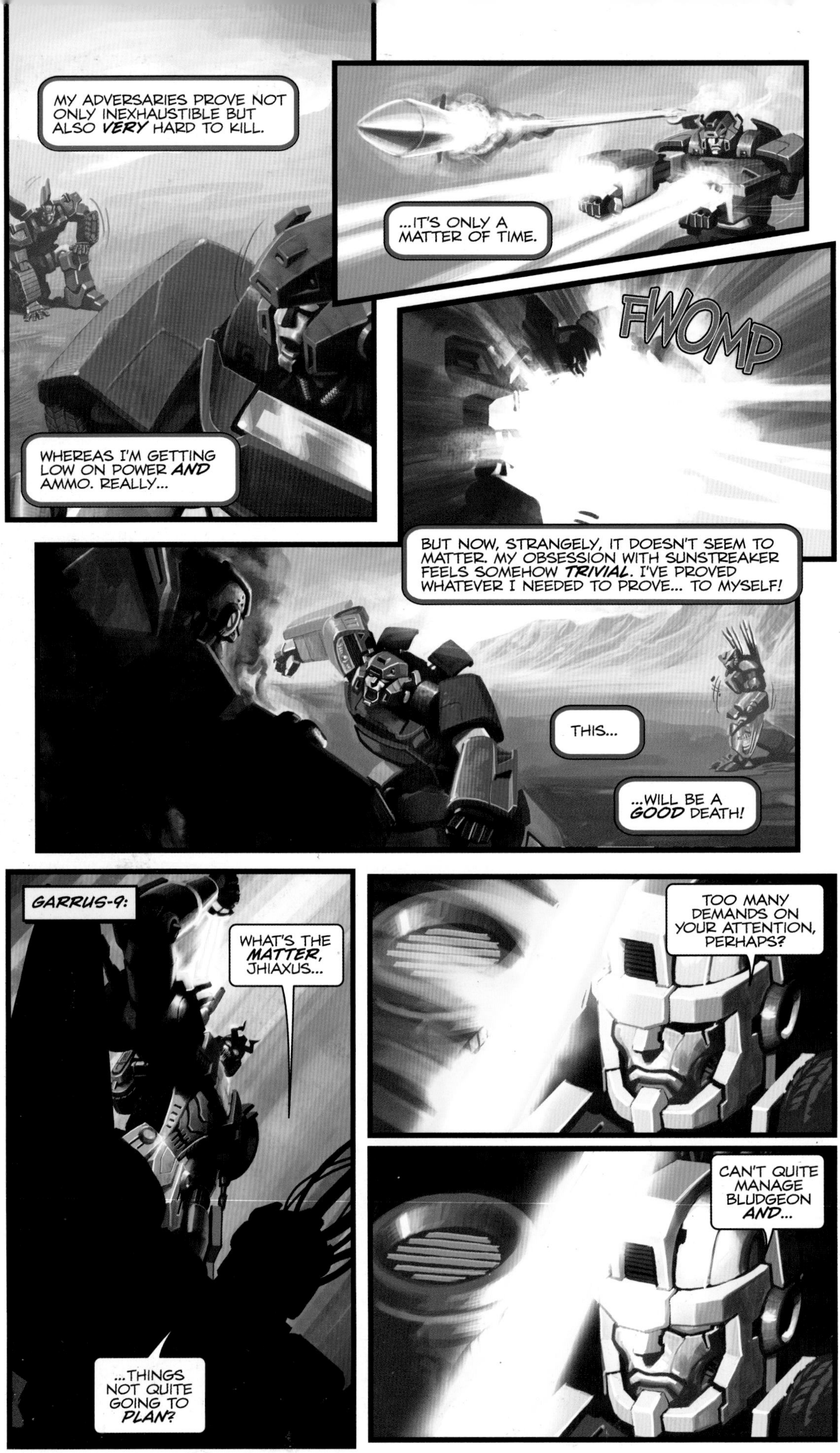
MY ADVERSARIES PROVE NOT ONLY INEXHAUSTIBLE BUT ALSO VERY HARD TO KILL.
WHEREAS I'M GETTING LOW ON POWER AND AMMO. REALLY...
...IT'S ONLY A MATTER OF TIME.
FWOMP
BUT NOW, STRANGELY, IT DOESN'T SEEM TO MATTER. MY OBSESSION WITH SUNSTREAKER FEELS SOMEHOW TRIVIAL. I'VE PROVED WHATEVER I NEEDED TO PROVE... TO MYSELF!
THIS...
...WILL BE A GOOD DEATH!
GARRUS-9:
WHAT'S THE MATTER, JHIAXUS...
...THINGS NOT QUITE GOING TO PLAN?
TOO MANY DEMANDS ON YOUR ATTENTION, PERHAPS?
CAN'T QUITE MANAGE BLUDGEON AND...

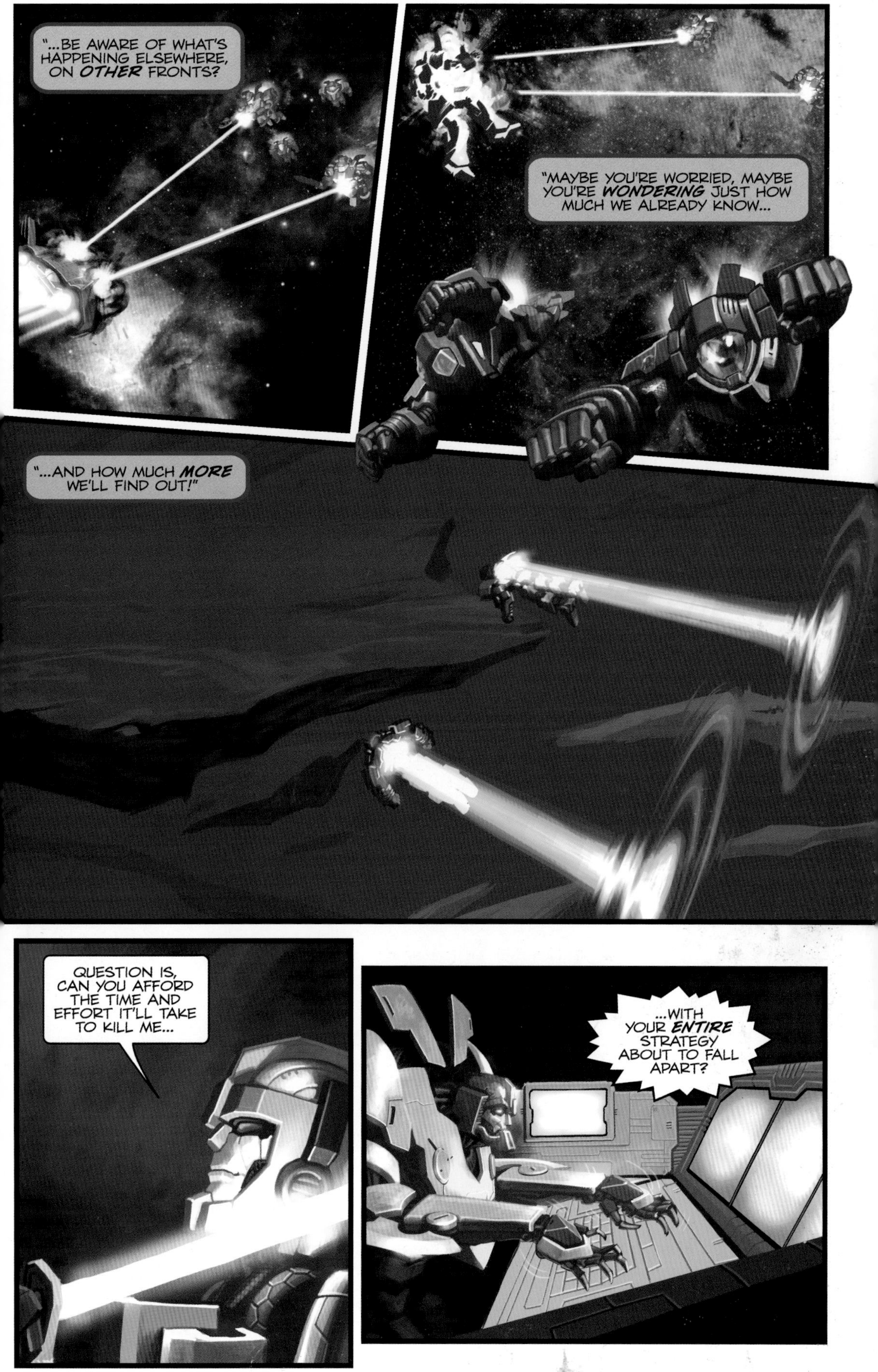
"...BE AWARE OF WHAT'S HAPPENING ELSEWHERE, ON *OTHER* FRONTS?
"MAYBE YOU'RE WORRIED, MAYBE YOU'RE *WONDERING* JUST HOW MUCH WE ALREADY KNOW...
"...AND HOW MUCH *MORE* WE'LL FIND OUT!"
QUESTION IS, CAN YOU AFFORD THE TIME AND EFFORT IT'LL TAKE TO KILL ME...
...WITH YOUR *ENTIRE* STRATEGY ABOUT TO FALL APART?

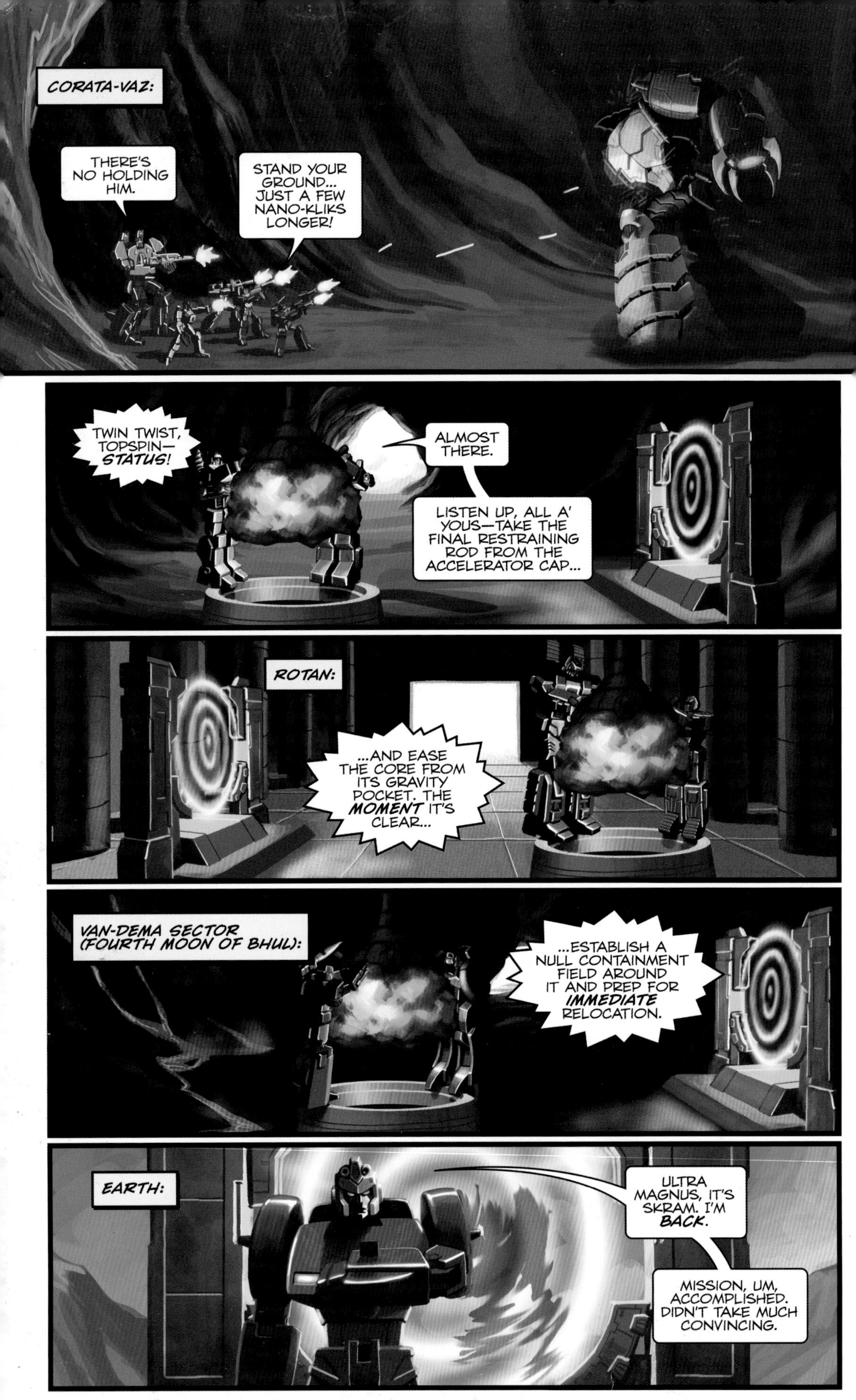

CORATA-VAZ:
THERE'S NO HOLDING HIM.
STAND YOUR GROUND... JUST A FEW NANO-KLIKS LONGER!
TWIN TWIST, TOPSPIN— STATUS!
ALMOST THERE.
LISTEN UP, ALL A' YOUS—TAKE THE FINAL RESTRAINING ROD FROM THE ACCELERATOR CAP...
ROTAN:
...AND EASE THE CORE FROM ITS GRAVITY POCKET. THE MOMENT IT'S CLEAR...
VAN-DEMA SECTOR (FOURTH MOON OF BHUL):
...ESTABLISH A NULL CONTAINMENT FIELD AROUND IT AND PREP FOR IMMEDIATE RELOCATION.
EARTH:
ULTRA MAGNUS, IT'S SKRAM. I'M BACK.
MISSION, UM, ACCOMPLISHED. DIDN'T TAKE MUCH CONVINCING.

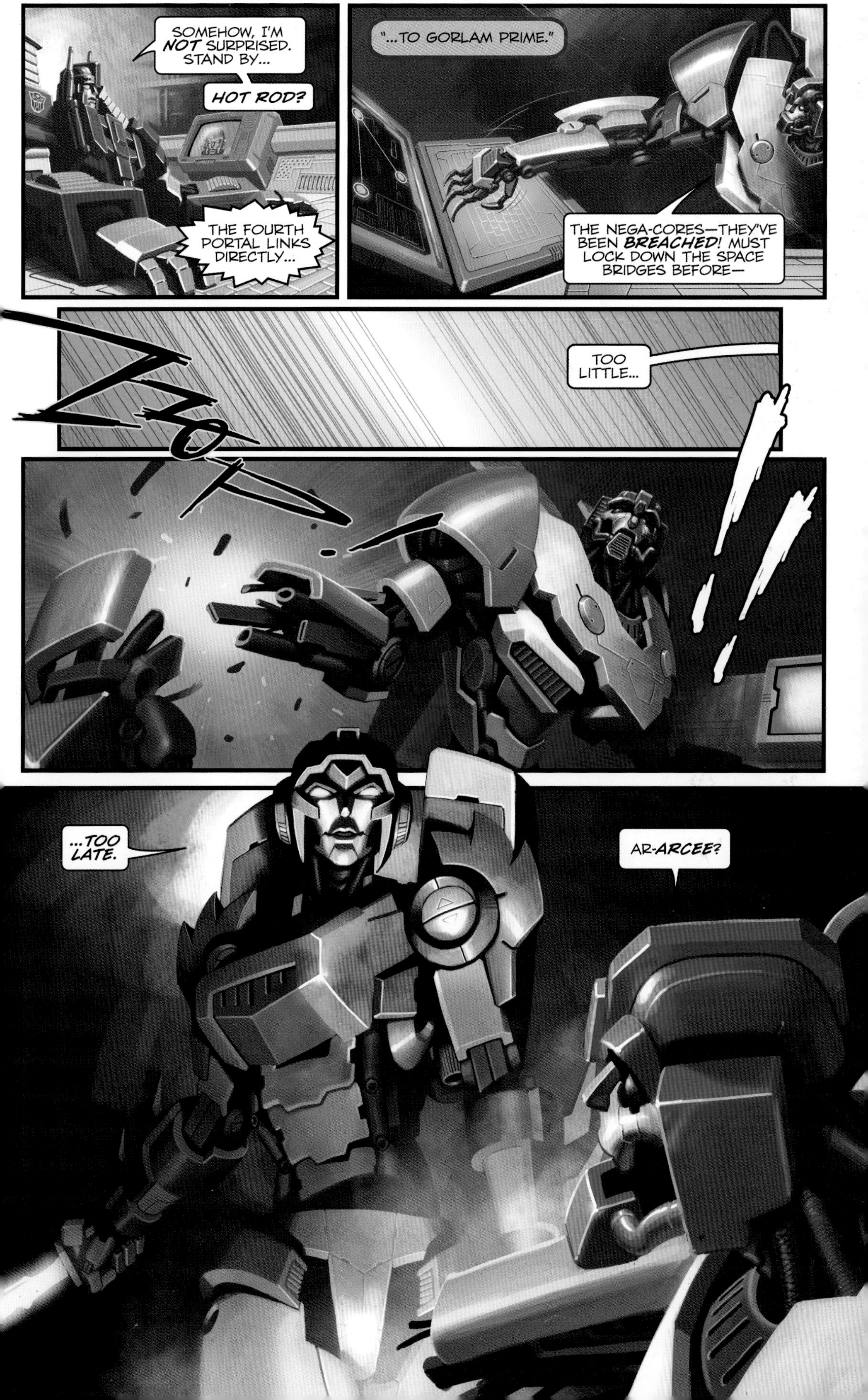
SOMEHOW, I'M NOT SURPRISED. STAND BY...
HOT ROD?
THE FOURTH PORTAL LINKS DIRECTLY...
"...TO GORLAM PRIME."
THE NEGA-CORES—THEY'VE BEEN BREACHED! MUST LOCK DOWN THE SPACE BRIDGES BEFORE—
TOO LITTLE...
ZZOT
...TOO LATE.
AR-ARCEE?

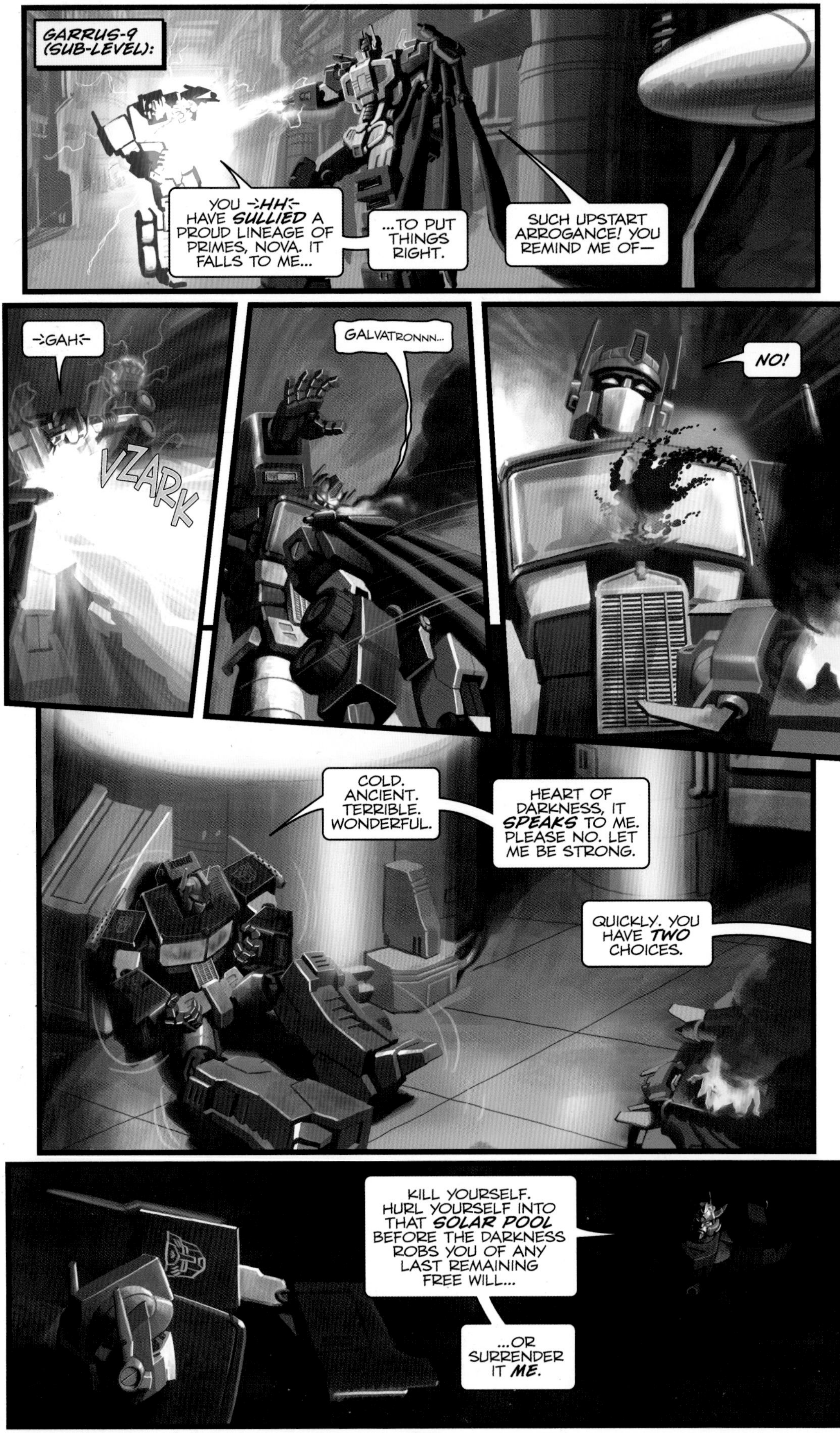
GARRUS-9 (SUB-LEVEL):
YOU -HH- HAVE SULLIED A PROUD LINEAGE OF PRIMES, NOVA. IT FALLS TO ME...
...TO PUT THINGS RIGHT.
SUCH UPSTART ARROGANCE! YOU REMIND ME OF—
-GAH-
VZARK
GALVATRONNN...
NO!
COLD. ANCIENT. TERRIBLE. WONDERFUL.
HEART OF DARKNESS, IT SPEAKS TO ME. PLEASE NO. LET ME BE STRONG.
QUICKLY. YOU HAVE TWO CHOICES.
KILL YOURSELF. HURL YOURSELF INTO THAT SOLAR POOL BEFORE THE DARKNESS ROBS YOU OF ANY LAST REMAINING FREE WILL...
...OR SURRENDER IT ME.

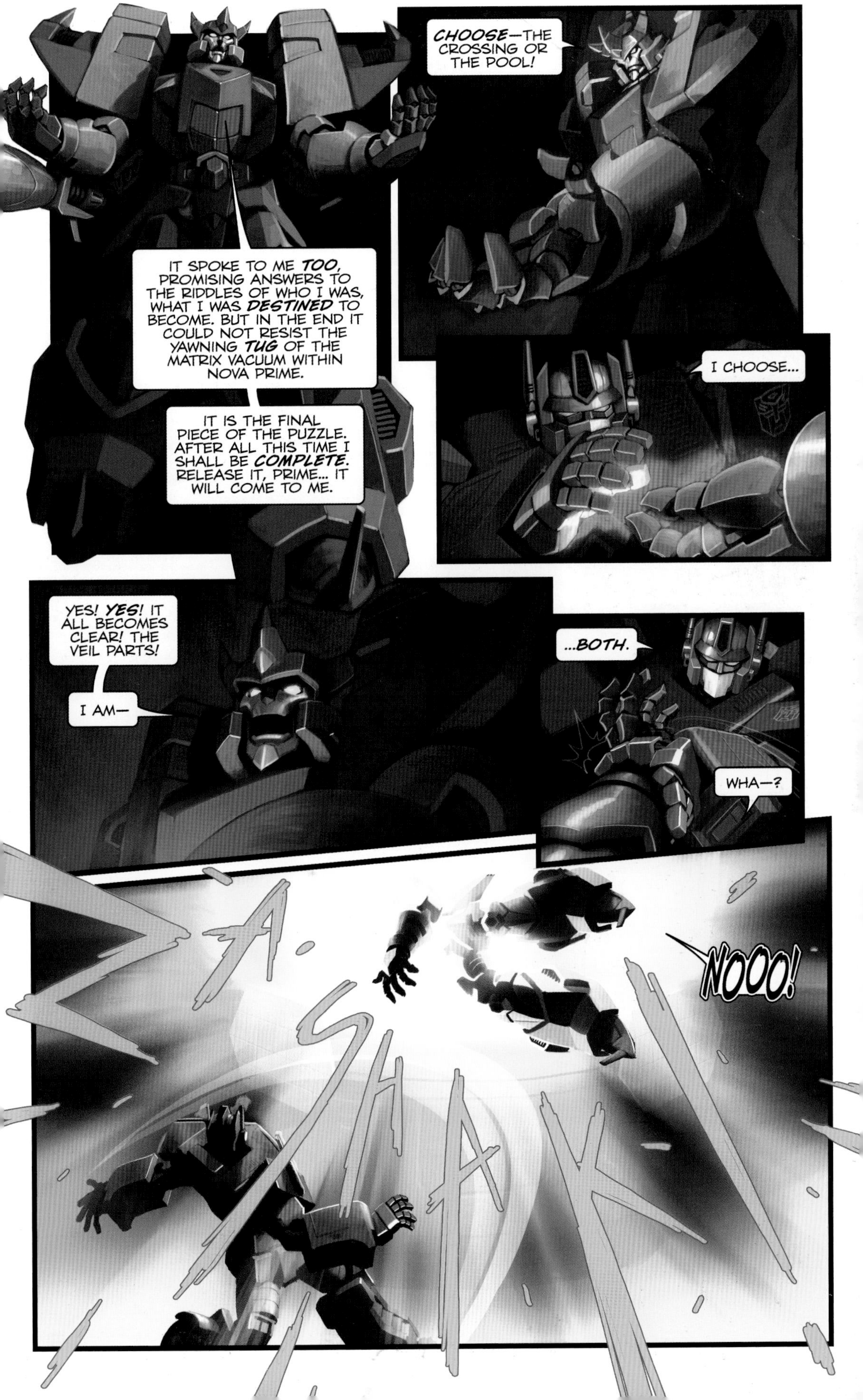
IT SPOKE TO ME *TOO*, PROMISING ANSWERS TO THE RIDDLES OF WHO I WAS, WHAT I WAS *DESTINED* TO BECOME. BUT IN THE END IT COULD NOT RESIST THE YAWNING *TUG* OF THE MATRIX VACUUM WITHIN NOVA PRIME.
IT IS THE FINAL PIECE OF THE PUZZLE. AFTER ALL THIS TIME I SHALL BE *COMPLETE*. RELEASE IT, PRIME... IT WILL COME TO ME.
CHOOSE—THE CROSSING OR THE POOL!
I CHOOSE...
YES! *YES*! IT ALL BECOMES CLEAR! THE VEIL PARTS!
I AM—
...BOTH.
WHA—?
ZA-SHAK!
NOOO!

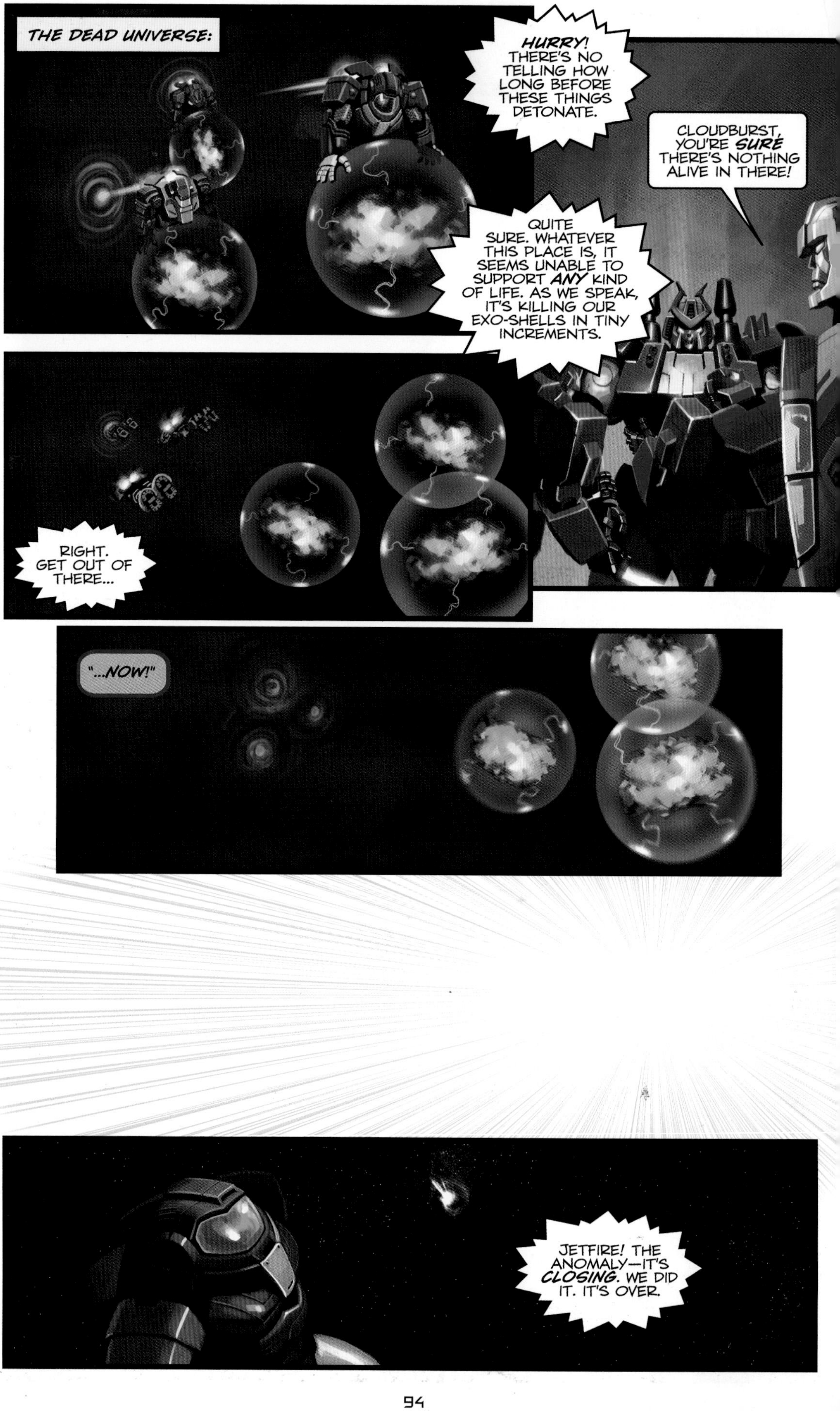
THE DEAD UNIVERSE:
HURRY! THERE'S NO TELLING HOW LONG BEFORE THESE THINGS DETONATE.
CLOUDBURST, YOU'RE SURE THERE'S NOTHING ALIVE IN THERE!
QUITE SURE. WHATEVER THIS PLACE IS, IT SEEMS UNABLE TO SUPPORT ANY KIND OF LIFE. AS WE SPEAK, IT'S KILLING OUR EXO-SHELLS IN TINY INCREMENTS.
RIGHT. GET OUT OF THERE...
"...NOW!"
JETFIRE! THE ANOMALY—IT'S CLOSING. WE DID IT. IT'S OVER.

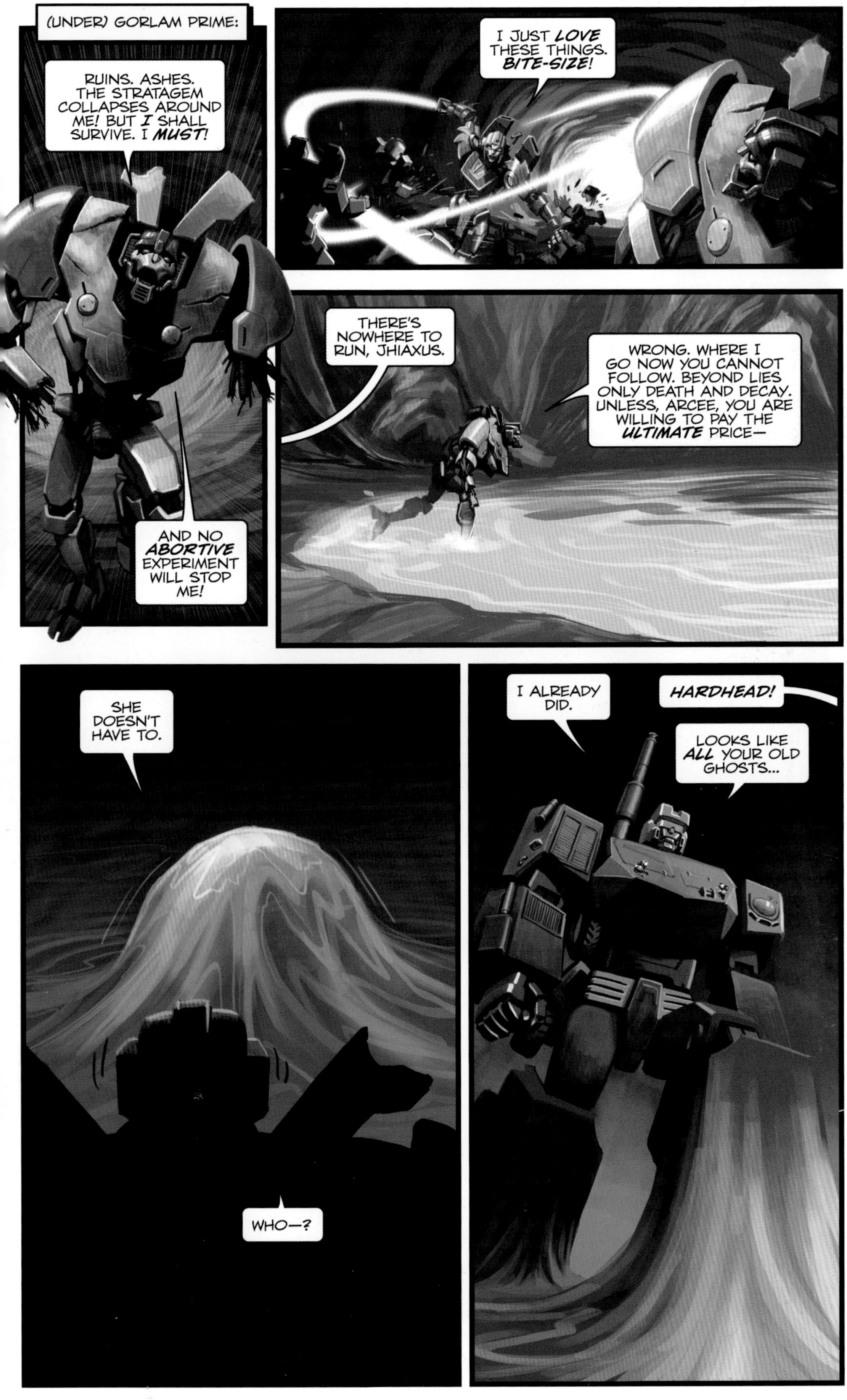
(UNDER) GORLAM PRIME:
RUINS. ASHES. THE STRATAGEM COLLAPSES AROUND ME! BUT *I* SHALL SURVIVE. I *MUST*!
AND NO *ABORTIVE* EXPERIMENT WILL STOP ME!
I JUST *LOVE* THESE THINGS. *BITE-SIZE!*
THERE'S NOWHERE TO RUN, JHIAXUS.
WRONG. WHERE I GO NOW YOU CANNOT FOLLOW. BEYOND LIES ONLY DEATH AND DECAY. UNLESS, ARCEE, YOU ARE WILLING TO PAY THE *ULTIMATE* PRICE—
SHE DOESN'T HAVE TO.
WHO—?
I ALREADY DID.
HARDHEAD!
LOOKS LIKE *ALL* YOUR OLD GHOSTS...

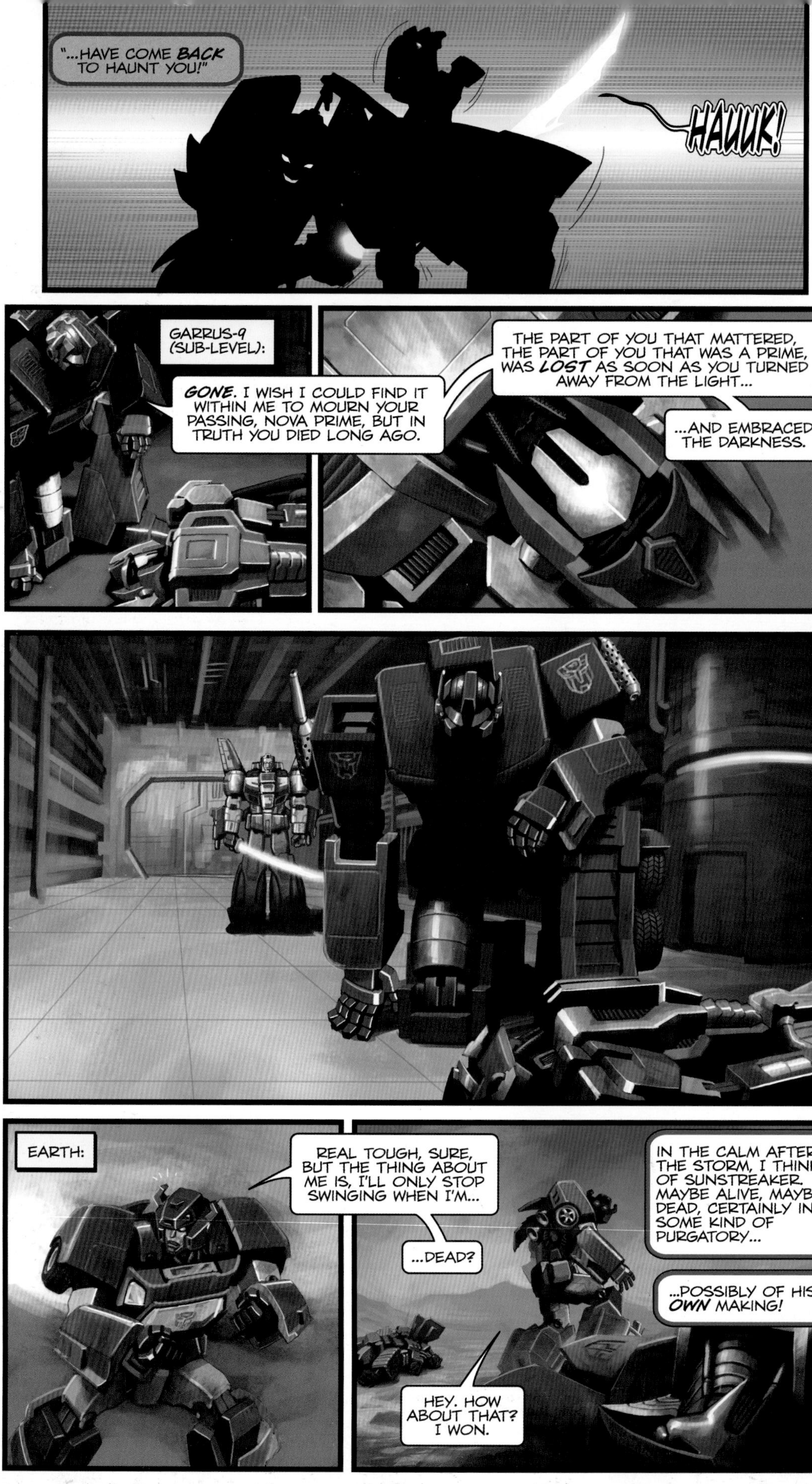
"...HAVE COME BACK TO HAUNT YOU!"
HAUUK!
GARRUS-9 (SUB-LEVEL):
GONE. I WISH I COULD FIND IT WITHIN ME TO MOURN YOUR PASSING, NOVA PRIME, BUT IN TRUTH YOU DIED LONG AGO.
THE PART OF YOU THAT MATTERED, THE PART OF YOU THAT WAS A PRIME, WAS LOST AS SOON AS YOU TURNED AWAY FROM THE LIGHT...
...AND EMBRACED THE DARKNESS.
EARTH:
REAL TOUGH, SURE, BUT THE THING ABOUT ME IS, I'LL ONLY STOP SWINGING WHEN I'M...
...DEAD?
IN THE CALM AFTER THE STORM, I THINK OF SUNSTREAKER. MAYBE ALIVE, MAYBE DEAD, CERTAINLY IN SOME KIND OF PURGATORY...
...POSSIBLY OF HIS OWN MAKING!
HEY. HOW ABOUT THAT? I WON.

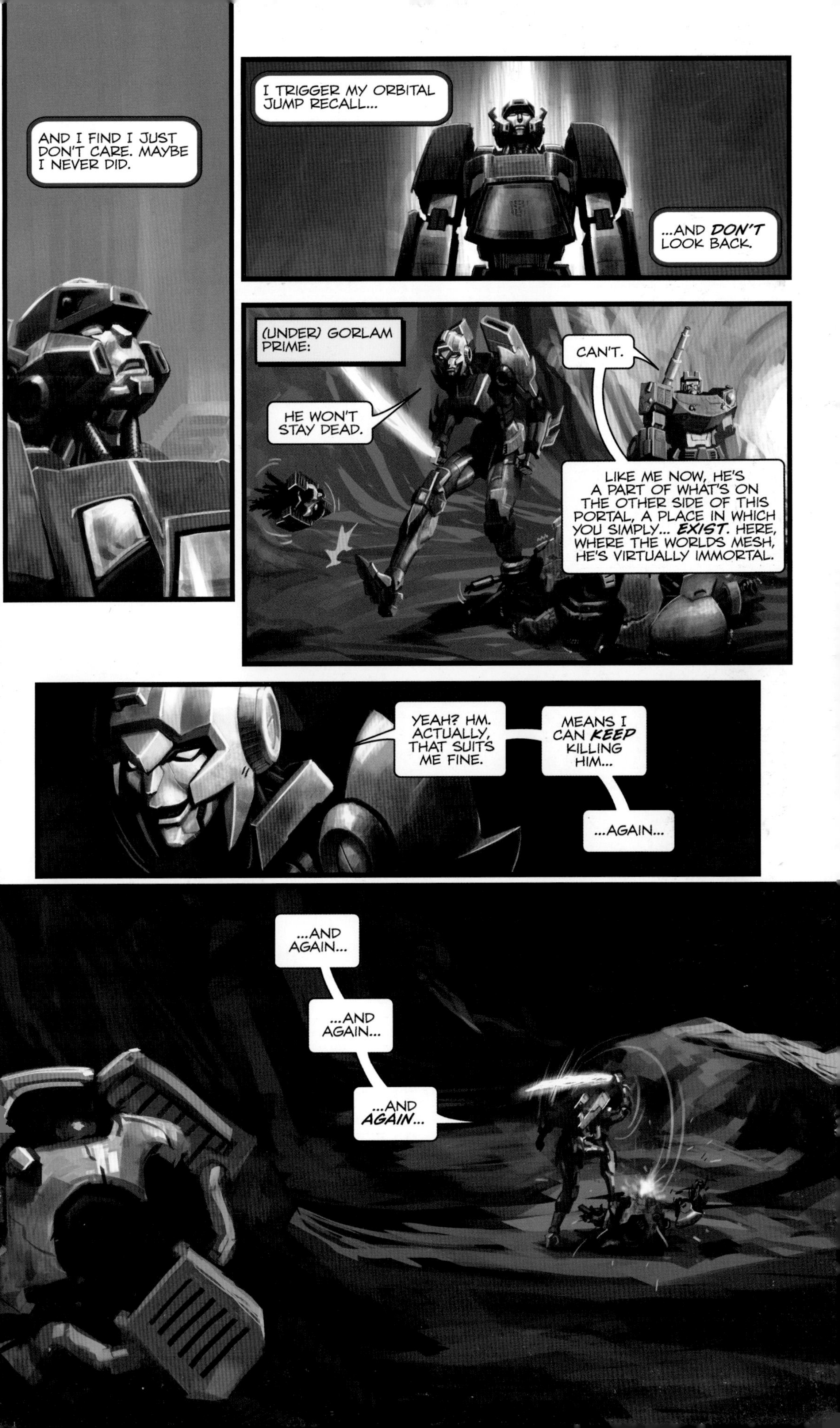
AND I FIND I JUST DON'T CARE. MAYBE I NEVER DID.
I TRIGGER MY ORBITAL JUMP RECALL...
...AND ***DON'T*** LOOK BACK.
(UNDER) GORLAM PRIME:
HE WON'T STAY DEAD.
CAN'T.
LIKE ME NOW, HE'S A PART OF WHAT'S ON THE OTHER SIDE OF THIS PORTAL, A PLACE IN WHICH YOU SIMPLY... ***EXIST.*** HERE, WHERE THE WORLDS MESH, HE'S VIRTUALLY IMMORTAL.
YEAH? HM. ACTUALLY, THAT SUITS ME FINE.
MEANS I CAN ***KEEP*** KILLING HIM...
...AGAIN...
...AND AGAIN...
...AND AGAIN...
...AND ***AGAIN...***

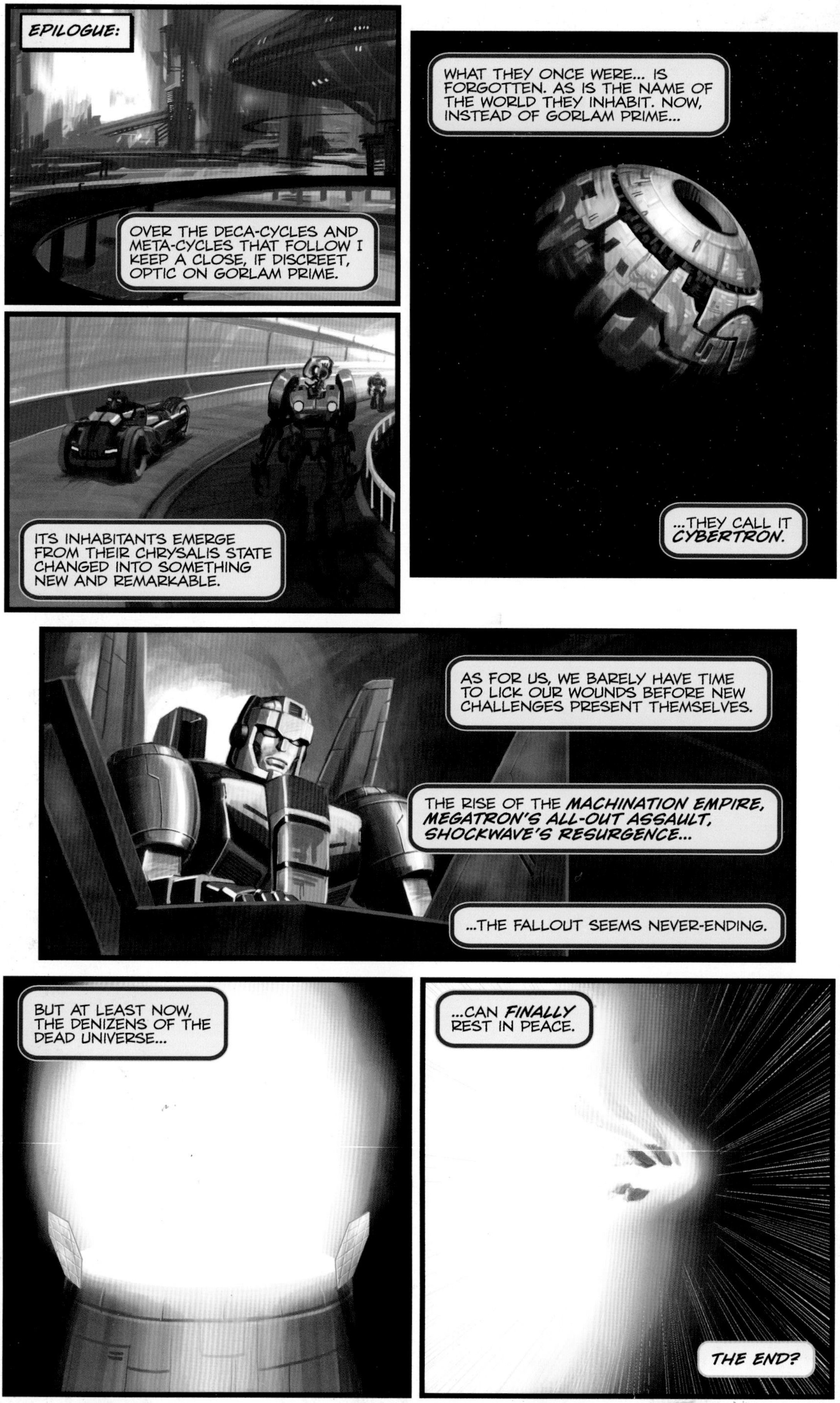
EPILOGUE:
OVER THE DECA-CYCLES AND META-CYCLES THAT FOLLOW I KEEP A CLOSE, IF DISCREET, OPTIC ON GORLAM PRIME.
ITS INHABITANTS EMERGE FROM THEIR CHRYSALIS STATE CHANGED INTO SOMETHING NEW AND REMARKABLE.
WHAT THEY ONCE WERE... IS FORGOTTEN. AS IS THE NAME OF THE WORLD THEY INHABIT. NOW, INSTEAD OF GORLAM PRIME...
...THEY CALL IT *CYBERTRON.*
AS FOR US, WE BARELY HAVE TIME TO LICK OUR WOUNDS BEFORE NEW CHALLENGES PRESENT THEMSELVES.
THE RISE OF THE *MACHINATION EMPIRE, MEGATRON'S ALL-OUT ASSAULT, SHOCKWAVE'S RESURGENCE...*
...THE FALLOUT SEEMS NEVER-ENDING.
BUT AT LEAST NOW, THE DENIZENS OF THE DEAD UNIVERSE...
...CAN *FINALLY* REST IN PEACE.
THE END?

rtwork by Nick Roche

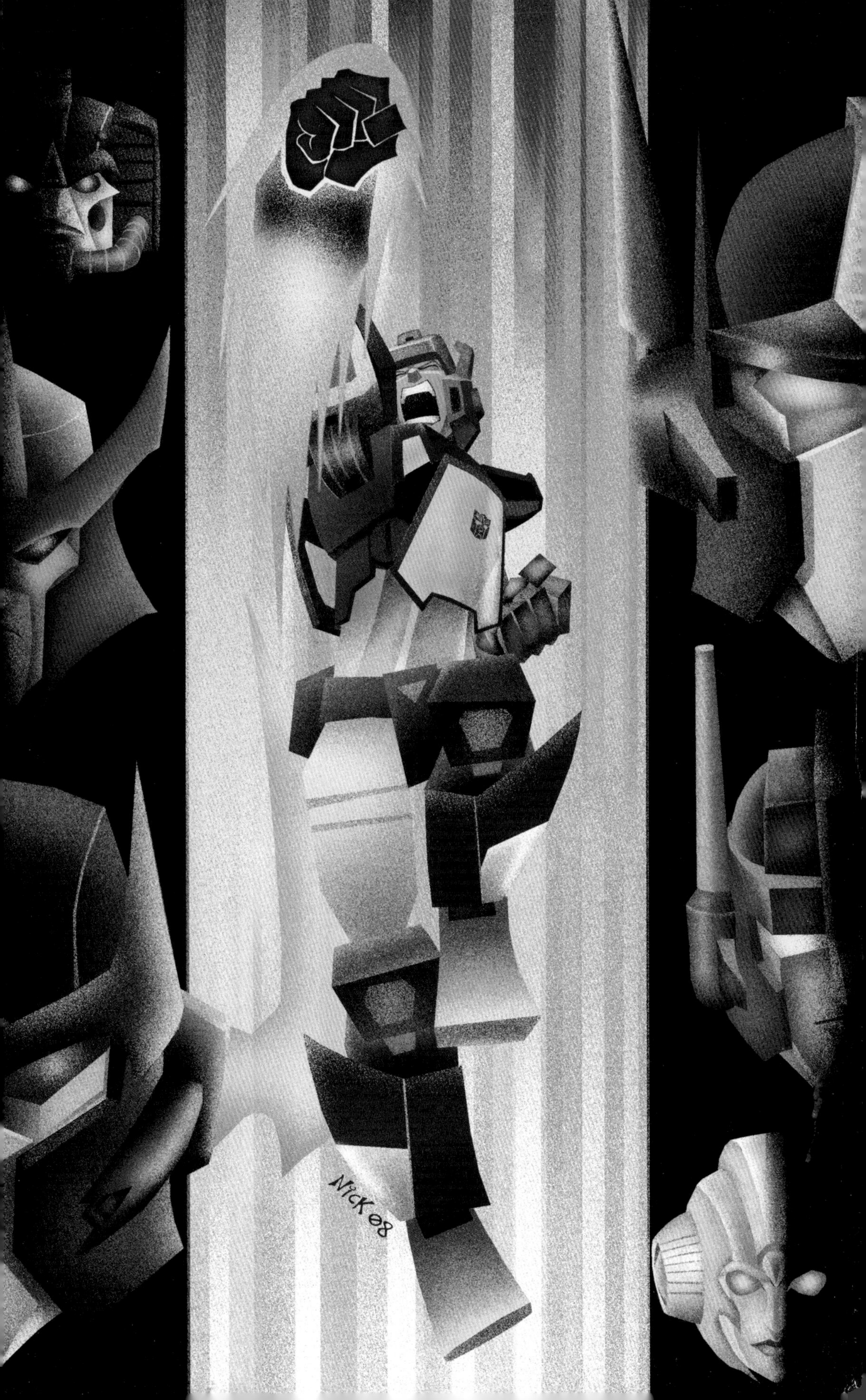
NICK 08

ART GALLERY

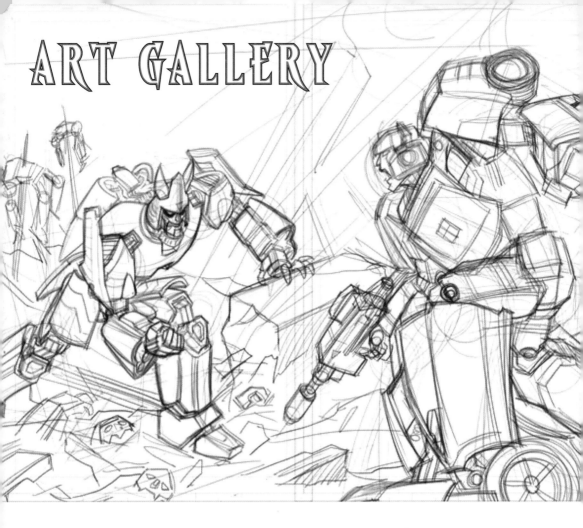

CYCLONUS

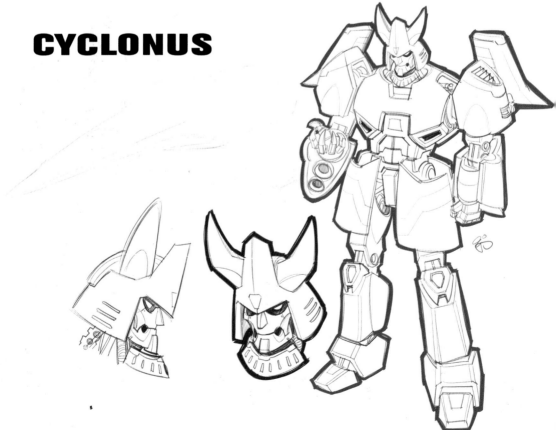

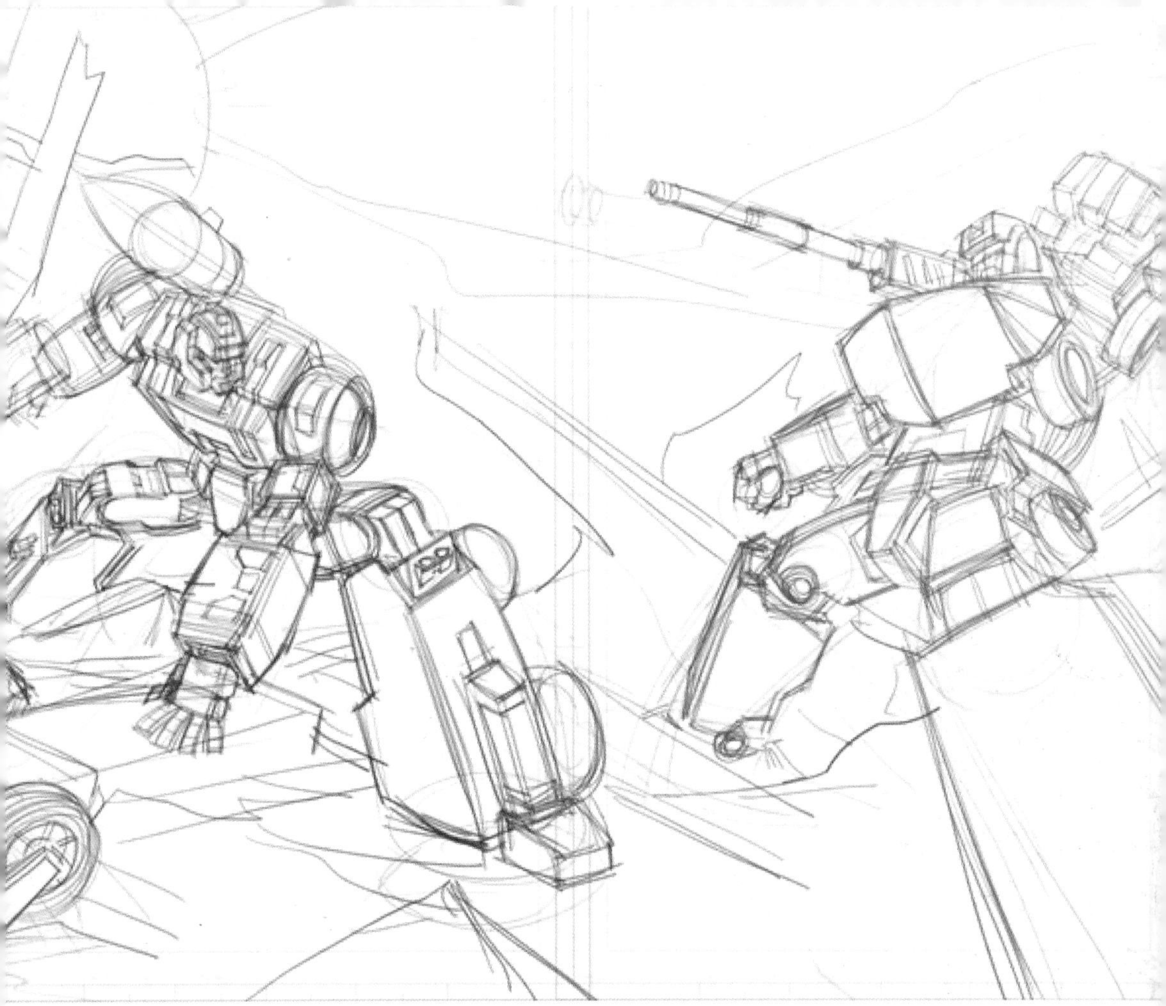

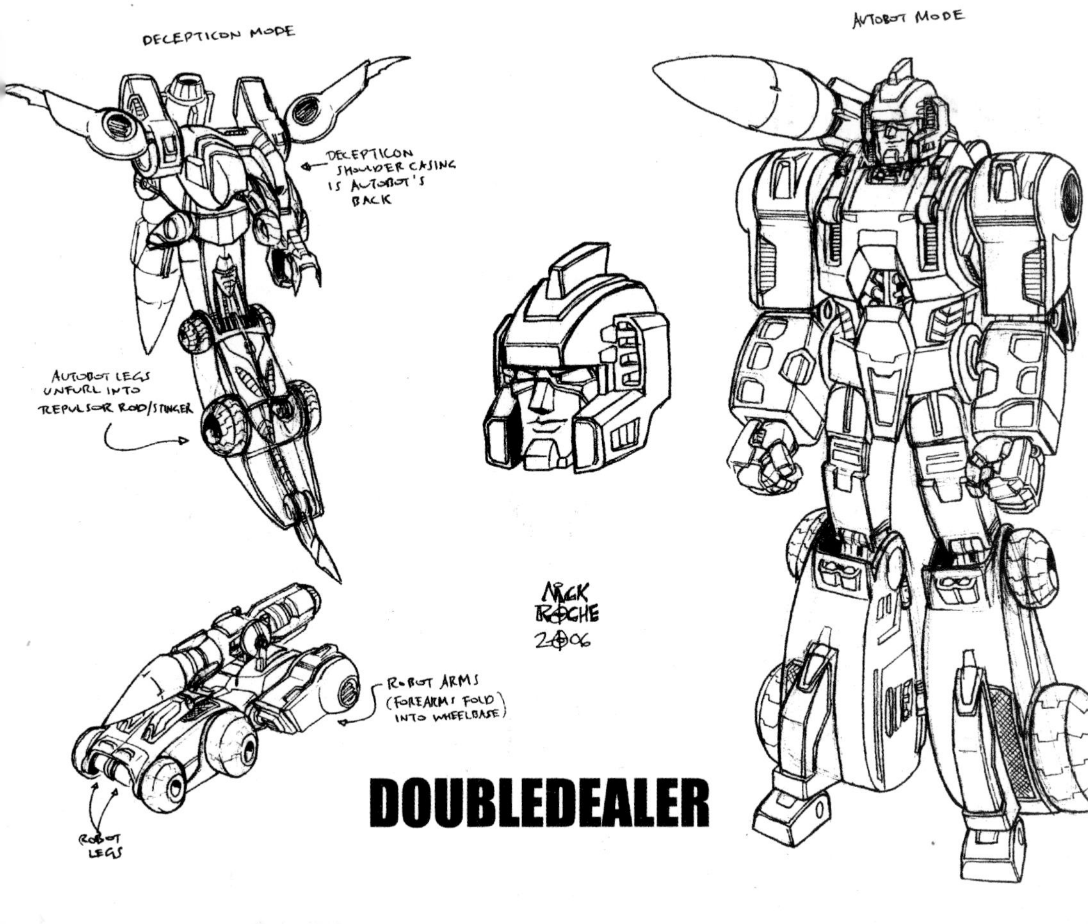
DECEPTICON MODE
DECEPTICON SHOULDER CASING IS AUTOBOT'S BACK
AUTOBOT LEGS UNFURL INTO REPULSOR ROD/STINGER
ROBOT ARMS (FOREARMS FOLD INTO WHEELBASE)
ROBOT LEGS
AUTOBOT MODE
NICK ROCHE 2006

DOUBLEDEALER

GRINDCORE

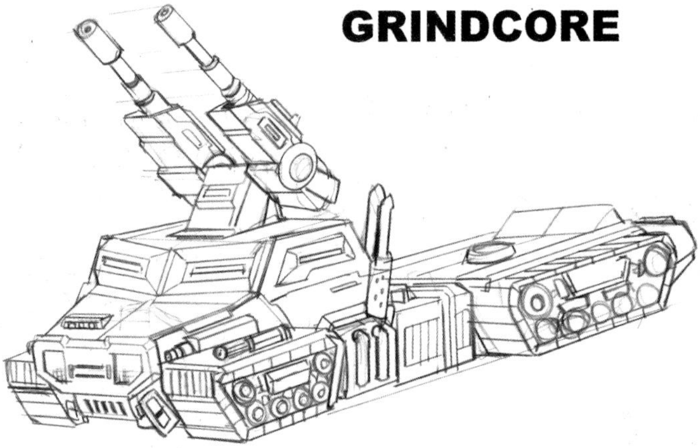

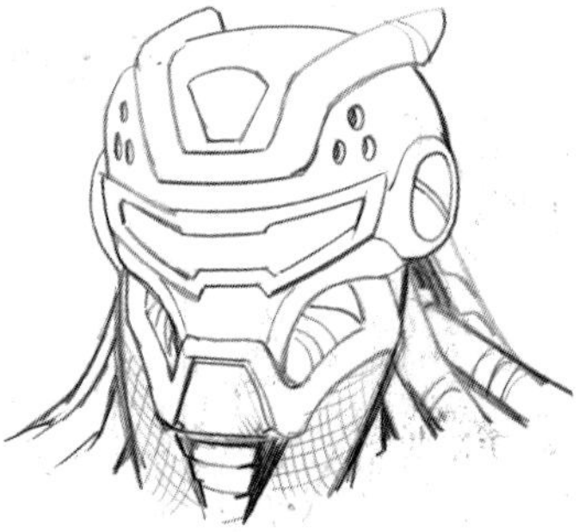

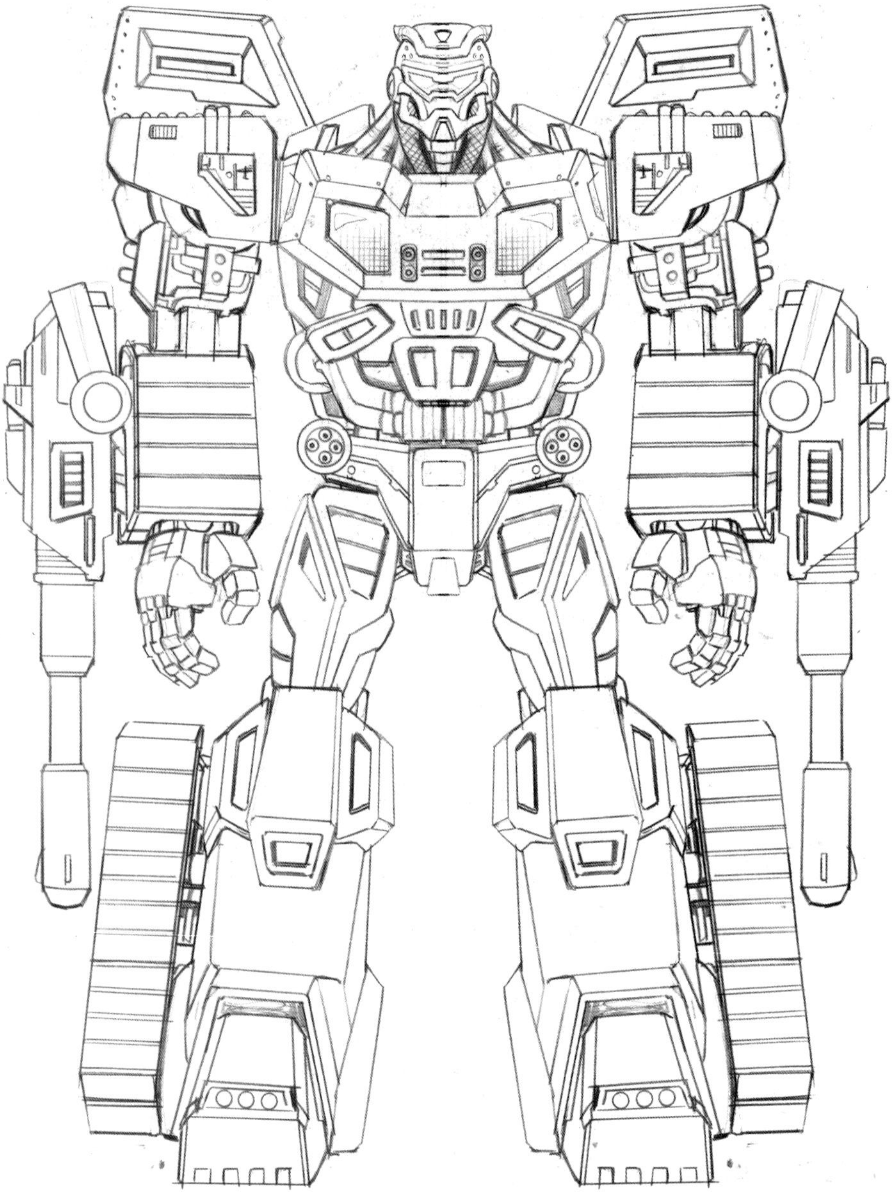

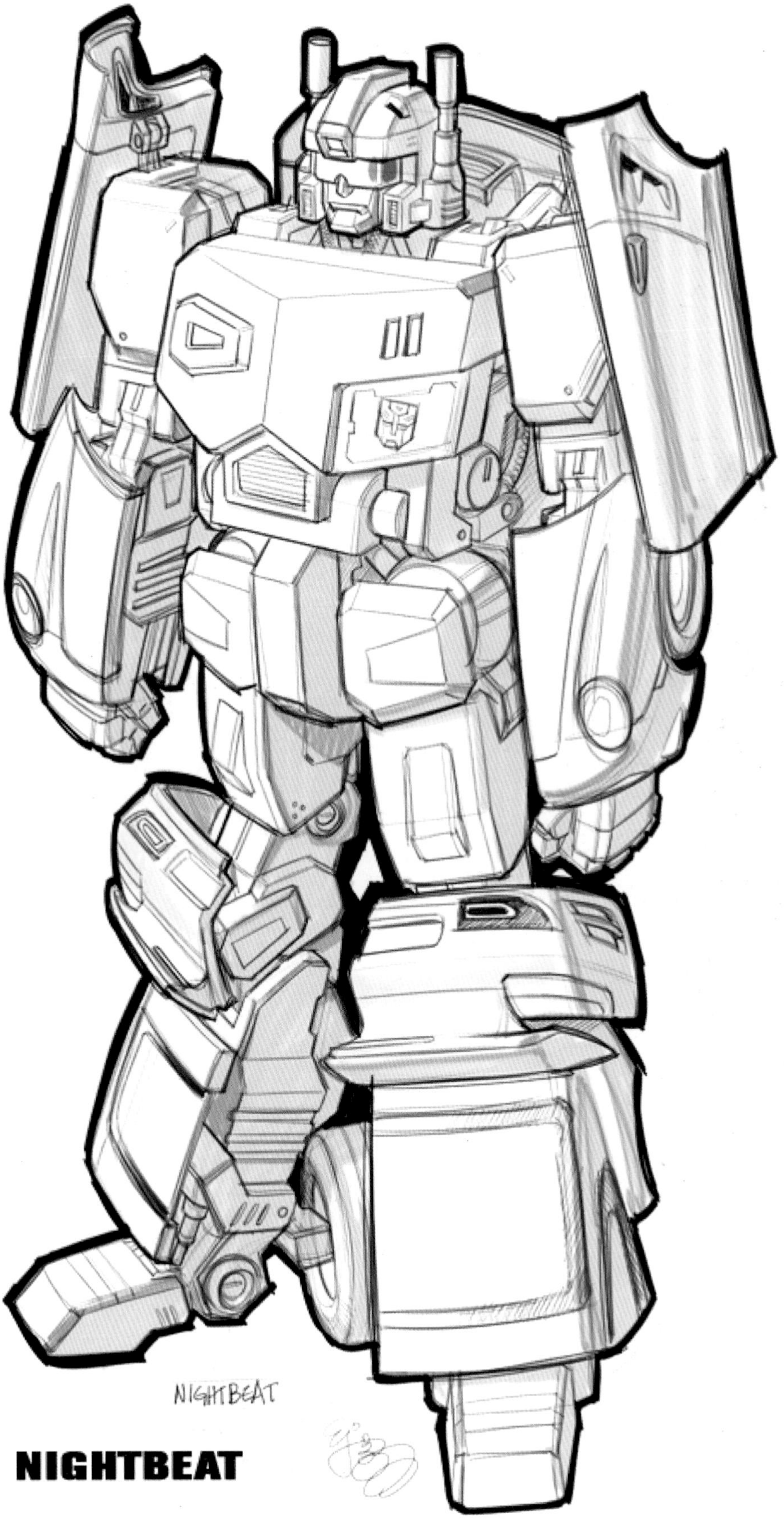
NIGHTBEAT

NIGHTBEAT

STRAXUS

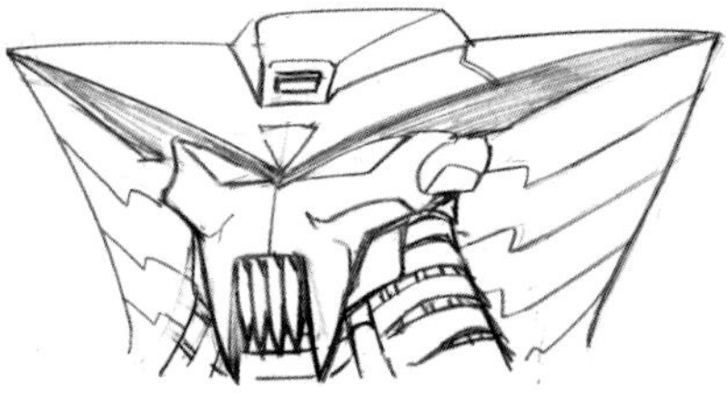

Battle Helmet

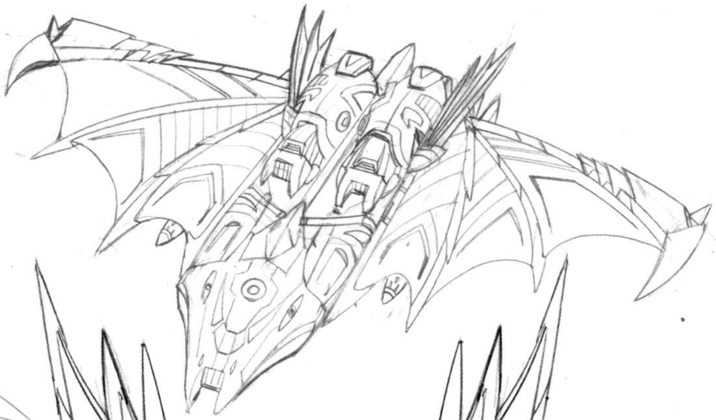

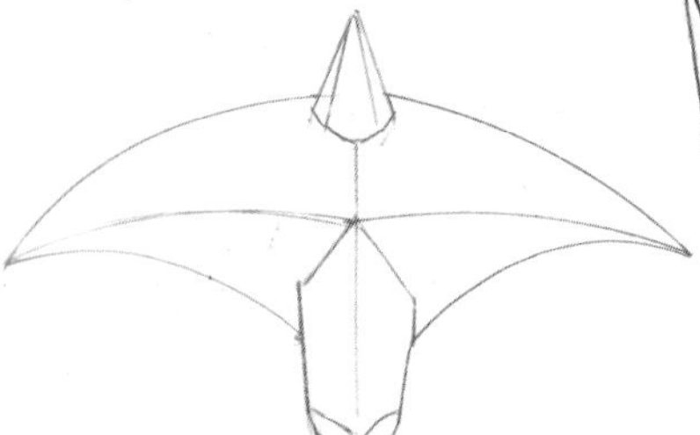

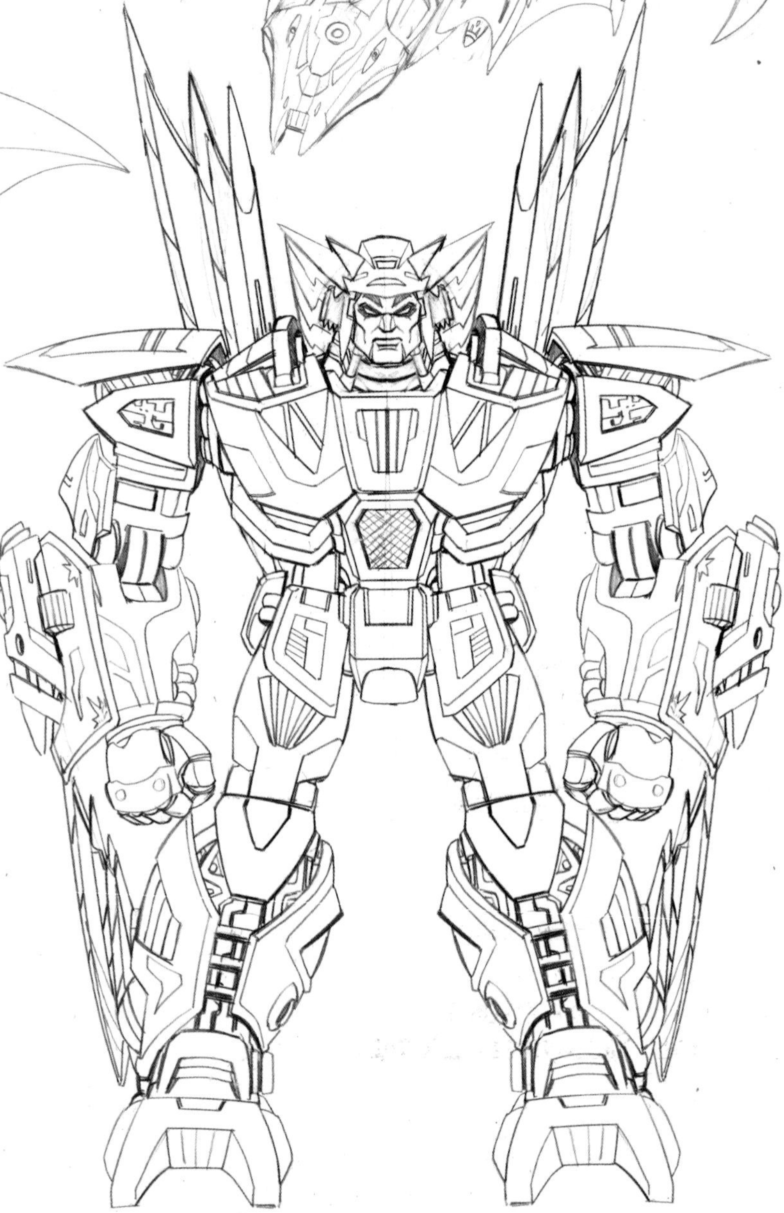